Roger Sessions on Music

Roger Sessions on Music

COLLECTED ESSAYS

Edited by *Edward T. Cone*

PRINCETON UNIVERSITY PRESS

PRINCETON, NEW JERSEY

Contents

v

Contents

Editor's Note

The essays that constitute this book are more accurately described as "collected" than as "selected." In reviewing Roger Sessions' output in this form—articles, lectures, addresses, spanning almost half a century—the editor found very little that should not be included. Some of the omitted items would have resulted in undue repetition: a lecture here that furnished material for an essay there, or an early attempt to deal with a subject that was superseded by a more definitive version. A few others were rejected as too narrowly topical or occasional. Into this category fall some book reviews and some program notes for performances of Sessions' own works. The last would no doubt be of general interest, but Sessions feels that there is inevitably an element of impermanence, if not of falsification, in all such self-explanatory attempts, and is loath to see them canonized, so to speak.

Naturally, it has not been possible to avoid all repetition, nor would that have been desirable. The present collection affords the opportunity to follow certain themes as the author develops them through various stages of his own musical and intellectual development. In particular, his view of the problems created by the course of musical evolution in the nineteenth century and of the ensuing twentieth-century crisis can be traced from his early "Music in Crisis" of 1933, through other essays in Sections I, IV, and VI, to the recent notes (1972) appended to "Schoenberg in the United States."

Other progressive themes, however, are not so overtly stated, but can be inferred by a comparison of the author's word with the composer's music. In this regard it is most interesting to read "To Revitalize Opera," an essay of 1938, in the light of Sessions' subsequent career as a composer of operas. With The Trial of Lucullus *(1947) and* Montezuma

Editor's Note

(1962) he brilliantly demonstrated that, like all his other speculation, his theorizing here had been based on intense personal conviction and was ultimately practical in its aims.

The division of the essays into sections should be taken in no rigid sense, although it is hoped that each section, read consecutively, creates a unified effect of its own. Certainly that is true of Section iv, most of which was written as a unit, and of Section v, which comments on successive phases of the world conflict of 1933-1945. But in other cases one might well argue against the chosen grouping. "America Moves to the Avant-Scene," for example, has close connections with Sections iii and v, although it is placed in Section i; and "Music and the Crisis of the Arts," although given the leading position in Section iii, might equally well be assigned to Section ii.

Within each group the essays are in general arranged chronologically. The only exceptions are the leading articles of Sections i, ii, and iii, each of which was chosen because it seemed to strike the keynote of the section so accurately. The chronological arrangement may at times seem too strictly applied, as when an early account of Oedipus Rex *is widely separated from the later remarks on Stravinsky. But one who reads the section in order will find that the sandwiching of the Schoenberg essays between those dealing with Stravinsky throws revealing light on the author's developing attitudes toward both composers.*

The essays are presented with a minimum of alteration from their original forms. A few references have been updated; a few topical allusions, now irrelevant, have been deleted. The dates assigned to each article are normally those of publication, but essays originally delivered orally are dated accordingly. Introductory material and footnotes are by the editor, except as otherwise specified.

EDWARD T. CONE

Preface

First of all, I wish to thank my dear friend Edward Cone for his initiative and his energy in collecting these various papers of mine, and his sensitive expertise in editing and classifying them. Those that were previously published, in some cases as much as fifty years ago—had to be sought out and gathered from a number of sources, in England as well as the United States; others were found among my own archives, often in the form of penciled sheets from which I originally read them, with no thought that they might eventually be published. Professor Cone has done a superb piece of work in selecting these, preparing them for readers, and classifying them in regard to their various topics. It is a happy privilege to express my warmest gratitude to him; and in view of his very high achievements both as a musician and a writer on music, I cannot help feeling very deeply honored.

It has been both interesting and, in a very personal sense, enlightening, for me to re-read these papers. They reflect the nature of my own musical reactions through the course of the years which they cover, and through the various places where I have lived. The oldest among them were written in 1927, in Florence where I had already resided for two years. Since the preceding autumn I had occupied the guest house on Bernard Berenson's estate, where I spent the following year as well. I was a frequent guest at the Berenson Villa, "I Tatti," where I met many people of distinction in the cultural world not only of Italy, but of other countries of Europe, as well as England and the United States. I became vividly aware of both the cultural and the political situation on the European continent as it was at that time.

My principal musical contacts at that time, however, were formed by occasional visits to Paris, to Vienna, and to the United States, where my First Symphony (composed in

Florence) was performed, in Boston, in April 1927. It was
not until I moved to the American Academy in Rome in
the fall of 1928 that they began to flourish in Italy. In Rome
I met, and saw frequently, leading figures in Italian music
of that time, as well as many visiting artists. A number of
these remained my friends during later years. One of them,
Otto Klemperer, persuaded me to visit Berlin, where he was
extremely kind; he not only introduced me to musicians but,
by virtue of his important position in the Prussian State
Opera, made it possible for me to attend, generally without
charge, virtually any musical performance that I wished.
Some of the most precious musical friendships of my life
—with Italian, German, Austrian, and French musicians—
have dated from that period. In most cases they continued
in the United States for many years afterwards; and in fact
they helped to sustain me through the most difficult years
of my musical career.

The years which I spent in Berlin, 1931-33, were those
which led to, and included, the advent of Hitler to power.
I had lived in Italy for six years under the rule of Mussolini; and above all during my years in Rome I had become
aware of the nature of Fascist rule and the kind of threat
it posed. In Berlin during that period, the prevalent economic and political chaos was visible on all sides. Though
musical life seemed relatively untouched by this until Hitler
actually assumed power in January, 1933, I was acutely
aware of it, partly because of what I had witnessed in Italy,
partly because of acquaintances which I had outside of
musical circles—including English and American news cor-
respondents. By the time I left Germany, three months
after Hitler became Chancellor, these implications had become quite clear and thoroughly alarming. When I returned
to the United States in June, 1933, I found myself dismayed
at the prevalent unawareness of the real situation in Europe,
and its potential menace to Western culture, including the
United States. I looked askance also at the rose-colored

Preface

spectacles through which some especially of the younger generation were casting glances at Stalinist Russia, about which I had heard in some detail, from contacts which I had enjoyed in Berlin with various individuals, both American and European, who had actually seen conditions there at first hand.

I record these matters here because many of the documents included in this volume date from those years, and were written against the background of those events.

The attentive reader will of course notice changes in my attitudes towards specific issues, both musical and of a more general nature, during the nearly fifty years covered by these papers. Some of these changes are the result of developing familiarity and understanding on the purely artistic level; in other cases they reflect a growing skepticism regarding certain aspects of our culture as they revealed themselves under the impact of world events in a period which, in the immensity of its turmoils and its problems, has no parallel in recorded history. I have however managed to retain an essential faith in the future, and believe this also must be clear from the contents of this book.

Once more, my deepest thanks to Professor Cone, to the Princeton University Press for its willingness to publish this book, and notably also to Margot Cutter who has been so cooperative in overseeing its publication.

ROGER SESSIONS

Princeton, New Jersey
March 1978

I

The Composer's Craft

The Composer and His Message
[1939]

Originally delivered as one of the Spencer Trask Lectures at Princeton University in the Fall of 1939. The series, entitled "The Intent of the Artist," also included lectures by Sherwood Anderson, William Lescaze, and Thornton Wilder.

THE fact that a composer, in speaking of music, speaks primarily or indeed exclusively as a practitioner, may easily seem too obvious to mention. It is a fact, however, that the critic, the historian, even the musical theorist are familiar figures on the American scene. With inevitably varying degrees of success, they fill the rôle of articulate mediators between the public at large and the wares offered it by a multitude of purveyors. In a very real sense, they form the conscious ideas of the public regarding music, and determine, or at least influence profoundly, the character of American musical life.

The composer, on the other hand, is a shadowy and often inarticulate figure whose activities and whose processes of thought remain mysterious and almost legendary. He speaks very rarely, except to his colleagues, about his art; when he does so, he frequently either, through lack of initiative, adopts the language and tone of the critic or the musico-literary rhapsodist, or speaks in terms accessible only to those versed in the technical mysteries. It is indeed difficult to avoid these extremes, since music, although at least as popular, and—as I shall try to show later—still more primitive in its sources than the other arts, is by its very

From *The Intent of the Artist* by Augusto Centeno (ed.) (copyright 1941 by Princeton University Press, extended to December 31, 2016), pp. 101-134. Reprinted by permission.

nature less obviously connected with the everyday experience of the layman, hence less easy of access. Even if the layman is so exceptional as never to have tried to express himself accurately and vividly in words, or experimented in at least the rudiments of design, modelling, or construction, these activities, closely bound up as they are with visible and conscious experience, are easily apprehended by him.

It is not however my object at this point to draw a distinction between the composer and his fellow artists in other fields, but rather to call attention to the fact that his activities, precisely like theirs, belong in the sphere of action and not of thought. He is, like them, a *doer* and a *maker*, not a *thinker*. He is therefore sharply differentiated in his approach to his art from the critic, historian, or musical theorist. In saying this I am not, of course, drawing attention to a purely professional distinction. Many composers have been active as critics and theorists, and in fact it is to composers that we owe a tremendous proportion of what has been most illuminating and most enduring in these fields. The composer's point of departure, however, is entirely different from—perhaps is even opposed to—that of the scientific scholar or thinker. It is based not on careful analysis, weighing, and comparison of facts, but at best on an insight, born of intense and active experience, into the nature of the materials and the creative processes of his art.

The insight of which I have spoken springs, however, from a very personal experience and may as a result be easily subject to the limitations of personality. A musical composition is a *deed*, and as such, the result of intense and single-minded conviction. Consequently the composer's judgments are often distinguished by intensity rather than breadth of vision; they are intuitions, rather than opinions, and derive their vitality as well as their evidential value from the very fact that they are born of intensely felt experience of artistic materials and impulses, just as the value of the critic's judgments derives from the fact that

4

they are, presumably, the reasoned products of an observation which has objectivity as one of its aims.

The composer is therefore, in his nature as such, a man of faith and conviction, in distinction to the critic or theorist, who is essentially, and in the original sense of the word, a skeptic. It is true that such distinctions can never be absolute; not only do pure types scarcely ever exist, but it is certainly not desirable that they should. A critic can scarcely form valid judgments in the absence of intense experience of the works with which he has to deal; he cannot form any judgments whatever in the absence of the values which result from the very faith which the artist embodies in his work. Conversely, the personality of the mature artist—and an artist cannot achieve real stature without maturity—is formed, like that of any other mature being, partly through reflection on both what he sees around him and what he has experienced within himself. It is for this reason that, contrary to an oft-quoted opinion, first-class artists are so often first-class critics, and that first-class critics are necessarily those who share the essential nature of the creative artist to an extent sufficient to enable them to understand him.

The composer, then, like his fellow artists, is essentially a *doer*, a shaper of materials. What are these materials, what is their essential nature and what are the shapes that result? What, finally, are the psychological processes that go into their making?

I do not, of course, intend to explore here the physical nature of sound, the mysteries of the musical ear, or the subtleties of musical language. These are matters with which only the teacher and the student need concern themselves, and in which we have ample evidence that slight knowledge is dangerous. I propose rather to make certain observations regarding the materials of music in their psychological essence; to give a few suggestions regarding what these materials mean to the composer and, by inference, also to his most enlightened audience. It is hardly necessary for me to point out that such a picture as can be given within the limits of a short essay can be scarcely more than a rough and incomplete sketch, which demands infinite qualification and nuance if it is to become even coherent.

What, then, is the essential element in music which differentiates it from the other "fine arts"? I do not wish to raise here questions which belong properly to the philosopher. I have sometimes wondered, however, whether the various human products generally grouped together under the term "fine arts" have as much in common as this classification would seem to indicate. What has the impulse of the painter or the architect really in common with that of the composer? and is literature, which seems on the surface, by virtue of its vast range, to include so much from all of the other arts, not in reality something essentially different from any of them? At all events, for the purposes of clear definition, I would like to dwell on their differences and to ignore for the moment the prevalent assumption of a common basis.

It seems to me that the essential medium of music, the basis of its expressive powers and the element which gives it its unique quality among the arts, is *time*, made living for us through its expressive essence, *movement*.

Music is apprehended through the ear; the visual arts, painting, sculpture, and architecture, through the eye. Is there not, more than a difference in function, a genuine and essential contrast in content, between what the eye sees and what the ear hears? I am speaking, of course, not in terms of science, but of ordinary experience. The visual arts govern a world of space, and it seems to me that perhaps the profoundest sensation which we derive from space is not so much that of extension as of permanence. On the most primitive level we feel space to be something permanent, fundamentally unchangeable; when movement is apprehended through the eye it takes place, so to speak, within a static framework, and the psychological impact of this framework is much more powerful than that of the vibrations which occur within its limits. For our experience the visual arts are undifferentiated in time. When we cease to look at a painting or a statue, it nevertheless continues to exist; it undergoes no perceptible change while we are looking at it, and we find it unchanged when we return to it after absence. We may contemplate it as long as we like, and though continued or repeated contemplation will make us familiar with more and more of its details or characteristics, these features have been present from the start, even to our eyes; it is our consciousness, following its own laws and not those of the object itself, which has developed. And when through these or other visual arts movement is suggested, it is through energy implied but not expressed.

Literature, to be sure, takes place in time, and in poetry and the drama time is, to a certain extent as in music, controlled. But even in poetry time is only a part, and a relatively small part, of the total expression; to a far greater extent than in music it is variable according to the will of the interpreter; its subtle rhythms, moreover, are subject to the laws of speech and of concrete literary sense. The real medium of literature is language, as shaped by the literary imagination. One of the expressive elements of language is rhythm, which is employed by the poet as an active, controlled medium in order to heighten its effect. I venture to say, however, that only in rare and fleeting instances does movement assume the whole or even the principal expressive burden.

In speaking of musical movement, on the other hand, we do not refer to rhythm alone, but rather to music as a complete and essentially indivisible whole. In this connection it is relevant to compare our ordinary experience of sound, the medium of musical movement, with the experience of space as I have described it above. If our visual experience is primarily of the permanent and static, sound, as we are ordinarily aware of it, is essentially of limited duration, fleeting and elusive—and the very essence of our adjustment to it is closely bound up with this fact. We cannot escape from it without fleeing its presence; and if it assumes anything like unchanging permanence this is such an exceptional occurrence that either we become quickly unaware of it, or it becomes intolerable. Sound for us, in other words, is naturally and inextricably associated with our sensation of time.

Time becomes real to us primarily through movement, which I have called its expressive essence; and it is easy to trace our primary musical responses to the most primitive movement of our being—to those movements which are indeed at the very basis of animate existence. The feeling for tempo, so often derived from the dance, has in reality a much more primitive basis in the involuntary movements of the nervous system and the body in the beating of the heart, and more consciously in breathing, later in walking. Accelerated movement is, from these very obvious causes, inevitably associated with excitement, retarded movement with a lessening of dynamic tension. The experience of meter has the most obvious and essential of its origins in the movements of breathing, with its alternation of upward and downward movements. The sense of effort, preparation, suspense, which is the psychological equivalent of the up-beat, finds its prototype in the act of inhalation, and the sense of weight, release, and finality produced by the down-beat corresponds most intimately to the act of exhalation. "In the beginning was rhythm," remarked Hans von Bülow; another distinguished musician remarked later that life begins, according to this above analogy, with an up-beat, the first breath of the newborn child corresponding to the preparatory anacrusis of a musical statement, and ends, like the most natural and satisfying rhythm, with a down-beat.

The other primary elements of music—melody and rhythm—derive from more complicated but only slightly less essential muscular movements, which, it has been fairly well demonstrated, are reproduced in miniature by the human nervous system in response to musical impressions. If we instinctively respond to a rising melodic pitch by a feeling of increased tension and hence of heightened ex-

8

pression, or a falling pitch by the opposite sensation; if an increase in intensity of sound intensifies our dynamic response to the music, and vice versa, it is because we have already in our vocal experiences—the earliest and most primitive as well as later and more complicated ones—lived intimately through exactly the same effects. A raising of pitch or an increase in volume is the result of an intensification of effort, energy, and emotional power in the crying child just as truly as in the highly evolved artistry of a Fedor Chaliapin or a Marian Anderson.

Similarly, our feeling for rhythm, in the stricter sense, derives from the subtle and more expressive nervous and muscular movements, such as occur in speech, song, gesture, and the dance. A melodic phrase, for instance, is analogous psychologically to a vocal phrase, even though, because of its range, its length, or its specific technical demands, it may be realizable only on instruments; it must be thought, by the interpreter as well as the listener, "in one breath"— that is to say, with a psychological energy and control, precisely analogous to that with which the singer or orator husbands his vocal resources and controls his breathing, according to the expressive curve of melody or rhetorical declamation. The association between music and dancing is probably even older than that between music and words, and needs no further illustration here; the point I wish to make is that the basic elements of our musical sense, of musical expression, hence of music itself, have their sources in the most primitive regions of our being. In this sense music is the oldest, just as in a quite other sense it is the youngest, of the arts; the primary sensations on which it is based antedate in human experience those of visual perception and, to a still greater extent, those of language.

On a still less primitive level than melody or rhythm as such, we meet with the one basic element of music which is not derived directly from movement. This element, harmony, has its origins in the nature of musical sound itself rather than in the impulses of the human organism. Already in speaking of *musical* sound we have moved far from the primitive elements to which I have drawn attention; we have in fact taken note of a stage in the process of their *organization*. When the ear has learned to discriminate between musical "tone" and undifferentiated sound, it has already achieved a high degree of refinement and begun to shape its raw materials into something approaching a controlled medium of expression. The musical tone, however, is not a simple sound but a complex of sounds. It is this fact which, apprehended by the musical ear at an advanced stage in its development, leads to the elaboration of an always more complex set of relationships between sounds, and thereby opens up still further and more decisive possibilities of organization. Speaking for the moment in historical terms, it was only about 1600 that the harmonic sense reached maturity: it was at approximately the same period that music loosed itself from exclusive association with words and gesture, and achieved complete autonomy. From the purely technical standpoint, it was the development of the harmonic sense which made this possible. For this enriched the composer's vocabulary by revealing to him new possibilities in the combination of sounds; through these possibilities, derived from the physical nature of the tone itself, it provided him with a point of departure which enabled the ear to find its way through the intricacies of a much vaster tonal design than had ever been dreamed of before. In other words, it added incalculable resources to musical expression, by making possible an infinitely more complex, more supple, and more finely differentiated musical movement.

Harmony, then, more than any other musical element, brings to music the possibility of extension, of larger design, by reason of the well-nigh inexhaustible wealth and variety of tonal relationships which it embraces—and these relationships, as I have said before, have their origin in the unity of the tone itself. I have no intention of entering at this point on a detailed discussion of what musicians call "tonality." It is one of the most intricate and elusive of technical questions, and today so problematical that the term itself must needs be exactly and carefully defined before any fruitful or illuminating discussion can take place. What is not problematical is the psychological need which the principle of tonality, or key, fulfills; the necessity for a unifying organization in the sphere of sound, just as tempo and meter constitute a unifying principle in that of rhythm. Movement becomes expressive only if its directions are clear. To this end points of reference are necessary; suffice it to say that each new development in music has created, on a convincing psychological basis, its own points of reference. Without them, music would hardly be possible. One of the most vivid and effective means by which this is accomplished in music is harmony, with all that this implies.

If the above be true, it will be seen that harmony brings into music its only inherently static element. I have stated that it rests in principle on relationships implicit in the nature of a single tone. The extension and elaboration of these relationships gives musical movement an endless variety and nuance. The unity from which they are derived, however, and their constant implicit reference to that unity, gives them a psychologically compulsive power, an inherent sense of direction which is one of the most compelling expressive means at the composer's disposal. The tensions which it creates in the minds of the hearer are of the very essence of musical expression, and serve admirably to illustrate the real psychological character of what I have called "movement" in music.

Let me take as an illustration the opening bars of the *Tristan* Prelude—an admirable illustration, because the composer has told us so clearly what the music intends to convey—hopeless, unsatisfied longing. Please observe these points: First, the expression is attained by raising the tensions of which I have spoken to the highest degree of vividness and force. Secondly, the tension is achieved not by purely harmonic means, but rather by the interplay of several other musical means, of which I have mentioned only the most essential. Finally, in their entirety, they constitute a coherent musical design, achieved through the cumulative growth of a harmonic impression, and through the association of musical ideas in the repetition of a musical pattern.

In analyzing these measures we must not forget that we are dealing with living materials, and that such analysis has therefore to do only with the effect which the music produces, not necessarily with the conscious intentions of the composer. The music is a *gesture*, the result of at least as many complex forces, impulses, and experiences, both individual and general, as every other gesture. Like every other gesture it is essentially indivisible, and while we can, obviously, note certain of its elements, we must nevertheless remain constantly aware of the fact that we are not thereby revealing its whole or even its essential meaning. Analysis, whether technical, historical, or—according to the latest fashions—psycho-sociological, may reveal some of the effects which art produces and some of the means through which these effects are produced. Beyond this it remains mere speculation, certainly without artistic and possibly without scientific validity. For art consists neither of devices, supposed "influences," nor mere reflections of the artist's inner life.

With due consciousness of such limitations, then, let us examine the passage in question.

Its four well defined sections are indicated in the present text by brackets. If the third bracketed section seems disproportionately long, it is nevertheless obvious that the repetition of the same notes in measures 11, 13, 14, and 15 illustrate clearly to the eye what is still clearer to the ear— the fact that these measures serve to prolong and intensify this musical moment, without introducing any essential changes. Measures 12 and 13, to be specific, repeat at a higher octave the two preceding measures, while measures 14 and 15, in the same two octaves, recall the concluding beat of the phrase and thus prolong still further both its harmony and its expressive effect. I shall refer presently to this prolongation and to its expressive significance.

Each of the four bracketed parts is based on the same musical phrase. This does not mean that the phrase is literally repeated or that, even in the second phrase, it is literally transposed. It means however that the general outlines, the accent, the inflection, are in each case so similar as to leave no doubt in the hearer's mind that each successive phrase is a repetition, with equal or greater intensity, of the same musical gesture.

Let us look, then, at the phrase itself in its original form. Note the long F of the 'cello at the beginning of the first measure, and the long G♯ of the oboe at the beginning of the second. Each of these notes is extraneous to the harmony, and each creates a feeling of suspense which is not resolved till the very end of the measure. The expression of the F is enhanced by the long crescendo which is so familiar to all who have heard this music; the G♯ by an accent and by the dissonant chord which accompanies it. In the third measure the dissonant A♯, again, slightly delays the note, B, which belongs to the harmony.

The effect may be grasped more vividly by looking at the underlying harmonies themselves:

The three notes in question—F, G♯, and A♯—not only give the melodic line flexibility and a certain degree of freedom; they also, by delaying in each case the entrance of the expected harmonic note, draw special attention to that note, and thus intensify both the note itself and the harmony which supports it. Above all, they help in these instances by their very length to create and sustain a feeling of suspense, which is the essence of the expression to which I referred above.

Let us look further, however, at the harmonies themselves. They form what musicians know as an "uncompleted cadence" in the key of A minor. This means that to the normal musical ear they produce the effect of a question which is left temporarily, at least, unanswered. We expect, after the last of the chords quoted in the preceding example,

the chord of A, and in its minor form. Why this is so I shall not attempt to explain here. The answer leads into the most fundamental problems of music, aesthetics, and even acoustics. Let me draw attention, instead, to the paramount importance of the final harmony in each phrase. Its position as the conclusion of the phrase makes of it inevitably, by the fundamental laws of rhythm, the goal of the harmonic impulse and thus the point at which the harmonic expression of the phrase is, so to speak, accumulated.

In the present case it may be observed that this final chord—E, G♯, D, B—leaves the hearer temporarily at least in a state of suspense, and that this is further enhanced by the long pause which follows. The E on which the chord is based is known to musicians as the "dominant" of A; among the tonal relationships which the composer, through the technical means at his disposal has set up, the E, at the interval of a fifth above A, is second in importance to the A itself; and through these relationships the listener has been given the almost instinctive desire, or at least the expectation, that the A will follow in the bass, along with the upper notes which complete its chord.

What does follow, I shall not describe in complete detail. The same processes within this phrase are repeated in their essentials in the two following phrases. The 'cello in each case takes its note from the final harmony of the preceding phrase, and each statement in its turn intensifies, through sheer repetition in the first case, through slight variation in the second, the expression of the initial gesture. But what is more important is the binding principle which, far more than the so-called "thematic development" of the phrase itself, welds the whole passage into a single gesture of much larger proportions.

In other words, the expressive meaning of these seventeen measures is embodied in a design which makes of them a single unit. It is fairly easy, for example, to follow the upper voice from each phrase to the following one, which begins with the same note on which its predecessor left off; the ear follows without difficulty the connection between the B in measure 3 and that in measure 6, between D in measure 7 and that in measure 10. It recognizes, in the first two notes (E♯-F♯) of measure 16, the notes of the preceding measures, to which I have already drawn attention. A closer examination of the passage as a whole would reveal other connections of the same type, attributable not so much to the "technical" prowess of the composer as to the absolutely unhampered and consistent intensity of his musical thought.

These, however, are only details in their relation to a large harmonic design, itself a prolongation of the "dominant seventh" harmony of A minor, to which reference was made above. I have already referred to the fact that the harmonic sense of a phrase reaches its point of greatest concentration in the final harmony of the phrase; and no clearer illustration of this fact could be given, than the passage included in the third bracket, where the final harmony is prolonged by repetition, first together with the measure which resolves into it (12-13), and then, by a double repetition of the melodic pattern of this final measure itself (14-15).

The emphasis on this harmony underlines the fact that we have here reached, so to speak, the harmonic climax of the whole passage—the moment of greatest tension. What has happened? The answer to this question may be grasped in the clearest fashion by repeating in close succession the final harmonies of the three phrases, the significance of which I have already noted. It will be seen that the basic notes of these harmonies progress in two successive steps from E, which we have already defined as the "dominant" of A minor, to B, the upper fifth and quasi-dominant of E, and that if taken together they form the chord of E minor, with B as its culminating point. The B harmony therefore creates, so to speak, a new level of expressive suspense which is intensified or, in the language of sheer design,

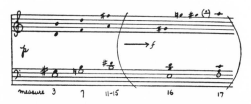

underlined, by the prolongation, described above, of the harmony in question.

The expressive process becomes quite clear in measure 16 where the entrance, *forte*, of the original E chord brings a temporary sense of resolution; a closing, so to speak, of the harmonic circuit. These sixteen measures may in fact be considered as a vast elaboration of this harmony, the "dominant seventh chord" (E-G♯-B-D) of A minor. This harmony, in other words, is developed in such a way that its inner structure is utilized with a maximum expressive effect, constituting not only the coordinating center, but the very expressive essence, of the passage in question.

I have dwelt at such length on the harmonic aspect of the passage simply because it is the most difficult to describe in words which convey a meaning except to the technically initiated. No less important to the whole effect is the steady upward unfolding of the chromatic scale, beginning with G♯ in measure 2, moving first from G♯ to B, B to D, D to F♯, and then through G♯ in measure 16. These sixteen measures may thus in a sense be considered, through this chromatic traversal of a complete octave, as in the upper or melodic voice, an elaboration of the G♯. This melodic effect is in actual fact, of course, inseparable from the harmonic effect already described. The G♯ is not only an ingredient of the dominant seventh E, G♯, B, and D but in a sense its most active ingredient, since it is the so-called "leading-tone" of the key—i.e., the tone directly below the key note or tonic, and one which, as musical theorists are wont to say, always tends upward to this key note—in this case of course A. In other words this G♯ in the upper voice enhances in the greatest measure the expressive effect of the "dominant seventh" harmony.

Both the chord and the G♯ find their resolution in measure 17. Here, however, one may observe another harmonic principle, which dominates the whole prelude, and which embodies still further the expressive principle of suspense. As I have pointed out, the expected resolution is, in the case of the G♯, the "tonic" A, and in the case of the "dominant seventh" chord, the tonic chord of A minor as illustrated above. By means of what is called the "deceptive cadence," however, the suspense is prolonged and heightened through the substitution of another harmony—in this case the chord of F—while the G♯ is resolved to A (preceded by B) in quite normal fashion. Examination of the whole Prelude will reveal the fact that the expected resolution never takes place, and careful analysis would show a profound connection between this fact, and the expressive impact and character of the whole.

I have brought forward this illustration in order to show certain aspects of what I have called "movement" in music, and in doing so, I have touched upon the question of musical expression. What is it, actually, that music expresses?

Let us consider for a moment the music to which I have just referred. It is associated in Wagner's drama with a definite situation, with definite characters—hence we are accustomed to say it "expresses" the tragic love of Tristan and Isolde. Is it, however, the music that tells us this? Does it tell us anything, in any definite and inevitable sense, of love and tragedy? How much of what is implied in this definition of its content is there by virtue of its association with the drama? Is this association an inevitable one, or is it in the last analysis arbitrary?

The music certainly tells us nothing specifically about Tristan and Isolde, as concrete individuals; in no sense does it identify them or enlighten us regarding the concrete situation in which they find themselves. Does it tell us, then, specifically, anything about love and tragedy which we could identify as such without the aid of the dramatic and poetic images with which Wagner so richly supplies us?

It seems to me that the answer in each case is, inevitably, a negative one. There is, in any specific sense, neither love nor tragedy in the music.

I have attempted a description of this music in terms of movement. I have tried to point out how intimately our musical impulses are connected with those primitive movements which are among the very conditions of our existence. I have tried to show, too, how vivid is our response to the primitive elements of musical movement.

Is not this the key both to the content of music and to its extraordinary power? These bars from the Prelude to Tristan do not express for us love or frustration or even longing: but they reproduce for us, both qualitatively and dynamically, certain gestures of the spirit which are to be sure less specifically definable than any of these emotions, but which energize them and make them vital to us.

So it seems to me that this is the essence of musical expression. "Emotion" is specific, individual and conscious; music goes deeper than this, to the energies which animate our psychic life, and out of these creates a pattern which has an existence, laws, and human significance of its own. It reproduces for us the most intimate essence, the tempo and the energy, of our spiritual being; our tranquility and our restlessness, our animation and our discouragement, our vitality and our weakness—all, in fact, of the fine shades of dynamic variation of our inner life. It reproduces these far more directly and more specifically than is possible through any other medium of human communication.

In saying this I do not wish to deny that there is also an associative element in musical expression, or that this has its very definite place in certain types of music. It must be remembered that the emergence of music as an entirely

separate art has been, as I have pointed out, of very recent
origin; that until the last three hundred years it was always
connected with more concrete symbols, whether of the
word or the dance. It is but natural, therefore, that this
associative element should form a part of the composer's
medium. It is, however, I believe, not an essential part,
especially since it consists so largely in associations which
have their basis in movement. Quiet, lightly contrasted
movement, for instance, may be associated with outer as well
as inner tranquility—the light rustling of leaves in the wind,
or the movement of a tranquil sea—just as agitated movement may be employed to suggest the storms in nature, as
well as the perturbations of the spirit. On the other hand, we
meet with associations of a far less essential nature—the tone
of the trumpet, for instance, suggesting martial ideas; or certain localisms—folk songs, exotic scales, bizarre instrumental
combinations, etc.—which are used for the purposes of specific and literal coloring. But one would hardly attach more
than a very superficial musical significance to associations of
this type. They belong definitely in the sphere of applied
art, and when they occur in works of serious import they
serve, in conformity with an expressed intention of the composer, in a decidedly subordinate capacity, to direct the
listener to more concrete associations than the music, in its
essential content, can convey.

The above considerations indicate why a certain type of
literary rhapsody seems to the musician quite amateurish
and beside the point, in spite of the fact that musicians
themselves—even great ones—have occasionally indulged
in it. At best it is a literary production, bearing no real
relationship to the music and throwing no real light on its
content, but expressing the literary impulses of the author
with more or less significance, according to his personality.
Thus it is that of three distinguished commentators on
Beethoven's Seventh Symphony—all three of them composers, and two of them composers of genius—one finds it
a second *Eroica*, another a second *Pastorale*, and the third
"the apotheosis of the dance." It must not be forgotten that,

for the composer, notes, chords, melodic intervals—all the musical materials—are far more real, far more expressive, than words; that, let us say, a "leading tone" or a chord of the subdominant are for him not only notes, but sensations, full of meaning and capable of infinite nuances of modification; and that when he speaks or thinks in terms of them he is using words which, however obscure and dry they may sound to the uninitiated, are for him fraught with dynamic sense.

So, in trying to understand the work of the composer, one must first think of him as living in a world of sounds, which in response to his creative impulse become animated with movement. The first stage in his work is that of what is generally known by the somewhat shopworn and certainly unscientific term "inspiration." The composer, to use popular language again, "has an idea"—an idea, let me make clear, consisting of definite musical notes and rhythms, which will engender for him the momentum with which his musical thought proceeds. The inspiration may come in a flash, or as sometimes happens, it may grow and develop gradually. I have in my possession photostatic copies of several pages of Beethoven's sketches for the last movement of his "Hammerklavier Sonata"; the sketches show him carefully modelling, then testing in systematic and apparently cold-blooded fashion, the theme of the fugue. Where, one might ask, is the inspiration here? Yet if the word has any meaning at all, it is certainly appropriate to this movement, with its irresistible and titanic energy of expression, already present in the theme. The inspiration takes the form, however, not of a sudden flash of music, but a clearly-envisaged impulse toward a certain goal for which the composer was obliged to strive. When this perfect realization was attained, however, there could have been no hesitation—rather a flash of recognition that this was exactly what he wanted.

Inspiration, then, is the impulse which sets creation in movement: it is also the energy which keeps it going. The composer's principal problem is that of recapturing it in every phase of his work; of bringing, in other words, the requisite amount of energy to bear on every detail, as well as, constantly, on his vision of the whole.

This vision of the whole I should call the conception. For the musician this too takes the form of concrete musical materials—perceived, however, not in detail but in fore-shortened form. The experience, I believe, is quite different for the mature and experienced composer from what it is for the young beginner. As he grows in practice and imagination it assumes an ever more preponderant rôle, and appears more and more to be the essential act of creation. It differs from what I have described as "inspiration" only in works of large dimensions which cannot be realized in a short space of time. It arises out of the original inspiration, and is, so to speak, an extension of its logic.

What I have described as inspiration, embodies itself in what is the only true sense of the word "style"; conception, in the only true sense of the word "form." Neither style nor form, in its essence, is derived from convention; they always must be, and are, created anew, and establish and follow their own laws. It is undeniable that certain periods —and the most fortunate ones—have established clearly defined patterns or standards which give the artist a basis on which to create freely. Our own is not one of these; today the individual is obliged to discover his own language before he has completed the mastery of it. Where such standards exist, however, they retain their vitality only as long as they are in the process of development. After this process has stopped, they wither and die, and can be re-created only by a conscious and essentially artificial effort, since they are produced by a unique and unrecoverable impulse, and are suited only to the content which has grown with them.

After inspiration and conception comes execution. The process of execution is first of all that of listening inwardly to the music as it shapes itself; of allowing the music to grow; of following both inspiration and conception wherever they may lead. A phrase, a motif, a rhythm, even a chord, may contain within itself, in the composer's imagination, the energy which produces movement. It will lead the composer on, through the force of its own momentum or tension, to other phrases, other motifs, other chords.

The principles underlying what is generally called musical structure are not briefly or easily formulated. We may, however, easily observe certain general characteristics which are always present in music and which seem inseparable from its nature as an art of movement.

Primary among these is the principle of *association*. I use the term here in a purely musical sense; certain features of the music must recur, and they gain their significance through the fact of their recurrence. The famous first four notes of Beethoven's Fifth Symphony, in spite of the various literary interpretations attached to them, have no possible significance by themselves. To be sure they remind us, who are familiar with musical literature, inevitably of Beethoven—but in the absence of all association they would have no meaning whatever. Musically, they begin to have significance only when they are followed by four other notes, similar in tempo, accent, and interval, but differing slightly in pitch and by this fact becoming, so to speak, the vehicle of movement. The accented E flat, in the second measure, is carried through this associative means downward to the D in the fourth measure. The sense of this motion is the direct result of the association of measures three and four with a parallel passage in the first two measures.

Obviously, such an example is rudimentary in the extreme and serves only to illustrate the principle in its simplest form; to show in some slight measure how association brings to music significance and coherence, and how, through its means, musical movement may be organized on a vaster basis than is possible within the limits of a single phrase. It would be possible of course to proceed with an analysis of the whole first movement of the Symphony and to show how, later, certain variations or transformations of the motif play an important and fateful rôle in introducing contrasts or in intensifying the dynamic outlines.

The Composer's Craft

It is necessary, I feel, to draw a careful distinction between the *psychological* principle of association and the purely material one of repetition, even though the former so often takes shape as the latter in its most literal sense. The classic composers had the finest of instincts in this respect and their art is incredibly rich in resource and variety of associative means. Some of their successors, unfortunately, are more literal minded, often substituting a materialistic principle of repetition for the creative principle of association, and later music finds itself in this respect as in others frequently caught in the toils of a sterile academicism. Artistic form has vitality and coherence only as long as its vitalizing principle is the imagination and impulse of the composer; it withers and dies as soon as the "materials" of music assume an independent existence—a condition which is possible only when the genuine creative impulse is weak.

Closely allied to the principle of association is that of *progression*. This is so obvious, in an art which has its basis in time, as scarcely to need mention. To say that in such an art each individual moment must be, generally speaking, of greater intensity and significance than the one which precedes it, is perhaps a truism. Less obvious and more difficult to describe are the infinitely various means through which progression is achieved. The two examples already given, however—the *Tristan* Prelude and the opening bars of the Fifth Symphony—illustrate the principle as clearly as possible; and, indeed, the analysis of each, even from quite different points of view, was largely concerned precisely with the gradual and progressive movement toward a clearly envisaged goal, and, especially in the case of the *Tristan* Prelude, the steady intensification of effect until this goal is reached.

In music of large design, the various elements group themselves into larger patterns. In the passage from the *Tristan* Prelude, we have seen how four short phrases contribute to the unfolding of a sort of superphrase, as clear and expressive in its highly organized outline as the simple primitive vocalization which is the origin and the basis of music. Such organization is, of course, indispensable to music of large dimensions.

I will mention, finally, a third principle, that of *contrast*. In the sense in which I use the word it denotes something quite other than what I have called progression. The latter term applies, obviously, to the development of a single impulse and is the process by which the impulse takes extended shape. When the impulse is complete, however, other necessities appear, and the need for contrast arises. What form the contrast shall take—whether the same materials shall be presented under different aspects, or whether a quite new departure is needed—such questions and the infinite degrees of difference which they include, depend upon the conception, the context, and the scope of the work in question. The large contrasts contained in a work of music, however, reveal its essential outlines and give it its largest rhythm, through the alternation of musical ideas with their contrasting movement, emphasis, and dynamic intensity.

From these remarks it may be inferred quite clearly that conception and execution are inseparable and in the last analysis identical. "Form" in music is identical with "content," regardless of whether the latter be significant or the former coherent. The actual process of composition remains mysterious—the composer is following, as best he can and with all the means at his disposal, the demands of his conception, listening for the sounds and rhythms which embody it, and giving them the shape which his creative vision prescribes.

The question is frequently asked, how far is the composer "conscious" while he is composing? Of what is he thinking, what are his feelings? The answer, I think, is contained in my opening remarks. Composition is a *deed*, an action, and a genuine action of any kind is, psychologically speaking, the simplest thing in the world. Is not its subjective essence intentness on the deed? The climber in the high mountains is intent on the steps he is taking, on the practical realization of those steps; if he allows his consciousness to dwell even on their implications, his foot may move the fatal half inch too far in the direction of the abyss at his side. The composer working at his music is faced with no such tragic alternatives; but his psychology is not dissimilar. He is not so much conscious of his ideas as possessed by them. Very often he is unaware of his exact processes of thought till he is through with them; extremely often the completed work is incomprehensible to him immediately after it is finished.

Why? Because his experience in creating the work is incalculably more intense than any later experience he can have from it; because the finished product is, so to speak, the goal of that experience and not in any sense a repetition of it. He cannot relive the experience without effort which seems quite irrelevant. And yet he is too close to it to detach himself to the extent necessary to see his work objectively, and to allow it to exert its inherent power over him.

For this reason I have always profoundly disagreed with the definition made by one of my most distinguished living colleagues who, elaborating Aristotle's famous definition of art, wrote that art on the highest level is concerned with *"der Wiedergabe der inneren Natur"*—literally translated, "the reproduction of inner nature." It seems to me on the contrary, that art is a function, an activity of the inner nature—that the artist's effort is, using the raw and undisciplined materials with which his inner nature provides him, to endow them with a meaning which they do not of themselves possess—to transcend them by giving them artistic form. Is not this what a far greater musician, Beethoven, meant, in the words quoted by Bettina Brentano: *"Rührung passt nur an Frauenzimmer (verzeih'mir); dem Manne muss Musik Feuer aus dem Geiste schlagen"*—"Emotion is fit only for women—for man, music must strike fire from his mind."

Music in Crisis
[1933]

SOME NOTES ON RECENT MUSICAL HISTORY

THERE can no longer be any question that music, like every other manifestation of Western culture, stands under the sign of crisis. The situation has been developing for decades; nearly a century ago the most sensitive observers were already aware that some such crisis was approaching. But what has, until recently, been visible only to the most far-flung spirits has since the war become an increasingly obvious and menacing fact, with the most concrete and actual implications. The reactionary tendency observable in every country during the past two musical seasons is only the latest and one of the most superficial symptoms of an underlying condition; though its intrinsic importance must not be over-estimated, it is obviously the reaction of a public which for the first time in musical history feels itself increasingly out of touch, not with this or that contemporary composer, but with "modern music" itself.

The active musical tendencies of the past ten years have all been, in their several ways, efforts in the direction of meeting this crisis. In speaking of them it should never be forgotten that the development of art is a living, organic process, not to be defined accurately in terms of "movements," "reactions," and "tendencies." Such definitions are for the most part approximations adopted, with a rather deadly concreteness, not by protagonists but by spectators;

From *Modern Music*, vol. 10, no. 2, pp. 63-78. Reprinted by permission of the League of Composers—International Society for Contemporary Music, U.S. Section, Inc.

in order to understand what is really happening one must get behind the definitions to facts, which then must be viewed in perspective. Such formulas have their practical usefulness, no doubt; but they have also the fundamental falseness of all attempts to classify matter which is stubbornly alive and constantly developing.

One must exercise a certain caution, moreover, in regard to the utterances of composers themselves. The creative activity is essentially practical rather than theoretical, and like all practical natures the artist is necessarily absorbed in his own problems, even though occasionally, as in the case for instance of Wagner, he is capable of making vital generalizations as well. But impersonality represents, for the artist perhaps even more than for others, a great effort of will and understanding; he is generally unable to foresee clearly what his future development will be, and at the same time must believe with fanatical seriousness in what he is doing, even though he may have quite other preoccupations as soon as he has surmounted the problems in hand. "Do I contradict myself?" wrote Walt Whitman; "very well then, I contradict myself." The testimony of a composer has the authority and the vitality of intensely lived experience but his interpretations of that experience are constantly open to revision, even by himself. Too much weight, therefore should not be attached to his reported casual utterances, nor should too important conclusions be drawn from them.

Perhaps the most obvious symptom of the present crisis is its "confusion of tongues"—the result of nearly a century of musical development before the Great War. What took place during this period was a gradual dissociation of the musical consciousness of Europe (rather, of the Occident) into a multitude of various components. This dissociative process, the last phase of which constituted the "modern music" of twenty years ago, represented for the non-German peoples first of all a breaking-away from the German domination of musical culture, and was the inevitable result of the then latest developments of German music which, as Nietzsche once so penetratingly wrote, had ceased to be "the voice of Europe's soul" and was instead degenerating into mere *Vaterländerei*. Bach and Mozart, Beethoven and Schubert were German composers, to be sure, but not in any sense purely German in significance; Bruckner and Reger, even Strauss and Mahler—even, as Nietzsche points out, Schumann—in a far more restricted sense, were. The "voice of Europe's soul," however, has never yet been truly recovered; the *Vaterländerei* of which Nietzsche saw the fatal beginnings in Germany began to reproduce itself elsewhere in a franker and even more accentuated form, in a quantity of national "schools" of picturesquely local significance; the common cultural heritage began to be abandoned in favor of localisms, until by the end of the century a very definite cleavage was perceptible.

The earlier years of our century brought definite signs of an even smaller division; a tendency toward an increasing number of purely individualistic and esoteric musical cults. Artists began to arise who no longer represented even a single land or a local culture, but rather isolated and even rootless yearnings of various kinds. "Prophets crying in the wilderness," unrecognized geniuses, the only defect of whose messages was their fatal subjectivity, appeared by the dozen; smaller spiritual stepsons of Wagner who, from an isolation essentially far deeper than that of Wagner, shouted their message to a fundamentally indifferent even though sometimes not wholly inattentive world, and who often strained and cracked their voices in the attempt to make themselves seriously heard. This was the age of "new possibilities," new technical devices, new and often quasi-religious aesthetic creeds, symptoms of a fundamental insecurity and a lack of any but a purely passive inner necessity. The artist, taken by and large, was no longer fulfilling a function as the voice of a real community of spirits; he had become rather a dealer in *articles de luxe* for a disabused aristocracy and a self-satisfied bourgeoisie. This type of music is well exemplified in the swollen and frenetically self-important works—not without a certain power—of a Scriabin; solitary orgies in which the once vital paroxysms of a Wagner are transported to a far thinner and more precious atmosphere. The more significant music of that time came to be representative of cities and of groups within cities, rather than of peoples. French music grew more and more essentially Parisian, German music to a certain extent polarized itself in Berlin and Vienna, even in Leipzig and Munich. But unlike the local Italian schools of painting in the Renaissance, these separate schools did not embody locally rooted expressions of a common human aspiration, but rather on the contrary, regional (often perhaps rather fortuitously regional) offshoots from a common background, a dissociative rather than a constructive movement. Many other factors contributed to this process; a constantly more complete rift between "serious" and popular music, the growth of a type of virtuoso whose ideals are more those of the "prima donna" than of the genuinely interpretative artist—all of them, needless to say, factors by no means isolated, but part and parcel of the structure and the very essence of contemporary musical life.

The characteristic music of the post-war years has represented a complete contrast to the tendencies above described, and to some extent, in a very real sense, a reaction against them. That is not to say that the earlier types did not continue to exist, or even to deny the possibility of important figures among them. J. S. Bach is not the only historical example of an artist who in a sense outlived his time and yet who has loomed in the eyes of posterity far larger than any of his "modern" contemporaries. But the general movement since the war has been in a quite opposite direction. The composer who is most truly of today, whatever his nationality or aesthetic creed, is no longer seeking "new possibilities" in the individualistic sense of the pre-war composers, but rather, in so far as he has a conscious program at all, submitting himself to the new *necessities* of his time, and setting himself the new tasks which these necessities demand. The popular classification of "tendencies" of which mention has already been made has served to call attention to the fact of various differences of approach to these problems, even though it has not always thrown a very clear light on their deeper significance.

It is idle to inquire when and by whom the somewhat sweeping and inexact term "neo-classicism" was first applied to certain contemporary tendencies. It has been applied rather disconcertingly to such essentially different composers as Stravinsky, Hindemith, and Casella—composers in each of whom a certain more or less conscious traditionalism (not a new thing in art) is apparent, but who differ widely both in the traditions which they represent, and in the roles which tradition plays in the composition of their styles. There is also sometimes a still more primitive failure to discriminate between the traditionalism which springs from an essential impulse and is animated by a real inner tension, and another traditionalism, also to be found in recent music, which represents the exact contrary of this —a manner, a mode, nourished on *cliché* and fashionable propaganda—a traditionalism of followers and not of independent spirits. It is obviously not the latter that comes into consideration here.

Let us abandon, then, the term "neo-classicism" and consider rather certain features which this term is commonly taken to represent. Many of these features are not traditionalistic in any necessary sense, nor were they so in their origins. The composers in Russia and France who, during the latter half of the last century, made the original break with the specific latter-day German tradition, brought into the varied general current of music a mass of new and at first sometimes not wholly assimilated materials which were in contact with that tradition, or rather with those of its phases against which the break was directed. A more transparent texture, a pronounced emphasis on rhythm and movement, a less emphatic harmonic style, and an instrumentation consisting of sharply defined rather than mixed *timbres*, were characteristic features of this newer music. What it lacked was first of all depth; it was very often music of association, of mood, of color, with relatively little essential and organic inner life of its own. Taken by and large it represented a collection of various *manners* rather than a style; an exploitation of certain nuances of color and sonority rather than a complete vision, a world in which all possible musical ingredients could find their place.

The true classical tradition of the seventeenth, eighteenth and early nineteenth centuries—the tradition which the Western world held in common under the leadership first of Italian and later of German musicians, was such a vision; and it was in a general sense to this tradition that musicians inevitably turned when they felt the need of a less limited and less external musical language and at the same time of that necessary connecting link with the past, without which art can never be more than a poor homunculus, essentially unnourished and incapable of organic growth.

This traditionalism, however, can in no real sense be called a "return to the past." Rather should it be considered in the light of a *reprise de contact*; and, in spite of its prophets, essentially nothing more than a point of departure. It was significant chiefly in that it marked the beginning of an instinctive effort to rediscover certain essential qualities of the older music with a view to applying them to the purposes of the new, an experiencing anew of certain laws which are inherent in the nature of music itself, but which had been lost from view in an increasing subjectivism and tendency to lean, even in "pure" music, more and more on association, sensation, and *Stimmung*.

This traditionalism, then, was essentially a part of a new attitude toward music—new at least for its time. Music began above all to be conceived in a more direct, more impersonal, and more positive fashion; there was a new emphasis on the dynamic, constructive, monumental elements of music, and, so to speak, a revaluation of musical materials. This revaluation has shown itself by no means only in actual compositions; it is perceptible among interpreters also. The function of the interpreter, in fact, has been to some extent reconsidered, and a far greater emphasis is today laid on fidelity to the composer's musical thought than was the case twenty years ago.

It would be inaccurate to define this current, as has been so often done, as an emphasis on "form" at the expense of "content"; it marks rather a change of attitude toward form and content both, which we might describe as a transference of the sphere of consciousness in the creative process. Whereas the earlier tendency was to be more and more conscious in regard to a "meaning behind the notes" and to construct the music according to principles derived from this indirect and not strictly musical source, the composers of the newer music proceeded directly from their musical impulses, seeking to embody these impulses in musical ideas which should have an independent existence of their own, and to develop these ideas according to the impetus inherent in them as musical entities. In other words, with the latter the *musical idea* is the point of departure, whereas with the former extra-musical considerations consciously determine the choice of the idea. The new attitude brought inevitably in its train a new and often laconic form of utterance which was sometimes interpreted as an abandonment of "expression." It was in reality, of course, a new manner of expression, a new sobriety and at its best, as in the finest pages of Stravinsky, a new inwardness. The grandiloquent and neurotic self-importance which characterized so much of the music of the years preceding the war has, in fact, practically disappeared and is only to be found in a few provincial survivals. The contemporary composer, when he wishes to achieve grandeur of utterance, does so by more subtle, monumental means.

It is assuredly false to conceive of music as having in any real sense moved away from "humanity." If it has in specific cases seemed to do so it is the result not of a false aesthetic but of a defect of temperament in the composer. Music—pure music—has, naturally, everything to do with humanity, with the deepest human emotions and experiences. But the nature of this connection has sometimes been apprehended only in the vaguest manner; it is in any case not always so literal or so flat-footed a connection as certain literary gentlemen like to imagine. Images and associations are certainly often aroused by music, especially in those who are unaccustomed or insufficiently gifted musically to enter completely into an inner world where tones are sufficient. To say this is not to deny the value or even the interest of such experiences, but only to insist on their purely subjective nature. The inner experience of the thoroughbred musician who writes "program music" is, of course, an entirely contrary one, being in fact the instinctive translation of non-musical experience into tones, instead of a translation from tones into concrete conceptual terms. The very power of musical emotion lies precisely in the fact that it attaches itself *directly*, without any associational medium, to the most intimate experiences of the hearer; here lies also its universality, since, once a musical idiom is clearly grasped, it is accessible to everyone who lives and feels.

Needless to say, however, a new attitude towards what is technically called musical "form" does not necessarily mean that form in the truest sense has always been achieved. Form in this sense is above all the full experience, to the point of complete fusion, of musical elements, and of the inner experiences behind them. It is present in a phrase, a rhythm, an instrumental trait, as surely as in a whole composition. In much contemporary music the inner experience is indeed there. The music is often *felt* and *heard,* by the composer; but how seldom is it felt and heard through to the limit! The experience behind it is too often explosive and spasmodic; it lacks the "great line" and the sharpness of contour which are the distinguishing—though not always immediately distinguishable—signs of a completely lived musical experience.

While by far the greater part of the more significant contemporary music composed outside of Central Europe, and very much of that composed in Germany as well, may be said to belong in a rough sense to the tendency above described, a large group of composers in the countries once included in the Austrian Empire, together with a perceptible number of Germans, have been following quite other lines. This so-called "Central European" tendency is chiefly embodied in the works of Arnold Schoenberg and his followers, though not strictly confined to them. Like the tendencies already described, it is an extremely complex phenomenon, composed of various contributing elements; while many of its features are of a strictly technical nature, too involved in their implications to be adequately discussed here. Nor must the qualification "Central European" be taken to imply an essentially local or geographical emphasis in the creed itself. Though in our belief it could, for historical reasons, have arisen nowhere else but in Vienna, and represents in fact an inevitable end-stage in Viennese musical culture, it claims for itself a universal validity, a more or less general monopoly, in fact, of what is significant in contemporary music. Far more than any other contemporary tendency it is dominated by a single personality, and its development is closely coincident with that of its leader.

A curious parallel with the beginnings of so-called "neoclassicism" may be seen in the definite formulation by Schoenberg of the constructive principles of his school—the well-known "twelve-tone system." The need for a fresh formal principle in contemporary music was felt, in other words, at very much the same moment by the leading spirits in the musical world and by composers of widely different feeling and background. The age of experiment was clearly over. New resources were at hand in profusion, many of them having been discovered by the very men who now felt the imperative need of absorbing them, organizing them, and wielding them into a new musical language.

The music of Schoenberg and his pupils is still very inadequately known, even to musicians, and at least as much on account of its extreme material complexity as of its emotional content, it will probably for some time continue to be so. It is par excellence music for the "initiated" and it is difficult to see how it can ever reach a "great public."

The "twelve-tone system" has often been decried as a purely cerebral construction; and there is no question that some of its features are extremely dogmatic. It can not be too much stressed, however, that a system of this kind has no real existence apart from the works which embody it; it is the works of Schoenberg and his followers that constitute what is vital in their contribution to contemporary music, not the system under which they are written.

It is necessary, then, to distinguish between Schoenberg, Berg, and Webern, the composers, and Schoenberg the musical theorist—perhaps again between these and Schoenberg the teacher, in personal contact with his pupils. It is to the enormous credit of the latter that his pupils show a wide divergence of styles, and that their work—naturally in the cases of those who have real creative talent and background—bears witness to a profound artistic discipline.

It is hardly necessary to point out that the art of Schoenberg has vital connections with the past. Close acquaintance shows how deeply it is rooted in the chromaticism of *Tristan* and *Parsifal*. This music may in fact be regarded as pre-eminently a logical development of that chromaticism, and the "twelve-tone system" as, in great part, a bold effort to formulate directive laws for its further development.

"Atonality," if its real and not its superficial meaning be understood, is merely another name for that chromaticism and not, as the term would seem to imply, a negation of the necessity for fundamental acoustic unity, based on laws which are the inevitable consequence both of natural phenomena of sound, and of the millennial culture of the Occidental ear. "Tonality" in the old, cadential sense, scarcely exists in any music of the present day, and where it can be said to exist in essence its nature has been so widened and modified as to render it unrecognizable to a composer of the last century. But the ultimate foundations on which the older tonal system was built, since they are inherent in the physical phenomena of resonance, remain unchanged; they can be enormously extended but scarcely modified.

All that is ambiguous and profoundly problematical in the music of Schoenberg is to be traced to its definitely esoteric character. A contemporary German musician whose pronouncements in such matters are as authoritative as they are brilliant and profound, has compared certain musical tendencies in present day Germany to the decadent Greek art of Alexandria, remarking that, "There is an Alexandrianism of profundity and an Alexandrianism of superficiality." "Alexandrianism of profundity," indeed, well defines the music of the Central European group in certain respects—its tortured and feverish moods, its overwhelming emphasis on detail, its lack of genuine movement, all signs of a decaying musical culture, without fresh human impulses to keep it alive. The technique of this music, too, is of a curiously ambiguous nature, and often represents an extraordinary lack of coherence between the music *heard* and, so to speak, its theoretical structure—another sign of an art that is rapidly approaching exhaustion. An orchestral movement, for instance, which is constructed according to the most rigid contrapuntal mathematics will turn out to be, in its acoustic realization, a succession of interesting sonorities without audible contrapuntal implications—an impression not to be dispelled by the most conscientious and sympathetic study of the score, the most complete familiarity with both its intellectual and its sonorous content. An opera whose remarkable feature when heard is its fidelity to the text, its responsiveness to every changing psychological nuance, proves on examination to be constructed in its various scenes on the external models of classic forms, without, however, the steady and consistent movement that gives these forms their purpose and their character. Such esoteric and discarded devices as the *cancrizans* variation of a theme, a technical curiosity which is admittedly inaccessible to the most attentive ear and which was used with the utmost rarity by the classic composers, becomes a regular and essential technical procedure. All of this goes to indicate the presence of a merely speculative element, tending to be completely dissociated from the impression actually received by the ear and the other faculties which contribute to the direct reception of a musical impression, and to produce what is either a fundamentally inessential *jeu d'esprit* of sometimes amazing proportions, or a kind of scaffolding erected as an external substitute for a living and breathing musical line.

Such reflections, however, are necessarily but approximative and by no means dispose of this music and the problems which it raises. A work of art is a positive reality and must be so considered, quite apart from the principles which are to be found within it. Thus one may reject many of Schoenberg's ideas and modes of procedure while acknowledging not only his historical position as the initiator of even more in contemporary music than is usually accredited to him, but also his work, and that of some of his followers, as in itself an important and fundamentally unassailable element in the music of this time.

Less strictly musical in significance than either of the general currents discussed above, but highly characteristic of our time and therefore worthy of some discussion, is the deliberate movement on the part of musicians, especially in Germany but also to a certain extent elsewhere, to seek a new relationship with the public and to form a great variety of new and direct contacts with it. The past ten years have witnessed the production of a vast quantity of music definitely written for purposes of practical "consumption," and though many of those purposes do not offer a precisely new field for musical production, new, on the other hand, is the scale and extent of the interest which musicians are taking in them.

As has been pointed out, the movement is to a large extent economic in character, and the necessities to which it responds are outer rather than inner necessities; but in several respects it is symptomatic and must command the attention of everyone who is interested in the way music may go in the future. For it represents a direct attempt to meet the crisis not only in its material but in several of its spiritual aspects as well.

The movement is therefore only in a partial sense an artistic one. It originated no doubt during the economic chaos in Germany just after the war, in the period of "inflation," when the economic breakdown of the German bourgeoisie led to a profound modification of the musical life of Germany, partly by reducing considerably the public able to attend concerts and operatic performances, and partly by taking the attention of the new generation away from cultural interests—a situation later made more acute by the political, intellectual, and moral unrest which followed. It was under the pressure of such realities that many musicians were forced to take stock of the whole place of music in present-day society and to seek new channels for their activity. They found these new channels in the constructive movements of the time, to which they sought to contribute the energies which music could give. Emphasis was laid above all on the practical purposes of the music thus produced; music was above all to cease to be an article of luxury or a primarily individual self-expression; to serve rather the ends of education, and especially of political and social propaganda. The same idea, far more drastically applied, will be readily recognized as that underlying the attitude of Soviet Russia toward art.

On perhaps a higher plane, the movement was undoubtedly in part the beginning of a renewed search for a fresh and more actively participating public. Composers busied themselves with the formation of a genuinely popular style, with rendering their music more accessible through a simplification of technique, with applying themselves seriously to the new problems offered by the radio, the cinema and mechanical means of reproduction. New ideals began to appear in the opera; younger composers began to produce works designed definitely for momentary consumption, works which were above all striking and "actual," designed to fulfill a momentary purpose and to be scrapped as soon as that purpose was fulfilled. They recognized, as did Wagner in a wholly different sense before them, the importance and the possibilities of opera in the creation of a public capable of the kind of participation which truly binds the composer to his world and his time.

The movement deserves close attention, as has already been said, not for its inherent artistic importance, but rather because of the questions it raises. Various ones among its enthusiastic promoters have deserted the ranks, and the movement itself seems to have settled down to its place as a more or less subordinate element in the musical activity of Germany. It nevertheless still exerts a strong influence, especially in the direction of opera, where it has undoubtedly influenced the character and quality of new productions by enlisting the services of the *avant-garde* of modern stage production.

Its chief interest, however, lies in the fact that by the very act of facing them, it has drawn attention to certain modern problems and dilemmas which may at any time become acute in other countries than Germany. A continuance and deepening of the present economic crisis cannot help bringing profound changes in the cultural life of every country; the universally reactionary movement in the musical life of the present season might easily be a mere foretaste of a greater tendency towards apathy and stagnation—a tendency which would be far more serious in any other country than in Germany with her incomparably more highly organized and ubiquitous musical activity. The composer will then be forced to conquer an entirely different public, potential or actual, than the one which is now prepared sooner or later to understand him. Under the circumstances the least that he can do is to examine carefully the moving principles of his relation to his art, and the relation of his art to the world, and to face both with a seriousness worthy of the occasion.

There is talk, nowadays, of a "return to expression"— talk the vagueness of which is slightly discouraging, it never being made quite clear what kind of expression is meant. Furthermore a certain crudity of understanding is evident in the implication that expression in any essential sense has been forsworn.

No doubt it was necessary—intimately and imperatively necessary—at a given moment for composers to rid their systems of certain poisons: of a rhetoric which had lost its vitality and degenerated into mere attitudinizing. No doubt it was necessary for them to become once more aware of music in its direct and sensuous aspects, to re-experience the simplest musical facts, in and for themselves, with a new freshness of sensation and perception. No doubt, too, this necessity no longer exists; many composers have gained through the experiences of the past ten years a fresh suppleness of style and of movement, a fresh sense of musical values, which they are able to apply with constantly greater freedom. The currents above described are all to a large extent characterized by a certain tenseness and lack of free movement which is inseparable at first from any far-reaching spiritual revolution or readjustment. But nothing could be farther from the truth than the idea that any art worthy of the name can be self-consciously guided in one direction or another, or that it consists in a series of short term "movements," "tendencies," and the like. Viewed in perspective the past fifteen years will appear as short and at least as inconclusive as any other fifteen years, and its fruits will be judged not by the fluctuation of the present fashions, but by living accomplishments, many and possibly even the most characteristic of which cannot yet have had time to become mature or in any sense definitive.

Thus far, then, a "return to expression" or any other new "tendency" has yet to become clearly defined—that is, it has not as yet incorporated itself in a vigorous new personality which shows clear and striking signs of having surmounted the inner conflicts necessary to fruition, and of having begun the apparently equally inevitable outer conflicts and struggles for recognition which every freshly authentic personality must face. This is not at all to say that no such personality will arise. There are still interesting and fresh beginnings from which much can be hoped and expected, and it must be remembered that a tortured and restless period like these post-war years—unquestionably, and for America as well as Europe the severest trial through which Western civilization has passed—is not one which favors the easy emergence of really commanding personalities, in art any more than in other fields. Yet it is obviously only through the emergence of such personalities that collapse can be avoided, or the crisis, even in its purely temporary aspects, be resolved. When it ceases to be a spiritual and moral crisis, it will cease to be in any but a very momentary sense a material one.

The above reflections are not precisely encouraging, perhaps; but the facts behind them are rather inescapable. To ignore these facts is to ignore fundamental realities of the present-day musical world—a sign of weakness or provincialism, and of a fundamental lack of contact with life. Awareness of them in some aspect or other is indeed the one common ground possible to contemporary composers. The various currents briefly sketched above have represented efforts, dictated by instinctive necessity, to meet these facts with positive achievements—perhaps they may eventually prove to be preliminary contributions to something like a common effort.

In the opinion of the writer of these reflections, such efforts have hitherto been incomplete, because based on an insufficiently profound and daring spiritual experience. It would seem to be obvious that a real community of spirits cannot be created in the realm of music alone, nor can it arise in music without a simultaneous or even previous stirring towards a new human solidarity.

Art is of course governed by necessities; it goes the way it must go. The artist needs all his faculties, then, in becoming constantly more fully aware of these necessities, in listening attentively to their stirrings in himself, and in meeting them with all of the forces at his disposal. He cannot make even the smallest vital contribution to the art which he serves unless he has the courage to remain unceasingly aware of the fundamental impulses within himself, and, from his own unshakable point of vantage, to participate freely in the vital impulses of the world of which he is a part. He must discipline himself to be content only with realities, in the deepest sense, since only on realities can a true culture, a true basis for human development and felicity, be built.

It may well be that the energies of the present day will, for some time to come, prove capable only of achievements of an intrinsically incomplete nature. But an age of confusion may be also an age of the greatest hope, and discussions as to the ultimate specific value of contemporary art are irrelevant and in the deepest sense amateurish. The truly mature artist does not ask himself such questions, since he knows that a life lived in an uncompromisingly creative spirit, or even the creation of a single genuine bar or phrase is a more exhilarating and essential experience than an infinite amount of "success," contemporary or posthumous. It is, however, hardly a matter of choice; in the absence of vital inner necessities, worthy the attention of a fully adult human being, music, or any other form of art, is scarcely worth bothering about.

The New Musical Horizon
[1937]

I HAVE been asked to comment on the musical ideals of the "present generation." What is meant by this phrase? To-day above all the most obvious characteristic of the musical world is the division of its ranks—its multitude of cross currents which may be, according to one's point of view, taken to indicate either a healthy ferment or a labyrinth of spiritual insecurity.

From a somewhat greater distance, however, one is struck by the completeness of a transformation which the entire musical horizon has undergone in the past twenty-five years. Contrasting personalities of the two periods—Strauss, Debussy, Ravel, Mahler, Scriabin, as against Schoenberg, Stravinsky, Hindemith, Berg, Bartok—give an indication of the extent of the change; an indication which is enhanced if we contrast earlier and later works of the same composers: the *Sacre du printemps* with the *Symphonie de psaumes* or Schoenberg's Five Orchestral Pieces with his Variations for Orchestra. Going further and examining critical pronunciamentos of both periods, we see the contrast at its greatest, partly because a really good work of art inevitably transcends the aesthetics of the moment which produces it, partly because of the ephemeral character of nearly all contemporary criticism.

There is, however, no doubt that a certain era is definitely past. A few pertinent if obvious facts. Twenty years ago, for instance, the virtuoso was still a glamorous, almost a legendary figure; and this was true not only of great performers but of the pianist, violinist, or singer as such. Today his hold on the public imagination has passed either outside

From *Modern Music*, vol. 14, no. 2, pp. 59-66. Reprinted by permission of the League of Composers—International Society for Contemporary Music, U.S. Section, Inc.

the musical field entirely, or at best to the conductor. Even a Toscanini, however, scarcely has the half-legendary prestige of a Paderewski or a Caruso or a hundred others; and there are signs that the prestige of the conductor is already slightly on the wane.

In the actual music produced the change is at least as striking. Twenty-five years ago the most representative composers were still writing chiefly program music; when not writing definitely illustrative music they were seeking first of all the characteristic, the evocative, the vaguely illustrative, and seeking new effects with an illustrative purpose in mind. Today, to be sure, opera and ballets are still being written, as indeed they always were; but the important instrumental works of recent years have all been sonatas, quartets, symphonies, concerti and the like, with program music confined to the musical Hinterland and to the movies where its well-worn devices are enjoying a somewhat too protracted usefulness.

The phrase "present generation" therefore has a very clear meaning if we accept it in the most inclusive sense. In my opinion the changes briefly noted above are the essential and significant ones, far more so than the various differences in outlook among contemporary composers. The following words pretend to be no more than scattered observations; the subject itself is a vast one, and generalizations are always subject to the charge of superficiality.

An abrupt change in artistic direction, such as has occurred several times in musical history, implies either the completed excavation of an old vein or the sudden discovery of a new one. A period of experimentation—a "romantic" period—is followed by a period of selection—a "classic" one—in which the new materials are tested and absorbed with whatever is inferior in creative potentiality eliminated.

Without undue exaggeration it is possible to characterize the nineteenth century as one in which the individual detail

or musical feature assumed constantly increasing importance, and in which synthesis, the real essence of musical
form, became in increasing measure a merely passive element
—a necessary evil, as it were, instead of the essence of the
music itself. This has often been noted; it has less often been
pointed out that it brought with it quite new conceptions of
harmony, rhythm, and melody; that such a change implies
also new ways of *listening* to music—not only adjustments
to the new idioms, but new and perhaps distorted conceptions of the music of the past. The "dissonances" in Bach or
Mozart have a significance, both "musical" and "emotional"
far different from that often lent them by hearers nurtured
on nineteenth- and early twentieth-century music, in which
dissonances are rather individual features than organic por-
tions of a musical line. Here the influence of the Wagnerian
leit-motif—more often than not extremely short and characterized by a single harmonic or rhythmic trait—is paramount. Its introduction is often motivated by dramatic, not
musical necessities and once introduced it intentionally dominates the scene, to the obliteration of what surrounds it.
The musical coherence is there, to be sure—but in a passive
sense; the detail is more significant than the line, and the
"theme" more important than its development. It is all too
seldom noted to what an overwhelming extent the reverse
is the case in the earlier music.

It is easy thus to see how the element of line, in every
larger sense of the word, tended to lose its importance, even
though it could not of course be abandoned altogether. In the
works of Debussy, Scriabin, the Stravinsky of *Petrouchka*
and the *Sacre*, the Schoenberg of the middle period, we
have, so to speak, the apotheosis of detail. Harmony, for
instance, instead of being as it had always been, until the
so-called "romantic period," an organic element in a flowing
musical line and even—so to speak—the determining framework of that line, has assumed more and more a purely coloristic function. According to the context it bears the weight
of pathos, of suggestion, of evocation, and an infinite num-

ber of new colors and new nuances of relationship are brought into it; but it achieves its effect no longer through its organic flow and interplay with other musical elements but through the color and the dynamics of individual sonorities. Hence the static quality of some of Debussy's harmonies, a single harmonic detail often serving as the basis of an entire section or even an entire work; hence the monotony of Scriabin who attempted to found a whole musical system on a single complex chord; hence the static quality of so much of the early Stravinsky where—as to a lesser extent in Debussy—the harmonies shift rather than flow.

It is a question, of course, whether the emphasis on evocation or pathetic detail was the result of program music, or whether on the other hand composers seized instinctively upon programmatic form and aesthetic as the result of the accumulation of new musical materials of which—either for reasons springing from the nature of the materials themselves or, more probably, because of the breaking down of older syntheses and the consequent expansion and scattering of human impulses which characterized the nineteenth century generally—the significance could not yet be made clear through musical means alone. "New possibilities" destroy or modify older necessities, and the fact that Beethoven —whose material was so much more complex than that of any of his predecessors—still achieves, not without a degree of effort unknown to any of the latter, a completely satisfying synthesis, inclines one to the latter view, since his successors, who claimed him as their master, failed to achieve such a synthesis but turned to program music instead.

The music of the past twenty-five years, then, is the result of an impasse to which music had come, in the constantly increasing refinement of detail, the increasingly static quality of musical language and perhaps above all the inevitable sacrifice of profundity and significance in musical expression to sharpness of sensation.

The Composer's Craft

We are told, then, that in contemporary music purely musical values predominate. What does this mean? To the critics of contemporary music it implies a denial of all "content." Such critics are I believe still under the spell of the older conception of music which persists in attaching concrete associational significances to each phrase and accent— the conception which persisted in counting the tears that fell on the hero's grave at the end of the Funeral March in the *Eroica*, and which revels today in Sibelius' evocation of "frosty northern landscapes." It loses sight entirely of the fact that to a musician or a sensitive listener a purely musical idea is at least as profound, as poignant, and as concrete in its significance as any associations which it might conceivably evoke. No associations or verbally definably "emotions" account for the effect of, say, Mozart's G-Minor Quintet nor can any words be found which adequately describe or even suggest it. It is, say, noble, tender, melancholy, poignant, but so are dozens of other works by dozens of other composers. It is the music which Mozart has written which is great, not the "ideas" which Mr. So-and-So can read into it, or the mess of verbiage with which he may regale himself and his readers the next morning. Likewise, Beethoven's ideas for or against the Revolution were precisely what he shared with millions of his contemporaries. What is great in his work is what he alone was capable of achieving—his music, the sounds, the musical shapes which he conjured up, of which the profoundly human significance transcends his specific preoccupations only somewhat less completely than it does the fundamentally meaningless pomposities of M. Rolland or Mr. Ernest Newman. The content lies—as Beethoven himself pointed out—in the tones, the lines, accents and contrasts, and not in the thousand experiences which, fused together in a single gesture, take composite shape as a musical impulse or idea. It can never be too clearly stated that if musical expression is something unique and untranslatable it does not therefore follow that it is without human significance.

49

Such a change in artistic aims brings inevitably a change in technical outlook and in some sense a reinstatement of formerly discredited modes of procedure. Even Debussy—strange as it seems today—is quoted as having been wont to express himself in round terms apropos of the tyranny of the tonal system, from which it was one of his declared aims to free himself. The writer remembers being taken to task shortly after Debussy's death by serious musicians for suggesting once that, after all, *Fêtes* is in the key of A major, *La Fille aux cheveux de lin* in G flat. It was considered not only as a grotesque misstatement but a slur on Debussy's memory. Today such an attitude is out of the question. While contemporary conceptions of tonality are far from being the same as those of a half century ago, musicians have nevertheless returned to the principle of a tonal, or, if you will, an acoustic center, around which tones and harmonies group themselves in clear relationship and in their various ways recognize the hierarchy of consonance and dissonance as it is furnished by the natural properties of the tone itself. This is, as should be clear to anyone but the musical illiterate, an inevitable result of the changes which I have attempted to describe. Tonality in the broadest sense is an inevitable product of the physical properties of tone, and as none other than Arnold Schoenberg has often pointed out, atonal music is simply uncoordinated music. As for Schoenberg's own "twelve-tone system," in which an additional set of relationships is, as it were, rigorously superimposed on those derived from the phenomena of resonance, it perhaps appeals to a quite special type of musical mentality, but its ultimate value will depend not on any question of abstract merit but on its efficacy as a vehicle for the imagination of those who use it.

It is inevitable that such a change as I have described should bring about changes in what may be all too inadequately termed the emotional content of music—the term is inadequate because it deals with what are essentially the intangibles of music. But precisely those intangibles are most striking to the average listener and changes of this kind have therefore, if anything, the widest repercussion. It is not difficult to see that the already noted preoccupation with detail went, as it were, inevitably, with an enhancement of keenness and intensity of sensation at the expense of profundity; concentration rather than development, contraction rather than expansion. It led thus to the exploitation of extreme and even exasperated moods,—the pathological exaltation of Scriabin, the shudders of the early Schoenberg, the expensive thrills of *Salomé* and *Elektra*, and, much later, the horrors of *Wozzeck* and *Lulu*. It would not, I believe, be too difficult to show that this is the inevitable development not only of a preoccupation with detail but of the peculiarly nineteenth-century conception of the artist as "genius"—a word which Mozart and Bach probably never heard, much less dreamed of applying to themselves. The nineteenth-century musician, on the other hand, performer as well as composer (and how well program music was adapted to his ends!) came before the public as a "personality," and became in turn a romantically lonely and tortured soul, a prophet, and a purveyor of thrills, delicate or violent as the case might be. Psychologically the sequence is logical enough if one considers the human experiences of the last century and a quarter and the relation of the artist to these. Logical also is the revulsion of the really contemporary musician who seeks emotional truth even sometimes at the risk of understatement and occasional gaucherie. From a similar impulse of revulsion also derives, at least in part, the now somewhat faded vogue of "Gebrauchsmusik," propaganda music, and the like—the exaltation of music which serves a "practical" purpose— which actually of course means a purpose wholly separate from the personality of the composer.

It is the above aspect of contemporary music which has most puzzled and even alienated so much of the public and that more or less articulate portion of it which writes books and articles on music. The public still demands "glamor," even though it no longer believes in it. The first of these propensities is still constantly raising false hopes, the second brings inevitable and invariable frustration. This will doubtless continue to occur until the public as a whole looks for values in art other than those of what is commonly known as "personality."

This is not to say that the contemporary musician does not wish music to be "personal," in the deeper sense, or even "characteristic." But here again he departs from conceptions till recently prevalent. This older aesthetic identified a composer's individuality with specific novel or frequently recurring traits in his style. Thus Debussy was the whole tone scale, Scriabin the "mystic chord," Schoenberg, for the period, extreme dissonance, and so on. Since the aims of the contemporary composer are different, so is his aesthetic; for him the composer's personality resides not so much in the material which he uses as in the individual accents which he brings to it. In a similar manner his nationality resides not in a self-conscious choice of "national idiom" but in the temperament which his work reveals. Both qualities are implicit in whatever music is real. But for the contemporary musician they are by-products in relation to his primary aim, which is musical expression—by-products as inevitable and fundamentally as resistant to conscious cultivation as the individual character of a gesture or a handwriting.

This is not to say that contemporary music is inherently better or more profound than what preceded. As Shakespeare's Hotspur noted and remarked, the spirits of the vasty deep do not always "come when you do call on them." The value of a work of art depends on quite other factors than the specific directions which a composer is following. What I have tried to show is some of the reasons, conscious or otherwise, why contemporary composers write as they do, and the causes which have produced them.

Song and Pattern in Music Today
[1956]

I N the course of many varied contacts and travels during these recent post-war years, one fact has struck me very forcibly; that is, the disappearance of sharply marked *localities* in our Western musical world. Everywhere one finds that musicians are discussing the same problems, and reacting to them in much the same ways. If, thirty years ago, one travelled from New York to Paris or from Paris to London or Berlin or Rome, one felt in each case that one was entering quite a different artistic climate. The differences in values, standards, and aims characteristic of the musical activities in these various centres were much more immediately striking than the resemblances. Today it is the reverse.

I suspect that this really represents a state of affairs which has been developing over a period considerably longer than thirty years, and it is clear that it runs parallel to the trend of our modern civilization in general. It is obviously not confined to the musical world as such, or even especially characteristic of it; and it is certainly the inevitable result not only of our modern means of locomotion but also of world-wide communication: not only of the motor car and the aeroplane, but of the telephone, the radio, the cinema and television in perhaps even greater measure. One of the incidental results is what is often referred to on both sides of the Atlantic as the "Americanization" of Europe. I hope that I as an American will not be suspected of undue sensibility if I point out that America too, has had, in this sense, to become "Americanized," and that the process, in our country also, has not been a completely comfortable one. Perhaps we are all undergoing a process not of Americanization but of modernization.

From *Score*, no. 17, Sept. 1956, pp. 73-84. Reprinted by permission of Kraus Reprint.

Let us return to music, however. The young composer of today, quite in contrast with his colleagues of, say, a hundred years ago, quickly finds himself faced with a public consisting not primarily of his neighbors and fellow townsmen, but of strangers in many parts of the world—a state of affairs reserved in former times only for those who had achieved an extraordinary degree of recognition in their own territory. In other words, he accustoms himself very early to the idea that he is necessarily speaking to the whole world of those who are interested in the music of his time. I do not think that this is true primarily because this world is, as is often claimed, smaller than it has ever been before. That may or may not be so. It is too often forgotten that the "musical public" of former days actually consisted of a truly small, and as we say, élite fraction of the population as a whole, and that in recent years, and above all since the introduction of the radio and the gramophone, this has ceased to be the case. At all events, the composer of today finds himself in the position I have described primarily because our modern means of communication have made a world-wide public available to him. It is one of the everyday conditions under which he is born and grows.

All this, of course, has a profound effect on the composer's relation to his own work. Naturally, in speaking of such things one is forced to generalize, and I am quite aware that I am doing so. Those of us, however, who come into daily contact with young composers, and are accustomed to take part in frequent uninhibited discussion of their problems, must be aware that this disappearance of *locality* as a conditioning factor in the musical life of today has confronted them with a set of premises quite unlike those faced by composers of any generation in the past, including our own just before them. In order to have music, we were obliged to go and get it, whether this meant being present at its performance, or—if we were to a greater or lesser extent musicians ourselves—performing or reading it from the printed page. The thought of music on any other terms

54

was a remote one; and while we could read or hear about what took place in other places and on other occasions, it was never a matter of intimate concern to us. If we were composers we might hope for performances of our music in distant places, and even on occasions at which we were not ourselves present; but such occasions, even if they took place very frequently, did not form a part of our own personal musical activity or experience. Their importance for us was of another kind. We were accustomed by the facts of our existence to regard such a development as a kind of projection of the locality to which we belonged; and in general we found a reasonable degree of inner security in such a state of affairs. Though the number of those who understood and responded to our music might be small, it consisted of people who had been born and nurtured against the same background as ourselves, and whose response to what we were trying to do was at best very warm, very genuine, and in the last analysis friendly in principle if not always in practice.

What I am trying to sketch is, of course, only a rough general picture of the facts which underlay all our assumptions about musical life, and which influenced to a large degree our conceptions of music itself. Such conditions have by no means been completely superseded, even now. But today everyone is brought into contact with a much larger territory—not only the composer, but all musicians and music lovers as well. The attention of the public, even that portion which is actively interested in the music of our own time, is far less preponderantly focused on what is being done in its own vicinity. A far wider range of interest is available to it, and it is inevitable and even natural that its sense of identification with its own immediate neighborhood is correspondingly weakened. This state of affairs is all too clearly manifested in the frequent attempts, which constitute a familiar phenomenon of present-day musical life, to promote interest in local composers; attempts which are none the less essential to our musical health for the fact that they often appear somewhat artificial—as is every effort to promote music for any reason other than a desire to listen to it for its own sake. At all events the young composer of today is quite accustomed to the idea of an absentee public, consisting of the people who are interested in music *throughout the world* or at least those parts of it that are familiar with Western culture; and he is more accustomed to this because he is quite aware that such people form an incalculably small, if active and determined, fragment of the enormous public mass which has some contact with what is called "serious" music. Once more it must be stressed that this mass public is something quite new on the musical scene, the result, even the creation, not only of mass means of communication, but, in a less direct if no less real sense, of other forces—economic and social and political—which have little or nothing to do with music or even with culture; and it is to a large degree still strongly swayed by these forces. So far it has not developed a tradition of its own; it is notably lacking in venturesomeness or curiosity; and in fact its lack of venturesomeness is one of the premises on which those who furnish it with its musical diet base their calculations. For the very concept of a mass public means that musical business enterprise is inevitably geared to the vast number of listeners whose interest is comparatively lukewarm, and that it must always tend to foster criteria which demand as little as possible from these listeners.

The young composer of today soon learns, therefore, that his own intense dedication to music has by its very nature little to do with the "taste of the majority," on which most of our contemporary organized musical life is based. He is born into a situation whose essential features have developed only in the course of the adult life of those musicians now in their fifties or older; and he is native to this situation in the sense that he has never known any other. It is inevitable, therefore, that he should react to it in a manner which can often baffle his older colleagues, and that the natural and altogether healthy tension between generations which has been characteristic of all vital cultures at all vital periods should today have acquired a quite new, and even highly problematic, character, through the circumstances which I have attempted to describe.

It is hardly necessary to point out that the resulting situation makes extraordinary demands on all concerned. It becomes constantly clearer that music is undergoing one of its major upheavals, at least comparable to that brought about by the discovery of polyphony in the ninth century or by the whole set of changes which took place roughly around the turn of the sixteenth. Future historians may quite conceivably find that the present transformation is more profound than either of the other two. Those, like our own, were coeval with vast changes in society as a whole, and in the inner life of Western man. Until we can be seen in perspective—until at least the change has become in some sense stabilized—it is perhaps idle to attempt to estimate its relative extent. What we can and must realize, however, is that all hitherto accepted values are being subjected to a constant and radical challenge, not primarily by individuals, but by conditions and events, and by the impact of these upon men and women. New values and new attitudes are in the making, and it is here that the most essential as well as the most difficult challenge lies. The challenge involves, that is, a searching reappraisal not only of traditional ideas, but even of those underlying assumptions which have always been taken for granted as irreducible; for such a situation brings with it inevitably a completely new set of requirements.

We may be sure that it is only the most fundamental questions which have any real relevance. We must distinguish clearly between those concepts which are in the final analysis to be considered merely as phases, however venerable, of our culture, and, on the other hand, those impulses which incline men and women toward music in the first place. Nothing is easier than to confuse the two. We have learned this not only from musical history but also from decisive events within our own lifetime, which any of us can remember if we have paid some attention to the musical scene over a period of years. Each successive generation has had to cope with such confusions on its own behalf; it is only that to-day, and to a large extent because of the factors which I have tried to throw into relief, they are more crucial than they have been for many generations. For it is precisely at the moment when the whole of our musical vocabulary is passing through a phase of radical, far-reaching, and still far from completely predictable transformation, that the new generations find themselves confronted by an unprecedented crisis, of which I have attempted to sketch the barest outlines, in the relations between those who are seriously dedicated to music, and society as a whole.

It is against such a background that we must ask our questions, having made it clear, I trust, that they relate to principles and criteria rather than to results. It is always necessary to remember that it is only results that count, and that principles, especially before the fact, are often quite misleading. But the principles nevertheless play their rôle in determining the nature of the results, and meanwhile it is necessary to make ourselves clearly aware of defects in principle, as well as to keep at the very least an open mind regarding the results. Quite unsound principles have often proved most fruitful as working bases for artists, including some of the very greatest.

With such precautions in mind we may well question some of the attitudes which are prevalent today. One of the most characteristic tendencies among our younger composers, for instance, is the urge to control and to account in advance for not only every note, but every nuance, every articulation, every *timbre*—in brief, every move that they make in the course of a work. Every gesture is to be subjected to the most minute control, in accordance with a design arbitrarily adopted or at least established by individual fiat. It would be a mistake to identify this mode of thought with any specific group or "tendency." As every-one must know who teaches or associates with young com-posers today, it is very widespread, and often amounts to almost an obsession, which excludes all other considerations and all other criteria. It is undoubtedly an inevitable phase of the drive towards new principles of organization, which every composer aware of today's musical problems knows very well. To some extent it derives from certain apparent implications of the twelve-tone method; I say "apparent," because they are based on an essential misconception of what the method implies. At times it seems as if certain composers had accepted the twelve-tone idea, not so much in terms of the method itself, of the artistic necessities to which it re-sponds, of the extensions implicit in its basic premises, as in terms of the criticisms which were and sometimes still are levelled against it. The system is accepted, in other words, not as a *means* of organizing the relationship between tones, and—what is at least as important—one which provides a multitude of new resources and new relationships deriving from such a method of organization, but rather as a prin-ciple possessing a kind of mystical validity and authority of its own. Organization as such becomes in these terms a *goal* and a value. The construction of intricate and quite ab-stractly conceived patterns, in which intricacy itself be-comes a criterion, in which every musical gesture is not only controlled but prefabricated in the interests of the pattern, becomes, not the unsympathetic caricature of an art which is misunderstood, not even a possible means to a broader and more inclusive artistic end, not even one of many possible modes of procedure which may conceivably lead to a satisfying result. It becomes frankly and quite out-spokenly the goal of music as such, and the ultimate prin-ciple from which musical criteria are to be derived; a prin-ciple which can and should be extended to include every classifiable element of music.

It is, of course, fairly easy to raise objections to such a principle. The value and even the existence of organization, after all, depends largely on what it is that is being organized, as it depends also on the whole which the organization produces. I do not wish to labour such objections at this point; there are answers to them, and the resulting argument is at best rather abstract and at worst sophistical. The real fallacy of such a conception seems to me to reside elsewhere, and to derive rather from certain pitfalls which are inherent in the traditional assumptions of musical theory. To be specific: we teach and study harmony, counterpoint and instrumentation; and in speaking of music we isolate as it were a number of other elements: melody, rhythm, line, metre, tempo, dynamics, texture, articulation and possibly other matters. We frequently speak of these things as if each of them were a separate and independent element, and as if a total musical impulse or impression could in actual fact be adequately analyzed as the sum and interplay of these elements, each proceeding according to its own laws. But surely it is our thinking that is in all essentials highly artificial. These elements are not even *ingredients*, but rather dimensions, facets, or aspects of an integral *musical* experience, and are inaccurately conceived in any other terms. In a genuine and complete musical impression no one of them pursues in any real sense an independent existence of its own, and the effect could only be destructive if it did. Each one of these various aspects derives its function from the total and indivisible musical flow—the *song* as I have adopted the term for the purposes of this article. Let it be quite clear that this term "song" as used here does not contain any specifically vocal reference, nor does it connote any identification with melody or "line." It is intended precisely to refer to the integral flow of music, and may be applied as well to the music of, say Anton Webern, as to that of Verdi or Mozart or Palestrina. The point that I wish to make is that music can be genuinely organized only on this integral basis, and that an attempt to organize its so-called elements as separate factors is, at the very best, to pursue abstraction, and, at the worst, to confuse genuine order with something which is essentially chaotic. It is surely quite naïve and even primitive to expect any other result. But such thinking would seem to be a logical consequence of the attempt to establish order on any other basis than that of a very clear and strong conception, in terms of sound and movement (or, lest I be suspected of belying my own premises, of sound *in* movement), of a given work as a whole. Such a conception will most assuredly call for the total organization of the music in all its aspects. But the control will be imposed ineluctably by the creative vision itself, and not by means of a pattern conceived *a priori* to determine every gesture. It should hardly be necessary to point out at this date that the twelve-tone method has nothing whatever to do with a pattern of this kind; that, like any system on which music has ever been based, its function is the indispensable one of defining a specific area of musical relationships; of giving, as it were, configuration to otherwise undifferentiated material. The musical imagination, over the framework of acoustical premises which result from such configuration, is as free to function as it ever was over the framework provided by the relationships embodied in, let us say, the tonal complex of C major. If we needed proof of these facts it would be necessary only to look at the mass of music already written which clearly owes something essential to the twelve-tone principle. It is no longer possible to identify the principle with the Viennese tradition as such or with any form of expression that can be considered as peculiar to that tradition. Though it originated in Vienna, it has attracted composers far removed from any specifically Viennese *cachet*, who have been able to use it for purposes which are completely their own. It has provided an essential part of the resources at the disposal of every present-day composer, to use or not to use, in any manner which musical imagination may dictate.

The drive toward the extremes of minute organization, which I have tried to describe and to which I have devoted much critical attention, is often associated with what must seem an exaggerated belief in the efficacy of musical analysis, and a misunderstanding of its function. Certain of its manifestations, in fact, bear the clear aspect of attempts to reproduce by conscious synthesis the kinds of results that are obtained analytically. While few would deny the practical use of musical analysis or even its efficacy in providing a sound basis for certain technical concepts, its limitations and its pitfalls should be kept clearly in mind. It deals by its very nature solely with effects, and cannot with any certainty provide more than speculative assumptions regarding the intentions or processes of thought which have led to them. One can discover, in other words, what a composer has done, and to a greater or lesser extent how he has done it; but one cannot discover with any certainty what has motivated him. Even the "what" and the "how" are discoverable only in terms of a given set of premises, which may or may not bear a valid relation to those of the composer himself. The rationalization of the data we obtain in this manner can sharpen our awareness of the music, and in fact the measure in which it accomplishes this will furnish us with the criterion by which we can judge the relevance of the analysis in question.

But in every real sense, it is not the music itself but our own aural and perceptive powers that we are analyzing. The analytical judgments we make have their basis in our minds and not in that of the composer. Any mature composer who is at all aware of his own processes of thought should be able to confirm this. He obtains his results through a stream of thought and impulse so intensely concentrated and fused that he himself, as he well knows, can give only the most fragmentary and helplessly insufficient account of its real consistency. But even assuming that we succeed to a large extent in gaining some insight into a composer's mode of thought—and we probably very often do succeed—it must be fairly evident that precisely what is most important to us, what gives the work its character and significance, is that which defies analysis either in musical terms or in any others. It defies analysis because it is nothing more nor less that the impact of the music on ourselves. It consists of the finest and at the same time the most complex network of subjective and objective elements, one which varies in colour and composition with every successive hearing; and even if some scientific mind of the future should find the means to dissect and classify all these separate elements, the fluidity of the process itself and of the relationships it involves would make his search for the ultimate artistic fact a futile one. It is for such reasons as these that a genuine musical work must always differ in its very nature from an exercise in technique, however intricate, and that the utmost that we can derive from analysis is the heightened awareness it can give us of the *results* of a composer's musical thought. That is already a great deal; but it is in no way the equivalent of, or a substitute for, that thought itself. It differs from the latter both in quantity and in quality.

An inevitable corollary of the tendencies I have described is the very widespread denial of the validity of what is called "expression" in music. Music, it is said, cannot and should not "express" anything whatever. It should justify itself as pure "material"; and on this material the composer should carefully avoid imposing his personality. Like many such slogans, past and present, this one has a valiant and important sound; it carries with it an odour of detachment and self-abnegation and lofty devotion. The only trouble with it is that it is difficult to understand exactly what it can mean. For the artist, like everyone else, "expresses something" in everything he does. Few people cultivate self-expression in their hand-writing, and yet hand-writing is inevitably so individual a matter that, try as one will to disguise it, an expert can detect a forgery and even to a large extent diagnose states of mind from the gestures which a hand-writing registers on paper. If music is to consist of organized material, the choice of musical elements and the nature of their organization are already "expression," and will inevitably bear the imprint of the individual who chooses or organizes them. If, in order to avoid this, one distributed the processes of choice and organization amongst several individuals, one could no doubt eliminate to some extent the element of individuality, but certainly not that of expression. The fact is that the production of a definite musical object (of any kind) is in itself an act of expression, and in the last analysis very little else. One cannot fill either space or time with an object of no configuration whatever.

Besides, one is forced to ask, what are the actual materials of music? Let us try to make our definition as broad as possible—broader in fact than any which I have implied so far. Let us, for instance, speak of "sounds" rather than tones. Can we say "patterns of sound," or do we not have to say "patterns of sound in time"? But patterns of sound imply contrast, as they most certainly imply organization. Organization in time implies movement, and thus movement, if our definition is correct—the movement of sounds and of organized groups of sounds—is inherent in the very definition of music; and awareness of movement is an indispensable element in either the organization or the perception of music. Perhaps it will have been noticed that I have avoided bringing into the definition such slanted terms as "expression" and "response." The materials of music, then, must include movement as such; and movement is, for good or ill, one of the stimuli to which our response is most instinctive, most immediate and most powerful. This is so true that awareness of movement is already, in essence, response to it, since such awareness derives from our most primary physical experiences. In perceiving it we already invest it with character, and cannot possibly avoid doing so. So here again we are faced with the ineluctability of expression whether we like it or not.

We now find ourselves confronted with another inescapable fact. It seems to be a characteristic of movement, or of any pattern in time, that it loses most of its force if it is exactly repeated. To put it in more concrete terms: nothing loses its interest for us so quickly as the mechanical repetition of the same movement. As soon as we realize that we may expect exactly the same inflexion that we have seen or heard before, we become bored; we become more aware of the repetition as such than of what is being repeated, and our awareness of movement quickly disappears. We know that movement is taking place but it ceases to make any impact on us. This I believe is the ultimate limitation of music that is mechanically reproduced—of which I would not dream of denying the many and varied uses; and I believe that it is also the ultimate problem of electronic music, of which I would certainly not wish to deny the enormous possibilities. It is not the only problem; there are others, of which some would not be irrelevant to the present discussion, if space permitted. But it is the one I have just mentioned that seems the most difficult to solve at the present time, except in the most arbitrary and irrational terms. It is also the answer to those who dream of eliminating the performer. For an incalculable service which the performer does for us is to invest each phrase, each gesture of the music, with fresh energy each time that he sings or plays it. Since it is a fresh departure each time, we never expect it to be twice exactly the same; and yet the variants which save the situation for us are motivated by a genuine conception of the movement itself in its essential features, and—assuming that the performer is competent—they are never arbitrary or accidental.

I trust it is clear that the objections I have made to certain widespread attitudes and trends of thought, especially among younger composers, do not imply an *a priori* judgment of actual works. Such an approach to music would be naïve and unpardonable. One cannot reiterate often enough the fact that the continued existence of music, as of everything else, is dependent on constant renewal. One of the conditions of such renewal is the sloughing off, by each new generation, of attitudes inherited from its predecessors

—attitudes which no longer meet the needs of the generation in question; and the replacement of these by new attitudes which may well seem strange to those who have not felt quite the same needs or been subject to the same influences. This in itself—and again one cannot insist on it too often—is a natural and thoroughly healthy symptom and as such should be welcomed.

What we may well ask in the present instance, however, is first of all whether the drive to divest music of all its human connexions is not a reflex gesture in response to the conditions which I tried to outline at the beginning—conditions which have accustomed the younger of our composers to become aware of a vast distance between them and their listeners, and which may inevitably make communication seem not only remote but even unreal. It is not to underestimate the difficulties or the problems of the situation if we argue that such a reflex action is not a healthy one, but rather a flight into self-pity, and that it runs a grave risk, as Roberto Gerhard pointed out in a recent article,[1] of "throwing out the baby with the bath"—which is after all only a polite metaphor for what is essentially an act of self-destruction.

One must also ask another and more searching question. An often outspoken and always implicit premise in the currents of thought which I have here attempted to describe is a denial of the validity, or even the existence, of imponderables, in music or anywhere else. It requires no special perspicacity to see in all this a flight into what is perhaps the besetting superstition of today—a tendency, amidst the insecurities of an age of transition, to take refuge in the chimerical certainties which a quasi-scientific approach to all problems seems to provide. That such "certainties" are in actuality chimerical, we are constantly being warned by the profoundest scientific minds. Such certainties as science can provide belong exclusively to the realm of measurement, not

[1] Roberto Gerhard, "The Contemporary Music Situation," *Score*, no. 16, June 1956, pp. 7-18.

of definition; to quantity—and quantity in the abstract—not to quality or character or even existence. If art as such denotes anything at all—even if we consider it quite simply as the construction of objects—science can be of no help whatever in removing it from the realm of imponderables. The certainties which art provides are not scientific certainties but empirical ones; they are inner certainties which belong to a realm of perception, of feeling, and of conviction, not of demonstrable fact. Objective "proof" in regard to them proves in fact nothing, for the simple reason that it belongs to quite another category. One could have learned this long ago with relation to such a scientific fact as, for instance, the over-tone series—a valid and extremely useful fact regarding the materials of music, but one which has led to grotesquely unsound results in the various and quite contradictory attempts which have been made to use it in "proving" musical values. It is *available*, and that is all that has ever been demonstrated; in itself it neither provides the composer with tools nor imposes obligations as to how they are to be used. These are provided and imposed by the composer's imagination, and in a sense also by the accumulated experience which we call tradition. But, as we should know by this time, neither clues nor obligations exist outside a given context, and they change completely when contexts are altered.

Certainly, in a period like ours in which the individual is so constantly made aware of his isolation, the urge to seek refuge in readily demonstrable facts is a strong and understandable one. One finds company more easily on the basis of ponderables than of imponderables, since as fixed quantities they carry their own compelling authority, and one can at least enjoy the comfort of disdain for those who refuse to accept them. Their toughness makes them an apparently trustworthy material out of which to build barricades. But in art it is imagination, constructive and otherwise, that is inexorable; the demonstrable facts lie completely within the realm of materials and means, which are quite neutral and, in the absence of imagination, lead precisely nowhere. If artistic values are sought elsewhere, there is every probability that they will prove more elusive than ever. The toughness which the artist needs is of another kind. It can be found only within himself, in the quality of his love for music and the strength of the conviction and imagination which he can derive from this source.

Let me once more make the position quite clear. None of the questions which I have advanced diminish either the reality or the force of the challenges inherent in the musical situation of today, nor do they limit the extent of those challenges. It is altogether possible that the years directly ahead will assume the aspect of a period of experiment, of rapid change, of trial and error, of exploration, sometimes into regions which are not only uncharted but in which curiosity and daring are the only possible guide. One hopes in fact that such an age will be based on premises derived from genuine curiosity and daring, and on slogans which look to something richer, not poorer, than what has gone before. Let us have organization, by all means, or, as it is sometimes stated, grammar; but if we are really to have it, it would be well to remember that grammar only arises, by definition, out of the need to say something with clearness and precision. In other words, it is what has hitherto been called "expression" which is at the core of the matter. If, as is quite possible, the term itself has become too stale to be of any further use, let us by all means find another one. But let us not dodge the real issue by taking refuge in negatives, devices, and materials worshipped as ends in themselves, as *Dinge an sich*.

There still remains the question of communication, and it is one that is perhaps easier to answer than to state in exact terms. If we ask to whom is the composer speaking, the answer may be either that he is not speaking at all, or, on another level, that he is speaking to anyone who cares to listen to him. The nature of artistic communication is in reality not so much that of speaker and listener as that of participants in an experience shared in common. In the article to which I have already referred, Mr. Gerhard stressed the fact that it is the "willing ear" that constitutes the real listener not only to the music of today but to that of the past as well. It could be pointed out—and I believe Mr. Gerhard would agree—that the "willing ear" implies something decidedly more than passive acquiescence; especially in the case of contemporary music, the ear must be at least gracious as well as willing, and sufficiently aware of the rewards which the music can offer, to be ready to meet its demands. There is nothing peculiar to contemporary music in this state of affairs. Is it not true of all genuine experience in any sphere and on any level, that one's rewards bear a direct relationship to the contribution one is ready to bring to it? Music is peculiar among the arts because it is physically possible to hear it without really listening, and to imagine that one is receiving its full impact without any of the concentration which genuine listening requires—whether the work is complex and unfamiliar or, say, an opera of Bellini. The only difference is that in listening to a work that is familiar, we can let our minds wander freely and be sure that whatever sensation we receive from it will not be unpleasant. We do not necessarily have to pay close attention in order to avoid being bored, as is the case with practically every other art, including the theatre. Such compensations are not offered us by music that is new or unfamiliar; if we are to win from this what it has to offer, we must approach it as we would approach a new acquaintance to whom we are attracted, or a new country which we are visiting and from which we hope to derive some impressions that are real and rewarding. Such listeners as this implies are rare if one measures them against the mass public, though they are probably as numerous today as they have ever been; and it is quite possible that their number may increase as the mass public develops in experience. But it is they that constitute the real public and, now as always in the past, the court of final appeal; for they are the truly interested ones.

The intensity of their love for music and their need for musical experience gives them an authority and an influence quite incommensurable with their numbers. For it is quite unlikely, at least in our civilization, that they will ever constitute more than a small minority, even though no-one is excluded from their number if he really cares to join them. The very existence of the mass public, however, has made it more difficult in certain respects for the composer to reach them, though this distance can be, and in fortunate cases is, already bridged to a certain extent by the possibility of mechanical reproduction.

I do not offer these considerations as providing in any way a solution to the serious problems that face every young composer. I do however believe that he should make himself as aware as possible of all that genuine communication actually demands, as far as his own music is concerned. But at the same time he should realize that his only real security, as an artist, lies in being fully himself, and in giving fully what he has to give. The fact that this has been said many times and throughout the ages, and that it is much easier to say than to do, does not make it the less true. But the willing listeners are there if one can reach them. They consist in the final analysis of men and women living and recognizable as such, not merely as part of an anonymous "mass public." They have a profound need for the experience that music can give them, and they are ready to receive what the composer has to offer. Once the composer becomes really aware of them, and realizes that they constitute the channel through which his music can eventually reach larger numbers, he may conceivably feel not so much alone.

Problems and Issues Facing the Composer Today
[1960]

---

*In the Summer of 1959 the Fromm Music
Foundation sponsored a Seminar in Advanced
Musical Studies at Princeton University, under
the directorship of Roger Sessions. This essay
first appeared in a special issue of the* Musical
Quarterly *(April, 1960) devoted to various aspects of the work of the Seminar.*

THE premises behind such an undertaking as was attempted in last summer's Princeton Seminar in Advanced Musical Studies were of course based on the obvious changes in orientation and outlook that are taking
place—and have for many years been taking place—in the
minds, attitudes, and intentions of the composers, performers, and even listeners of our day. It is hardly necessary to
point out in these pages that change is inevitable at any
period whatever in the development of an art. The history
of the art is itself primarily an account of such changes and
an attempt to fathom both their wide-ranging causes and
their equally far-reaching effects, and to formulate terms in
which these can be adequately grasped. The History of Art
likewise seeks and provides criteria by which the main periods of change may be compared with one another in character and extent.

The history of Western music reveals at least two phases,
and possibly three, that may well have seemed to those who
observed them as contemporaries to shake the art of music
to its depths and to raise questions of the most fundamental
kind—questions, that is, not only as to the character and
trend of current developments, but as to the function, the

From *Musical Quarterly*, vol. 46, no. 2, Apr. 1960, pp. 159-171. Used
by permission of G. Schirmer, Inc.

significance, and even the ultimate nature of music itself. The beginnings of polyphony, the late sixteenth and early seventeenth century, and possibly the thirteenth and four-teenth—if this be not indeed considered as a late phase of the first-named—were such phases. They were periods of ap-parent crisis, during which long-established values were brought into deep question and challenged both on the most profound and the most superficial levels; "experimental" periods in the sense that many things were tried which soon proved abortive, while others, soon discarded, seemed to find justification at a much later date; but periods of intense creativity not only by virtue of the music of genius that survived them, but because they tapped new veins, uncover-ing the resources out of which the music of the following three or four centuries was to be built. In each period the musical transformation was coeval with a far-reaching trans-formation in Western society, and undoubtedly related to it, though the exact nature of this relationship seems—at least to this writer—far more difficult to penetrate and to clarify than it is frequently assumed to be.

The period in which we live has at the very least much in common with these earlier ones. For well over a hundred years each successive generation has seemed to many of its members to contain within itself the seeds of the imminent destruction, not only of a great musical tradition, but pos-sibly of music itself. Though this had happened at earlier periods also, it has happened at a steadily increasing tempo since, roughly, the death of Beethoven. Each generation has, to be sure, at length become assimilated, by and large, to the "main stream"; the "revolutions" have in each case been discovered eventually to be not so revolutionary after all, and the revolutionaries of one generation have become sym-bols of conservatism and eventually clubs with which to beat their revolutionary successors of the next. But, with each succeeding phase, this has come about a little more slowly, and there is no doubt an easily discernible reason for this. It is true that in our time the situation of all the arts, and in all of their phases, has been rendered far more complex, first through the development of mass media, and the consequent immeasurable expansion of the more-or-less interested public, and secondly through various economic factors, including not only the decline of private patronage and the consequent and inevitable increase in commercialization, but drastically rising costs in virtually every phase of musical production. It is however no less true that, precisely at this moment of economic and, if you will, social crisis in the arts, the inner dynamic of music itself should be leading to developments of which the eventual result can at best be only dimly sensed.

One symptom—or result—of this, of course, may be seen in the increasing articulateness of musicians themselves in regard to their own artistic principles. Since the early years of the nineteenth century composers have felt more and more inclined to express themselves in print regarding music and all of its phases. In the case of earlier composers—Mozart and Beethoven, for instance—one must rely on correspondence, on reminiscences, and on a few sibylline and perhaps problematic quotations that have become traditional, and no doubt often distorted, if one wants to discover their working principles beyond the evidence of the music itself. From Carl Maria von Weber on, however, composers have devoted considerable effort and energy to criticism, later to theory, and more recently still to teaching. This is certainly due in very large part to the fact that, in a period of artistic upheaval, creative artists find themselves first of all sharply aware of their own relationship to their traditional inheritance and to the directions in which they feel impelled to extend or even to reject it. Secondly, they find themselves, in a period in which the formulated notions regarding musical esthetics, musical theory, and musical syntax have long since lost the vitality they once possessed, impelled or even obliged to arrive at what are at least working formulations of their own. If they are not to remain in relative solitude they are also likely to communicate these formulations. Since the cultural pessimism of our time abhors solitude—once considered a decidedly honorable state for an artist—and demands "news" at almost any price, they may even find themselves virtually compelled to do so.

One has only to open practically any European periodical devoted to living music in order to become aware of the intellectual ferment that characterizes the musical life of today. One will find there, as one finds in fact on all hands, serious and often acute discussion of every phase, from aesthetic attitudes in general to the most precise and esoteric matters, and on a level that the conscientious artist of mature age, or the ambitious one of more tender years, cannot wholly ignore except at the price of an inherent lack of adventurousness which in itself bodes somewhat ill for his achievement as an artist. I of course do not mean to imply by this that he is bound to accept all or even any of the ideas he will find urged upon him. If he is genuinely adventurous he will accept anything whatever only strictly on his own terms. But he will find himself, certainly, challenged at every point, and obliged to find his own answer to the challenges thus presented to him; and if he is young and gifted he will welcome these challenges as a test of his creative conviction, if not as a source of direct stimulation along the lines of his own expression. At the very least, he will have the opportunity to become more aware of his own musical nature, and at the best he will learn to be untiring in his effort to avail himself of that opportunity, and to pursue his own creative efforts accordingly.

That the situation as I have described it contains its own peculiar pitfalls is, of course, obvious. I am not referring to the comment one frequently hears to the effect that a period in which musicians think and talk so much about their art must necessarily be a sterile one. As a matter of fact the present-day habit of drawing broad inferences of such a kind—apparently plausible but inherently far-fetched—is one against which we should guard ourselves in the name of elementary logic. It is not my purpose here, however, to propose value judgments on contemporary music, but merely to comment on facts and phenomena as they exist. But the least one can do is to point out that contemporary music, and in fact any music whatever, is to be judged in terms of music itself, not of circumstances with which no clear connection can be convincingly demonstrated. One cannot insist too strongly or too frequently that, in the arts generally and in music in particular, it is only productions that really count, and that only in these—music, written or performed—are to be found the criteria by which ideas about music, as well as music itself, must finally stand or fall: not the converse. This is a refrain that will recur repeatedly in the course of this discussion, as indeed it must in the course of any valid discussion of music.

The generic pitfall at which I have hinted is precisely this one. In an age in which theoretical speculation in either the aesthetic or the technical sphere has assumed the importance it has in our own, there is always the danger that it may be over-valued, and assumed to furnish criteria in itself, and not regarded simply as a means that may prove useful in helping composers to achieve the artistic results they are seeking—in the realization, that is, of a genuine musical vision. Again, one finds oneself obliged to emphasize that the primary function of the composer is to possess, develop, and with the utmost intensity to realize his own particular vision—a vision which, if it is genuinely vital, will be found to contain both general and specifically personal elements; and that theory and aesthetics can have validity for him only in so far as they can find roots in this vision. Otherwise they can represent only a flight away from music, or at a very dubious best, a crutch on which a faltering musical impulse can find some measure of support.

It is in fact fairly easy to recognize the pitfalls characteristic of those past musical periods with which we are most familiar. To a certain extent they are mirrored in the way in which these periods are regarded by the succeeding generations, which rebel against them. The characteristic pitfall of the nineteenth century was undoubtedly that of literary association and the manner of over-emphasis—sentimental, violent, or pretentious—just as that of the eighteenth was a certain type of elegant and formal conventionality. Our own particular brand of emptiness is perhaps beginning to emerge in a variety of clichés, derived both from so-called neo-classicism and from serialism in its earlier as well as its later phases. In each case we are dealing with a manner that has become generalized through lack of substance, and not with ideas in any positive sense. What is necessary, if the pitfalls are to be avoided, is that composers in the first place should always retain the courage of their own artistic vision, that teachers should emphasize the supremacy of real musical imagination, and that listeners, of whatever category, should, by holding themselves open to whatever genuine and even unexpected experience music can bring, learn to discriminate between what is authentic and what is fictitious.

Thus far I have spoken at length of a general situation in the musical world, and of some of the questions that situation raises as such, without attempting to deal with the situation itself, its background, or its nature, other than to characterize it in the very generalized sense of the decay of one tradition and the gradual movement towards new factors capable of superseding it. The ultimate shape these developments will assume is still by no means definitive in its outlines; but both their causes and their present trends are in certain respects quite clear, as are the specific questions posed by the latter.

It seems clear, for example, that the development of harmony as we have traditionally conceived it has probably reached a dead end. First of all, composers have for many years felt able to utilize all possible vertical combinations of tones, and have so abundantly availed themselves of that possibility that any new discoveries in this regard are virtually unthinkable. Even this fact, however, tells only a part of the story, since the possibilities are not so rich as

this purely statistical assumption would indicate. As more and more tones are added to any chord, each added tone contributes less to the character of the chord, or, in other words, to the factor that differentiates it from other combinations of tones. The decisive development of harmony, therefore, depends overwhelmingly on combinations of a relatively small number of tones; beyond that number, so to speak, the ear refuses to interest itself in strictly harmonic effect. It is not so much a question of possibilities as such, as of possibilities that are in any way decisive. The real point is that composers seem by and large no longer interested in chords as such, and that this is a tacit recognition that there is nothing left to be discovered, in the sphere of harmony, that arouses any feeling of excitement on their part.

Something similar had of course taken place already in regard to functional harmony. Based very clearly on a triadic premise, the principle of root progression had given way before the proliferation of "altered chords" that was so characteristic a feature of harmonic evolution in the nineteenth century. The process is a perfectly familiar one which need not be summarized here. Suffice it to say that what is often called "atonality" was a very gradual development—so gradual, in fact, that, aside from the literal meaning of the term itself, it is impossible to define with any precision whatever. It is in other words impossible to show exactly where tonality ends and "atonality" begins unless one establishes wholly arbitrary lines of demarcation in advance.

This is not the main objection to the term, however. "Atonality" implies music in which not only is the element of what is defined as "tonality" no longer a principle of construction, but in which the composer deliberately avoids all procedures capable of evoking "tonal" associations. Actually this is virtually impossible, owing to the mere fact that we use tones, and hear them in relation to each other. In other words, whenever a series of tones is heard, the musical

77

ear assimilates it by perceiving a pattern composed not only of tones but of intervals; and neither the process nor the sensation is different in any essential principle from the process by which one assimilates music that is unimpeachably "tonal." I am reliably informed that Anton Webern himself insisted on this point, and even on specifically tonal references in his own music.

Whatever real sense the word "atonality" may have derives from the fact that the further a chord departs from a strictly triadic structure, the less unequivocal it becomes in terms of a specific key; and that, in the proportion that such harmonies become predominant in musical usage, it becomes more difficult to establish genuine tonal contrast, and the effort to do so becomes more forced. As the cadence, in the early years of this century, came to acquire for composers more and more the aspect of a cliché, and as the composers found themselves more and more obliged to discover other means of achieving musical articulation, they found themselves obliged to discover new principles of contrast as well. They discovered that in the absence of strictly triadic harmony it was virtually impossible to establish a feeling of key sufficiently unequivocally to make possible a genuine and definitive change of key, and that hence tonality was for them no longer sufficient as a principle of structure. It was this discovery perhaps above all that led to both the adoption of the serial principle by Schoenberg and the attempt to find ways towards the revitalization of tonal principles that was embodied in the "neo-classicism" of Stravinsky.

The above does not mean, of course, that harmony has ceased to exist in any music, or that it has become an element that can be ignored. Our harmonic sense is essentially the awareness of one of the dimensions of music; having acquired that awareness, we cannot do away with it, and it would be ridiculous folly to try to do so. If art is to develop, awareness of every aspect of the art must increase rather than diminish. But harmonic effect as such has clearly ceased to be a major interest of composers, just as tonality has ceased to be an issue or a point of reference against which issues can be adequately discussed. To be sure, the question still arises constantly in the public discussion of music; but such discussion can have no meaning except on the level of very precise technical definition. We are dealing with facts, not with slogans, and the facts have to be referred to basic aesthetic and acoustical considerations, rather than to specific historical embodiments of these. If by "tonality" we mean, in the most general terms, the sense of pitch-relationship and of the patterns and structures that can be created out of such relationships, the word "atonality" can have no meaning, as long as we use tones. If we mean, on the other hand, a precise set of technical principles and hence of procedures, it is easy to see in retrospect that the very vitality with which it developed led ultimately beyond the principle itself.

If the cadence, as conventionally defined, came finally to seem to many composers, in the context of their own music, little more than a cliché, it was because they came to feel a definite disparity between the harmonic vocabulary native to them and the harmonies necessary to establish the cadence. While the composers of the late nineteenth century—one senses the problem already in the music of Wagner—succeeded in overcoming this disparity, often through sheer technical ingenuity and sometimes with visible effort, their successors often found this impossible to achieve without stylistic violence. It was necessary either to turn backward or to seek new principles.

As we all know, a similar development took place in the rhythmic sphere. It took place more quietly and with far less opposition, if indeed there was any appreciable opposition whatever. There is no need to dwell on the rhythmic question here. Though the changes that have taken place have been equally far-reaching, they have been in a sense less spectacular and less esoteric, if only for the reason that they owe so much to the influence of popular music and of

Gregorian Chant. They have found incomparably more ready acceptance, both from musicians and from the general public, than the developments of which I have spoken in the realm of harmony. Furthermore, the rhythmic aspects of music are bound closely and inevitably to the other elements of the musical vocabulary; in this sense one can say that the development of music away from the tonal and cadential principle has also created a whole new set of rhythmic premises and requirements.

In any event, the focal point of the more advanced musical thought of today is polyphonic, and more concerned with problems of texture and organization than with harmony in the hitherto accepted meaning of the term. Once more, this does not mean that composers have ceased to be acutely aware of vertical relationships between tones, of progressions from one vertical conglomerate to another, or even of the patterns formed by such progressions. But it is certainly true, I think, that they tend more and more to think of these matters in terms of texture rather than harmony as hitherto defined. The current trend is to refer to such vertical conglomerates as "densities" rather than as "chords" or "harmonies"; but it must be stressed that there is no satisfactory substitute for awareness of the entire musical context, and that the replacement of one term by another is useful in so far as it increases that awareness, and does not connote the evasion of one issue in favor of another.

It is of course fashionable to regard Webern as the patron saint of the dominant contemporary trend, and to invoke his name as a rallying point for all that is most aggressively anti-traditional in contemporary music. As is so apt to be the case, there is a discrepancy at many points between Webern the symbol and Webern the actual figure. The latter, however individual his musical style, was of course as deeply rooted in the Viennese tradition as Schoenberg himself, and probably more narrowly; and without in any sense meaning to detract from his musical stature, one can say that he remained a loyal disciple to the extent of being more Schoenbergian than Schoenberg himself. In the last analysis he was at least as much the Romantic Expressionist as Alban Berg, if not more so. Above all, and most important, he was a musician of the ripest culture, at once the most daring and the most realistic of artists. The teacher who at times finds himself obliged to stress the fact—so easily lost from view in the heat of speculative enthusiasm —that musical values are, first and last, derived from tones and rhythms and the effects they produce, and not from their theoretical consistency or analytical plausibility, can find no better or more demonstrable evidence in his own behalf than that furnished by almost any score of Webern.

At the same time, however, one may find oneself impelled to question the sufficiency of the post-Webernian trend as a firm and comprehensive basis for new departures in music. This brings us to the large question of serialism, which I have deliberately postponed till after discussing some of the factors that have given rise to it. One cannot, of course, stress too much that serialism is neither the arbitrary nor the rigid set of prescriptions that it is often supposed to be, not only by its foes but unfortunately also by some of its friends. It is rather the result of many converging trends of musical development, of which I have mentioned a couple of the most important and the most general ones. Above all, perhaps, it is the result of the decreasing validity of the harmonic principle as an organizing force, and the necessity of adopting consistent relationships between tones, which can serve as a constructive basis for the organization of musical ideas, along both the horizontal and the vertical dimensions.

Quite as important is to stress that serialism is in full process of development, and that the shapes it has taken are already manifold. It is no longer the exclusive possession of any one "school" or group of composers, nor is it bound to any one mode of expression, Viennese or otherwise. Need one cite evidences, at this date? In other words, it is a technical principle that a wide number and variety of composers have found useful for their own purposes, both because of the organizing principles they have derived from it and because of the musical resources it has opened up for them. Like any other technical principle, it yields nothing in itself; it is always for the imagination of the composer to discover what it can give him, and to mold it to his own uses. Like any other technical principle, it has to be thoroughly mastered, in terms of the composer's creative vision; a half-baked relationship to it in this respect can produce only less than half-baked results. For this reason the young composer who has not grown up with it from the beginning—there are already a number who have done so, and to whom it is, so to speak, native—would be well-advised to avoid it until he has become sure of his own musical identity, and can grow into it in full conviction and genuine musical maturity. It does not provide answers to all musical questions or in the last analysis to any; it is only a vehicle and a means, which, let us reiterate, many composers find useful. Once more like other technical principles, it has acquired its own brand—several brands, in fact—of academicism, and many varieties of cliché, which are none the less recognizable as clichés for being derived from a technical principle that has been in active existence for little more than forty years. Its value lies wholly in the music of the composers who have seen fit to adopt it, and the value of that music resides in the imaginative, emotive, and constructive force inherent in it, not in the ingenuities with which the system is applied, except in so far as these are the inherent result of a musical conception.

The serial organization of tones must be, and for the most part is, today regarded as a settled fact—the composer is free to take it or leave it, or to adopt it with varying degrees of rigor, as he may choose. The results it can yield are open to all to see and judge as they see fit. More problematical are some attempts that have been made to extend serial organization to other aspects of music—notably to that of rhythmic values and that of dynamics. Any discussion of these matters must emphasize once more that it is only results that matter; that the human imagination works along channels that are frequently unexpected; and that a critical scrutiny of technical premises does not release one in the slightest degree from the responsibility of holding one's mind, ear, and heart open to whatever may reveal genuinely new vistas of musical expression and experience.

With this caution in mind one can easily observe that tones are, for the musical ear, fixed and readily identifiable points in musical space, and that the progress from one tone to another has a clear point of departure and arrival. This is partly the result of the fact that within the octave there are only twelve tones, with which the musical ear has familiarized itself over the course of many centuries; and the additional fact that our musical culture has taught us to regard as equivalent tones that occupy the same position within the various octaves. A, for instance, is recognizable as A whether it be played on the open A string of the double-bass, of the 'cello, or of the violin—or, for that matter, in the high register of the flute or the piccolo. Time values, on the other hand, are by no means fixed; their range is to all intents and purposes infinite. This does not at all exclude the possibility of adopting an arbitary series of time values for the purposes of any single composition, but it does raise very valid questions regarding the serialization of time values as a general principle. The serialization of dynamics, however, raises questions of a much more fundamental nature. Dynamic values are by their very essence relative, both in an objective and a subjective sense. They have quite different meanings for different media and under different conditions. How can we regard as equivalent, except on the most practical level of balance, a given nuance on, say, the oboe and the violin, or for that matter, the same nuance in different registers of the same instrument; or on the same note on the same instrument, sounded in a small room, a large concert hall, and the open air? What does the indication p actually mean, and how can we as listeners distinguish in clear terms a transition from mf to f, or even from mp to ff?

The basic question of all is of course—as is often the case —"Why?" The principle of so-called "total organization" raises many questions and answers none, even in theory. First of all, what is being organized, and according to what criterion? Is it not rather a matter of organizing, not music itself, but various facets of music, each independently and on its own terms or at best according to a set of arbitrarily conceived and ultimately quite irrelevant rules of association? Was the music of Beethoven, or whom you will, not totally organized in a sense that is much more real, since it is an organization of musical ideas and not of artificially abstracted elements?

The subject of "total organization" leads naturally to the consideration of electronic media, since the latter make possible the exact control of all musical elements, and make possible in a sense also a partial answer to some of the questions I have raised. Since the potentialities of electronic media in the realm of sound are, at least to all intents and purposes, infinite, it is possible to measure all musical elements in terms of exact quantity, and in fact necessary to do so, since such measurement is the very nature of the instruments and the method by which they are used. A dynamic nuance thus not only can, but must, become a fixed quantity, as can and must, also, any tone in the whole range of pitch or color gradations. Every moment of music not only can but must be the result of the minutest calculation, and the composer for the first time has the whole world of sound at his disposal.

That electronic media will play a vital and possibly even decisive role in the future of music is not to be doubted. I must confess however to skepticism as to what that precise role will be. Two questions seem to me to be crucial. First of all, it is not sufficient to have the whole world at one's disposal—the very infinitude of possibilities cancels out possibilities, as it were, until limitations are discovered. No doubt the limitations are there, and if not there they are certainly in human beings. But the musical media we know thus far derive their whole character and their usefulness as musical media precisely from their limitations—stringed instruments derive their character and utility not only from the fact that they are stringed instruments, that the tone is produced by stroking strings, but from the fact that they are not wind or percussion instruments; and we have learned to use them with great subtlety of effect and power of expression because of that. The dilemma of electronic musical media is a little like that of the psychologist who is reputed once to have said to one of his friends, "Well, I have got my boy to the point where I can condition him for anything I want. What shall I condition him for?"

The other question has to do with the essential nature of music itself. Is music simply a matter of tones and rhythmic patterns, or in the final analysis the organization of time in terms of human gesture and movement? The final question regarding all music that is mechanically reproduced seems to be bound up with the fact that our active sense of time is dependent in large degree on our sense of movement, and that mechanical repetition mitigates and finally destroys this sense of movement in any given instance; it destroys also our sense of expression through movement, which plays so large and obvious a part in our musical experience. This is what lies behind the discussions of the element of "chance," which has so bothered the proponents of "total organization." But the element that "total organization" leaves out of account is not chance at all. It is the organic nature of movement as such, of the fresh and autonomous energy with which the performer invests each musical phrase, every time he sings or plays it, and which gradually disappears for our awareness if we listen so often to a mechanical reproduction of it that we become completely familiar with it, to the point of knowing always exactly what is coming next. It is more than the element of mere "surprise"; rather, if the expression of movement is to become effective, we require not only the evidence of movement from one point to the next, but a sense of the motivating energy behind it.

To raise these questions is not in any sense to reject the principle of electronic music as such. In the first place, composers are beginning to feel the need for new instruments. The existing ones, for all their technical perfection, are beginning at times to seem vaguely obsolete as far as some of the composers' musical ideas are concerned. The possibilities electronic music suggests are altogether likely to make this situation more acute.

In my own opinion, electronic media more than justify their existence if only by the new insight one can gain from them into the nature of sound, musical and otherwise, and above all by a vast quantity of fresh experience they can provide, on the purely acoustical level. They are still in a clearly very primitive stage and it is impossible to say what they may contribute in the future. But they raise the above questions and many others, and the questions will certainly become more acute as the media develop.

One hears a good deal, these days, of the developing "dehumanization" of music and the other arts; and specifically in regard to the tendencies we discussed in detail at the Princeton Seminar last year, and which I have been discussing in these pages. This is all very well, and not without its plausibility; but we are speaking of a movement that is widespread among the younger composers of Europe, that has begun to take root in the United States, and that above all is in constant development and evolution. Many ideas are being tested, and many are quickly discarded. If we regard certain manifestations with raised eyebrows, that is our privilege as members of an older generation, as it is always our privilege to point out flaws in logic. But if it is also our prerogative to insist on the primacy of the creative imagination, and to minimize the decisive importance of theoretical speculation, we are at the same time obliged to abide by our own premises and look towards artistic results rather than towards the ideas by which these are rationalized. By the same token it is well to remember that art, considered on the most objective level, reflects the attitudes of the individuals that produce it. The danger of dehumanization is a real and patent one, and the individual can, and certainly should, resist any dehumanizing tendency with all his strength. But this cannot, and must not, blind us to the claims of whatever is genuinely new and vital in the arts, or, once more, cause us to forget that the product, not the process, is of real importance, and that the creative imagination, at its most vital, has revealed itself through many and often surprising channels. There is no reason to believe that it will not continue to do so, as long as creative vitality— which for musicians means above all the intense love of music—continues to persist.

Style and "Styles" in Music
[1961]

*A lecture delivered at Reed
College in Portland, Oregon*

I AM sure that I have been asked to speak to you as a practicing representative of the arts, in which role I pretend some competence, and not of either aesthetics or history, in which, in spite of occasional contacts and even dabblings, I pretend none. If I trespass on territory where I do not belong, my intentions are quite innocent, and I apologize in advance. I will try to speak strictly as a musician, and a practical one. I owe enormous debts to scholarship—especially musical scholarship, and to the experience which I have received from the visual arts, from literature, and from the non-musical as well as the musical theatre— and I should be repaying these shabbily indeed if I were to regard my competence in any of these subjects as comparable to that which I claim in the creative activity to which I have primarily devoted my life.

I therefore hope that what I have to say in regard to music may have some general relevance, even though I cannot always see exact parallels in other fields for the distinctions I wish to make with specific reference to music. Some parallels, certainly, I shall assume, and above all, and most obviously, that of the problem of style itself.

It seems to me therefore natural to open a discussion of style in terms of the artist at work. How does the problem present itself, and by what means does he achieve a satisfactory result? Let me stress the point that I am attempting to speak of the artist at work, while he—or she—is in the actual process of what we call artistic creation, or invention, and not of the observations he may make regarding either the process or the result, necessarily at times when he is not directly engaged in it. The latter, however acute, may or may not be relevant to the subject of discussion. They are certainly always to be taken in a specific context, since both the artist's training and his activities lie properly in the realm of immediate experience, and he is likely to have little interest or ability in the realm either of abstract generalization or of precise conceptual or even verbal formulation.

To the artist at work, at all events, it would seem highly unlikely that the problem of style should present itself in abstract terms; unlikely, even, that he would even think very actively of style as such. But, assuming that he is a mature artist, possessed of a genuine conception, it is precisely in the direction of style that his efforts are directed.

Let me try to be specific in terms of my own art. Aside from such strictly technical matters as have to do with the effective realization of a musical work in performance, a composer will first find himself preoccupied with such questions as unity, coherence, rhythmic balance and balance of contrast, consistency of idiom. He may conceivably ask himself what has to be done in order to bring highly contrasting ideas into a coherent musical picture; how an envisaged climax is to be prepared in such a way as to give it the desired force; or, conversely, how, having prepared a climax, he is to develop the latter sufficiently to balance the expectancy aroused by the preparation. He may find himself dissatisfied by a given sonority which would be either so bland in its context as to create a sudden gap in the general texture of sound, or on the other hand so harsh as to create a violent contrast and therefore an accent at a point or in a context where none is needed, or otherwise out of the picture as he conceives it.

Secondly, a composer will certainly find himself deeply involved in questions which may be grouped under the general heading of continuity. Does the movement flow smoothly and consistently in the direction he has conceived, or does it proceed by unmotivated jerks? Does the music, as we may say, breathe properly, or should the phrases be a little more widely spaced here, or tumble on each other a little more closely there? Does a given contrast require an elaborate transition or an abrupt one? Or, how must the rhythmic pattern established be developed in such a way as to move naturally, under its own momentum, into the next one?

At other moments the composer will be engaged by the problem of clarity. Is the instrumental or vocal texture well defined—as transparent or as dense as he may wish? Has the composer succeeded in eliminating non-essentials which can only impede the flow of the music? Is the effect which he is producing as light or, conversely, as weighty as he intends? Is the choice or spacing of instruments or voices the one which will bring his ideas into sharpest relief? Is the phrase structure, with its preparations and its cadences, clear, and in balance?

One could of course go on further, and speak of the matter of conciseness, of tightness or looseness of construction, of elaboration or non-elaboration of detail. In any case, I have not of course wished to give an exhaustive or even summary account of the process of composition, but simply to exemplify some among many of the composer's conscious preoccupations (concrete and presumably quite unverbalized) while he is actually at work. They are, obviously, considerations of an overwhelmingly practical nature in the service of which he has developed his technical resources, and which these resources will make it possible for him to meet in his own way.

It will no doubt be noticed that I have thus far not mentioned the most important preoccupation of all, as far as the artist's drive toward style is concerned. This omission has been due to the fact that it is both a much less tangible and even a not necessarily fully conscious preoccupation. It is, however, the ultimately determining ingredient of style itself. Of course I am referring to the specific musical ideas which form the basis of a musical work, and the conception, which will determine the character of the work in all of its features. One may say that the matters of which I have up to this point spoken all involve questions of practical execution—and often, in a very real sense, of calculation. In connection with all of them the experienced composer will have learned to depend heavily on a faculty of judgment and almost routine intuition which is scarcely to be distinguished from that which, on a different level, we call technique. His craft will have developed, through experience, to the point where the knowledge of what he wants is scarcely to be distinguished from the process of achieving it, and where his dominant energies are brought to bear on the ideas themselves, in terms of concentration, of precision, and of profile. These properties, in fact, will tend to inform his whole work, and to the extent that they succeed in doing this, he will have achieved style. And indeed, style may perhaps be very accurately described in the not too happily alliterative, but nevertheless inevitable terms, profile and precision. In musical terms, the word style, properly understood, implies that the composer has achieved sharpness of definition, not only of his musical ideas but of their embodiment in a musical composition. Every note, and indeed every phrase of the work, performs a clear function in a definitive design and is in the place in which it belongs, to a degree that we often speak of "inevitability."

What I have thus far tried to give is of course only an indication of the process of style from the point of view of the artist at his work. If we approach the matter somewhat differently it becomes obvious that there are other earmarks, at which I have scarcely hinted. To be sure, I have used the word "profile" and related it to the artist's underlying conception of a given work. Behind this specific conception, which the artist embodies or, as we say, realizes, in a specific work, is his vision of his art as a whole. In a real sense the central objective of his life as an artist has been the development of this vision, from his early efforts toward self-discovery through the refinements and the expanding areas of insight which his artistic experience brings him. The identity which he achieves is inevitably the result of a total effort, that is to say, one which engages the whole of his artistic energies. Unless it does this it is obviously incomplete. Genuine style, therefore, will bear the earmarks of such an identity; and its profile will be essentially that of its author.

Thus I believe we can note a few of the inherent characteristics of genuine style. Not only will it be characterized by sharpness and precision of outline, but that outline will delineate a real visage, always recognizable as such; in other words, once more, an identity. Or, in still other and oft-repeated words, the style is in an entirely true sense the man.

Let me admit freely at this point that the word "style," even in much the terms that I have thus far outlined, may be entirely legitimately used in contexts which transcend the work of the individual artist. I wish however to dwell a little longer on its individual aspects, simply for the purpose of defining a few corollaries and perhaps even hinting at some widespread fallacies.

First of all, if it be true that "the style is the man," it follows fairly logically that we can also say "no man, no style." Lest this seem a trifle obvious, let us only recall the efforts which are to be noticed in every period, and perhaps especially in our own, to define and even to solve the problem of style in terms which leave the human being largely or even completely out of account. In this category belong most obviously, of course, the various attempts which we witness from time to time to base aesthetic theory on so-called "objective" criteria, sometimes derived from the materials of art rather than from artistic expression itself, sometimes from sources, scientific, mathematical or otherwise, which have no real relationship to the art in question, or even to art as such. I do not mean at all by this statement to condemn all efforts to gain from any source whatever, the technical insight which such a source may provide; I would insist only that the values proper to an art are derived from the experience which the art provides, and that the search for them elsewhere than in terms of that experience is bound to be a futile one, productive only of confusion and wasted effort.

Let me draw another inference, and a much subtler one, from the conception of style which I have tried to outline. In defining the style as the man, we are stating what is by implication essentially an inclusive and not a restrictive concept. According to this concept, style is in essence the imprint of an individual on the whole range of artistic material within his ken; it is not at all to be defined in terms of a selection of a part of that material and the exclusion of another part. The distinction is an important one, I believe, and one which has, at least in our musical life, many varied applications. One of these was first made clear to me by my teacher Ernest Bloch, who later became an illustrious citizen of Oregon. The incident took place the first time I ever met him, as a young student. After pointing out the obvious fact that, in my music, there were influences from many sources, he made it clear to me that it was of no real importance that these were present. This was natural in the work of a young man; the important thing was that I also should be present, and my own imprint upon it. In other words, individuality and, carried one step further, style is achieved by virtue of a quality which is present in the music, and not by virtue of what is absent.

So too, for instance, when a young music student asks his teacher whether the fugue the latter has assigned is to be written "in the style of Bach," the teacher might quite justifiably if a little pedantically answer that this is impossible because Bach's style, like that of any other truly great composer, stretched the limits of the musical vocabulary of Bach's day, whereas, since our present-day vocabulary has expanded far beyond that of Bach, one cannot today write really in his style. While Bach constantly used all of the musical resources known to him, we, in imitating his results, must inevitably restrict the use of the resources available to us. For us, the process of imitating the "style" of any master of the past means moving in the opposite direction from that followed by the master in creating it. I of course do not mean to imply that this kind of imitation is to be shunned or condemned; it can have at the very least, in some cases, a real pedagogical value. What I do mean is simply to take note of the fact that if we use the word "style" in this connection, we are denoting not the profound essence of style itself, but merely its rough external appearance. In order to capture its real outlines, we would be obliged to find ourselves somehow in the same relationship to the musical vocabulary of the composer's time as that in which the latter himself stood. For one thing: in imitating the style of an artist, we find ourselves obliged to establish or postulate a norm, with clearly understood limits beyond which it is a violation of style to pass. The original artist was bound by no such fixed limits. The work of most if not all great artists—composers, at any rate—is certainly characterized at times by what we consider as exceptional flights of daring, consisting sometimes of exceptionally poignant or dramatically accented contrasts, sometimes of subtleties so refined as to puzzle not only the composer's contemporaries, but even succeeding generations, until their secret is finally discovered. In enumerating all these possibilities I have of course specific instances in mind, which I would cite here if time permitted and if making my point clear did not involve an extended musical program. Of another type of daring, however, I would cite the opera *Die Zauberflöte*, in which Mozart brought together elements of palpably diverse character. Were it not for an overwhelming and unmistakable imprint of character which not only stamps every phrase with Mozart's signature, but informs it with the strong and unique character or atmosphere of the work itself, one might gravely question the unity of style. It is true that there are still those who find the work disturbing. Ferruccio Busoni, the great

Italian pianist and composer, who was certainly one of the keenest musical minds of his time, is said to have remarked that musicians could be divided into two groups, those who find *Die Zauberflöte* an inferior opera based on an absurd libretto and those who find it the greatest of all operas, based on a text which, with Mozart's music to animate it, proves to be the most satisfying and inherently dramatic libretto ever set to music. Busoni indicated that he belonged to the latter group. So do I—and we have on our side Beethoven and in a sense Mozart himself, along with a host of others. Whether or not one agrees literally with Busoni, however, *Die Zauberflöte* could scarcely today be considered a controversial work; and my object in citing it was simply to point out the immense daring of its creator, one of the supreme men of genius in the whole history of the arts, in bringing together in one work elements so apparently disparate that in the hands of a lesser artist the result might well have been a hopeless mixture of styles. In Mozart's case, however, the worst that can conceivably be said is that it presents a somewhat problematical mixture, not of styles but of *genres*.

I spoke in my preceding paragraph of the "strong and unique character and atmosphere" of *Die Zauberflöte*. This brings me to another point which I consider relevant to the present discussion. Reverting to the question of imitation, it is clear that even the rough external appearance of a style is far easier to imitate in the case of some artists than in that of others. One can see this very clearly in the products of a type of *tour de force* which used to be fairly prevalent at one time: the practice of writing, on a given theme, variations in the manner of different composers. What I have always found striking in works of this kind is that while the variations, in the case of certain composers, actually succeed in conveying an idea of the manner, or style, of the composer in question, others invariably either are modeled clearly on one specific work, or fail to give a convincing suggestion of the composer. The composers are in nearly all cases the same ones: Chopin, Schumann, Debussy, for instance, in the former group, and Beethoven, Mozart, and Wagner in the other.

And yet no one in the least familiar with the work of any one of the three last-named composers would dream of finding his style lacking in identity. One recognizes the gesture and the accent of Beethoven or Mozart as infallibly as one does that of Chopin or Debussy, and recognizes it in every phrase of every work. The style, however, in both of these cases is certainly far less easy to define, and attempts to describe the creative physiognomy of either one of them are generally ludicrous in their insufficiency. The same is certainly true of Wagner and many others. For these composers all possessed, in an amazing degree, the faculty of creating a new and unique musical world with every important work. I have already spoken of *Die Zauberflöte*; but the very point I was trying to make is that the musical profile of *Die Zauberflöte* is not only consistent, but completely individual—as different from that of *Figaro*, or *Don Giovanni*, or *Così fan tutte* as these are from each other. The same may be said of Mozart's instrumental works. It may also be said of *Tristan, Die Meistersinger, The Ring of the Nibelung*, and *Parsifal*, as it can be said of the symphonies, quartets, and sonatas of Beethoven. This cannot be said in anything like the same degree of Chopin, of Schumann, of Debussy—in our own time, of Anton Webern, or, in the eighteenth century, of Domenico Scarlatti.

It would seem that we can distinguish here two well-defined tendencies in the development of style. One type of artistic sensibility develops, we may say, in the direction of range, the other in that of refinement. Of course these terms are ridiculously inadequate if not both qualified and rather carefully defined. In the first place, no artist can ever attain considerable stature without a very considerable measure of both range and refinement. The refinement of Beethoven is of a totally different nature from that of Chopin and, so to speak, differently located, but it is nevertheless

formidable; and Chopin's very personal world was popu-
lated by a great richness of individual types. One has only
to hear a performance of his complete set of Preludes, as
I did recently, to be aware that his range, too, was enormous, as was that of each of the other composers that I
have mentioned.

Nor must one fall into the error of regarding the distinction I am attempting to define, as one of stature or
quality. While I believe it is true that the artists whom we
regard as supreme belong with the Beethovens rather than
with the Chopins, it does not follow at all that a difference
in type indicates a difference in stature. Tchaikovsky, for
instance, was a composer of great range who, like Wagner
and Beethoven, created a variety of what I have called
musical worlds. One has to remember his ballets and his
operas, as well as his symphonies and his quartets; while
Brahms, in spite of his large canvas and the variety of his
conceptions seems, to me at least, in the respect of which
I am speaking now, far closer to Schumann than to Beethoven or Mozart. A comparison of Brahms's songs, taken
in the aggregate, with those of Schubert seems to me to
illustrate this point very clearly. Yet I think that few mature
musicians, even perhaps in Tchaikovsky's native country,
would regard Tchaikovsky as an artist of quite the stature
of either Brahms or Chopin. I am indicating a difference
in type and direction, and not necessarily in stature.

Nevertheless, I find the distinction an important one,
especially today. I say "especially today" because I see today
a very prevalent confusion regarding the whole matter of
style. The confusion which I have in mind can perhaps be
roughly summarized in an overvaluation of what I have
called refinement, coupled with a very fundamental misunderstanding of its real nature. I fancy that I see evidence
of the trend, though certainly not of the confusion, in the
work of one very great composer of this century who
seems to me to have carried the process of refinement so far
that his music, precisely at the period of his career when

it became most palpably characteristic, seems to me to have lost a great deal of its original force. The composer of whom I am thinking has been dead for nearly twenty years; his is a figure whom I revere greatly, and with whom I was personally acquainted on the most friendly terms. I am also stating a personal and at this point a distinctly minority opinion. I therefore prefer not to name him, at least not publicly. The confusion of which I have spoken is of course on a quite other level. At bottom it is the ancient confusion between ends and means, between material and substance, between appearance and reality, between dogma and principle. Its underlying motivation is certainly to be found in the human situation of today, and the insecurities which this situation engenders.

Precisely for this reason it seems to me necessary to recognize and to assert as boldly as possible that what I have defined as refinement is the result of a process of intensification, of the vital impulse toward precision and toward genuine profile, and not toward exclusiveness or impoverishment.

Properly understood, style is a living process, in every case a process of development and of boldness; and I often think that the most fitting motto for the young artist should be that of Danton: "De l'audace, toujours de l'audace, et encore de l'audace." If this motto is to be efficacious, however, the word "audace," boldness, must be understood in its primary sense; the artist must, as we say, "stick his neck out," and insist on being himself at all times and at all costs. It has nothing to do with the compulsion to seek novelty before all else; the novelty that is thus attained is inevitably perishable in the extreme, for the obvious reason that nothing is new more than once. Nor has refinement, any more than has originality, anything to do with what one excludes; it is achieved by growth and experience and concentrated artistic effort. All of these qualities—novelty, originality, refinement—are as it were by-products of this effort, even though they are certainly also earmarks of high artistic achievement. It is certainly a fact that the novelty which makes a real and permanent impact is of a quality which never disappears and which strikes one with undiminished force even in such a familiar work (but perhaps after all, never quite familiar) as Schubert's Unfinished Symphony, or Beethoven's Fifth, when the conductor has taken the trouble to study them afresh and when the hearer really listens. It is not merely novelty, in other words, but abiding uniqueness. In a similar vein, nothing could be further from the truth, or more exhaustively contradicted by the facts of at least musical history, as the still widespread picture of the "genius" as a young man who begins where his predecessors left off, toppling the established order at an early age, and then later settling down in benign and respected maturity, having turned out to be not so dangerous after all. No doubt, the intense vitality and personal force of the highly gifted artist is often—perhaps always—discernible from the start, though not always recognized in exactly these terms. But the really decisive—or, if you like, revolutionary—artistic achievements have always been the products of artistic maturity and not of adolescence. Let us freely admit, as we must in any case, that Schubert and, in particular, Mendelssohn reached an early artistic maturity that appears little short of miraculous; and if I may be permitted one short and somewhat haphazard foray into my neighbor's orchards, the names of Masaccio and Keats and Rimbaud also come to mind. Maturity achieved phenomenally early is still nevertheless maturity, and as the word itself denotes, it is the result of a process of development which is ineluctable.

I have devoted the bulk of my paper to a discussion of "style" in connection with the individual artist; and as I look back a little ruefully to my title I wonder if my listeners are inwardly reproaching me for neglecting the second half of my subject. In answer to them let me say that, when confronted in this connection with the most difficult problem which I as a composer perennially have to face—

namely that of coming to a decision on a title for my lecture, I was tempted to call it, not "Style and Styles," but "Style versus Styles." I chose the former by reason of the (I trust) obvious fact that Styles, or if you like, a Style is not the enemy of Style as such, but the result of it. It is also obvious that a style—and the article, definite or indefinite, is of the utmost importance here—can embody the visage of an epoch, a culture, or a tendency, perhaps more problematically even of a nation, as clearly as that of an individual. What I would insist on is that one can speak definitively of *a* style only after *the* style is complete, when its development is ended and when one can view it in its totality. Certainly, we all of us, and I as much as anyone, use the term colloquially and to a certain extent even carelessly —a procedure which is inevitable, useful, and even harmless provided we keep the fundamental distinctions clearly in mind.

For the artist, however, the healthy state of affairs is that he strive, in terms at least similar to those I have attempted to describe, constantly in the direction of style, and that he remain on his guard against the temptation to search for, or to conform to, *a* style, against the demand, which he will hear frequently voiced, that a young composer should have this as his aim, and even against the idea that this can be accomplished, in the above terms. Instead, he has the far more exacting task of being himself, of discovering and writing the music which is really his own authentic voice, the music, let us say, which he is most anxious to bring into existence. I would go a little further and say that until he begins to have a sense, however elusive or fragmentary, of what this music may be, he has not yet begun really to compose, however many notes he may have put on paper. For the comfort of such young composers who may happen to be present, let me quickly add that this is not so cut-and-dried a process as it may sound, and that—once more—it is not an exclusive process; it involves first of all honesty with oneself, and may involve, too, the avoidance of unshakeable commitments to anything one may choose to try until one is convinced that one is genuinely captivated by it.

For the artist, in his constant striving for the achievement of style, is pushing in a direction strictly opposite to that implied in the definition and classification of styles. In stating this so categorically I do not intend to imply any denigration of the latter activity. Definition and classification of styles is an indispensable phase in our understanding of the past, both distant and immediate, and in the process which we call tradition. But tradition, on the other hand, can be considered vital only in so far as it includes a vivid awareness, as well as understanding, of the living process of style itself.

Possibly the underlying distinction—whether or not I have succeeded in making it clear—and the understanding of the distinction, is of the utmost moment for the effective survival of the arts, of culture, perhaps even of civilization. Under present circumstances we can almost regard it as having some bearing on the survival of man himself. For styles—and I believe this statement is as valid for the individual artist as for a cultural tradition—styles decay and degenerate if their vitalizing elements are forgotten, and even if they are not constantly renewed by fresh blood and by evolution. If not superseded by the fresh and positive impulses which are the life-blood of style, their decay and degeneration may easily constitute a fateful symptom of the drying up of the living germ of human aspiration.

II

The Composer and His Audience

Art, Freedom, and the Individual
[1957]

To celebrate its centennial, the University of the South in Sewanee, Tennessee, held two symposia on the subject of Christian Civilization. The first, on October 19, 1957, was devoted to the Humanities; the second, on April 19, 1958, to the Sciences. This paper was read at the first symposium.

I HOPE you will bear with me a little at the outset of my talk if I take a few moments to explain myself and my relation to my subject. I am, first of all, a practicing musician—a composer. While I claim considerable competence in my own field I am, becomingly I hope, quite modest in regard to any real competence in the other arts. I have some knowledge of them, it is true; I have known painters and poets and sculptors and architects and novelists. I believe the matters of which I have to speak are of as great interest and concern to those interested in other arts as they are to music lovers, and I confidently hope that what I have to say may ring a bell for them. However, I will be necessarily speaking with primary reference to music, since it is there and only there that I can support any claim to be standing on solid ground. If in some instances my remarks should seem to relate only to music, I would be both willing and interested to be challenged. The general picture, however, applies to all of the arts, and in its fundamentals even extends beyond the artistic sphere.

There is, I should think, no doubt that the arts have been taking a beating in recent years. The beating comes from no single source, nor does it seem to have any single point

From *Sewanee Review*, vol. 66, 1958. Copyright 1958 by the University of the South. Reprinted by permission of the editor.

of attack. For years—possibly since even before Tolstoy's famous tirade—we have been told that the arts today are in a state of crisis, and we are constantly being regaled with proposals of the most varied character, looking to a resolution of that crisis.

Let us here perhaps take leave of the word *crisis*, which implies a situation of many facets, and problems of many sorts, but take account simply of a certain nervousness in regard to the arts, which has been widespread for quite a while. The nervousness, manifest on several fronts, has to do with the relation of the artist and the public, the gulf which in varying degrees separates the one from the other, the implications which this has for the future of art and of culture itself, and the real worth of the art of today. Very frequently, perhaps most frequently, the responsibility for this state of affairs is laid squarely at the door of the artist himself, in terms which vary considerably from instance to instance. The contemporary artist, we are told by one, is not living up to his responsibilities as a member of a democratic society. It is his duty to meet his public halfway, by providing the public with products which it wants and which it can understand. He is accused by others of making a fetish or a criterion of obscurity for its own sake, and assuming that because artists of the past were misunderstood during their lifetimes, the safest path to immortality is through insuring that he himself will suffer the same fate. Again, composers are told that the mere writing of serious music today is historically untenable, and the result of a dream—illusory and, if I may add my parenthetical comment, quite infantile if true—of following in the footsteps of Beethoven, yearning for a glory that is no longer to be had, since the future of music and the only musical vitality of the present, lies with popular music. Or the conclusion is drawn, quite simply, there are no great composers living, and valid music is a thing of the past.

Since I am not here before you for the purpose of pleading the cause of contemporary art I shall certainly not linger over arguments in disproof of the above·assertions, regarding which my comments would range from "sheer fantasy" to "true only in some individual cases." I do believe, however, that it is not irrelevant to record my own conviction that the period in which we live is not, as is commonly assumed, an artistically lean one; on the contrary—and I must say I have arrived at this conclusion to my genuine surprise after having for years assumed the opposite—on the contrary, I believe it is an extraordinarily rich one. I do not mean by this that we have necessarily produced any composers of the stature of Bach or Mozart or Beethoven. I do not know whether we have or not, and neither does anyone else. There is, for some time to come, no way of knowing; time will tell. Furthermore, our period bears no resemblance at all to the times in which those men lived. On the other hand, during the short space of fifty years since I first began to be aware of the musical world, music has undergone a major transformation which bears all the earmarks of one of the decisive changes of musical history, and which is obviously here to stay.

Let me, however, return to my point. Whatever the value of contemporary art, the gulf certainly exists, and is related, certainly, to a whole set of other facts, facts which have no organic connection whatever with the arts as such. Once more I must take my illustration from music, but I have little doubt that the situation is analogous throughout the cultural field.

The situation is of course a complex one, which has its roots at least as far back as the overthrow of the Old Regime and the consequent rise of the middle classes—two historical events which profoundly affected not only the nature of the artistic public but also, certainly, the development of the arts themselves. Limiting ourselves to the present century, however, we see very plainly two forces at work: on the one hand, the development of mass communication— especially the radio and phonograph; and on the other, the gradual decline of private patronage and the enormous growth of commercial enterprise in the musical world. I am speaking of course primarily of the United States; but the European picture, though different in some respects, reveals by and large the same trends and the same forces at work.

Let us first of all roughly compare the public of, say, 1913, with that of today. In the earlier years of this century—before the beginnings of public broadcasting, or of so-called "classical" recordings, the effective public for serious music embraced at the most a very few thousands, scattered mainly here and there in our large centers. It consisted in overwhelming measure of people who possessed an active and devoted love for music, and who in most instances had some experience of playing or singing—people, that is, whose primary experience of music came from the intimate contact gained through making it themselves, in however crude or inadequate fashion.

After the mid twenties, however, a decisive change took place, one which is still in full progress. The radio and the gramophone made serious music suddenly available to a much larger mass of people—consisting of many millions —most of whom had had little or no previous experience of it; and it was inevitable that our large musical enterprises —our opera companies, symphony orchestras, and concert agencies—should not only gear themselves to this vastly increased public, but should, according to the natural dynamics of business, seek to expand it still further, and keep expanding.

There were of course other forces at work, and in pointing up the process in these terms I do not mean to imply that it is to be deplored—the contrary, obviously, and especially in the long pull. Some of its short-term consequences, however, may be described as at least problematical. In order to attract and to hold an ever-increasing number of listeners to music, the fare offered to them must be such as can be assimilated easily or at the very least such as can be effectively sold to people whose interest in music is rela-

The Composer and His Audience

tively lukewarm, and who could easily be alienated if too much were demanded of them. I am speaking not only of logical consequences but of abundantly demonstrable facts. The more thoughtful among musicians, both here and abroad, find less and less to interest them in our public musical fare, and are more and more rarely to be seen at concerts or operatic performances. The classical repertory tends to shrink, and music of a semi- or quasi-popular type tends to claim a larger share of our programs. The composers admitted to be the outstanding personalities of our time are known chiefly and in overwhelming measure through early works of a relatively familiar and undemanding character: Schoenberg (born in 1874) through his *Verklärte Nacht*, written in 1897, Stravinsky (born in 1882) by *The Firebird*, written in 1909, and Béla Bartók by his Concerto for Orchestra, a late work but an essentially uncharacteristic one. The works on which the real fame and the all-pervading influence of these composers is based are seldom heard. I am speaking of course of a generation of composers of whom the last surviving representative is celebrating his seventy-fifth year—composers not only of international reputation but of universal influence on the work of their successors—as we say, the men at the very top. The case of these composers is interesting because, by and large, their position is unchallenged, at least by musicians, and their influence ineradicable and all-pervasive. Their more characteristic music is available, and may be expected to become little by little more generally and more intimately known, by means of the gramophone and the radio, in which fields a different set of factors operate, to some extent, in a direction quite other than the one I have described. Here too, however, and inevitably so, art is essentially at the mercy of economic forces; and one must take special note of the fact that these economic forces operate as it were automatically, quite independently of the wishes of those who hold positions of power in our economic machine. There are many individuals involved in the active running of the music business who do whatever they can both to maintain (and even to raise) artistic standards and to provide opportunities for new music to be heard. The hard economic facts, however, remain; the efforts of these individuals are of the utmost value in specific situations regarding composers and their works, but they cannot affect the general picture.

To explain the fundamental problem in the above terms does not, however, alter the fact that the gulf between artist and public exists and that, as I believe, it is symptomatic of dangers presently inherent in our whole culture. Several of the factors which I have mentioned—and others can be adduced which add to them—make it entirely reasonable to doubt whether the number of people interested in contemporary art is even proportionately smaller than it has been in any other period. What ours has done has been to bring into contact with the arts vast numbers of people who in former times would have had nothing to do with them. What is still more significant is that the public is no longer composed—as it always has been in the past—of people who passionately love the arts, therefore are close to them, and therefore to some degree adept.

But the basically problematical fact does not lie even here. It lies on the one hand in the conflict between artistic value and quality, and the economic forces of which I have spoken; and, on the other, in the conflict between the interests of the minority which is passionately devoted to the arts, and the demands of mass culture. It lies perhaps above all in the kind of hidden ideological drift which these conflicts engender, and the implied impact of this ideological drift on the autonomy of the individual, and in a more remote—but perhaps not so remote—sense, upon freedom itself. What I have in mind may be illustrated quite clearly if we consider once more the various indictments which are a very familiar feature of at least our musical life, and which have even on occasion—in my opinion contemptibly and even in the last analysis rather dangerously—been brought by certain artists against their colleagues; and if we compare them with the similar indictments which are invariably brought by totalitarian governments against those artists who show signs of independence or individuality. The indictment is always the same: the composer by showing such independence is, for one discreditable reason or another, deliberately cutting himself off from his fellow men and even by implication excommunicating himself from the human community, by indulging in the essentially private luxury of individual expression. His real obligation is to adapt himself to the tastes of the mass public which he serves, and which, he is told, is the final arbiter of the destinies of art.

Not everyone will be pleased with my phrasing of these last sentences; some will find it unfair, and indeed it is an attempt at a composite statement which tries to summarize a number of attitudes which all tend in the same direction and ultimately towards the same goal. It is a statement of what all these attitudes have in common—a statement of the claims of the mass against the individual, and a denial of the latter's essential right to exist except, at best, on sufferance.

It is individuality, in other words, which is under attack, both through the business dynamic of which I have previously spoken, and through the ideological drift toward mass criteria. The results, if the trend is allowed to continue, are quite predictable. Under the impact of criteria based on the taste of the majority a gradual lowering of standards is inevitable. Authors are already asked at times to make changes in their works, or to find attractive titles, designed to make them more accessible and hence more saleable. I know of at least one case in which an author, who had already published two moderately successful books and whose command of prose had received generally favorable comment, was confronted with a fully published book which he had written under contract but which had been rewritten before publication without his knowledge or consent; he was thus faced with the problem of deciding whether the changes in style and thought which resulted were serious enough to induce him to attempt to force the book's withdrawal, or letting it stand over his signature in garbled form, in a style which he could not recognize as his own. Such instances not only bespeak an erosion of respect for intellectual property, but what is more serious, a trend which if followed consistently is limitless in its implications. In its beginnings, the trend does not mean inevitably bad art; rather, since it is plainly and even bluntly anti-individualistic, it favors the merely good at the expense of the best, and the colorless at the expense of the individual and therefore possibly controversial; it also means, by its inherent momentum, an inevitable progressive decline. Once the principle of individuality has been effectively violated, there is nothing whatever to stand in the way of its further and complete violation, and little to stand in the way of total domination by the tastes and even the whims of a numerical majority.

It is hardly necessary, of course, to point out that the individual is no longer the lordly being that he once was, or that he once could believe himself to be. At a thousand points, and in a thousand ways, he finds himself hemmed in by forces which are not only beyond his control, but apparently only very imperfectly controlled by mankind as a whole, even though they are forces which mankind itself has unleashed, sometimes quite blindly and even inadvertently. With very little if any exaggeration we can say that individuality today is an act of faith; and implicit in our whole Western creed is the determination that it shall not become, as could so easily happen, an act of martyrdom.

If this is true, the well-being of the arts must be a matter of serious concern to us. For individuality, in the deepest sense of the word, is their very life-blood; the source from which they derive their vitality if not their ultimate rationale. I believe I need not explain that I am not at all referring to "individuality" in a certain romantic sense, as a quantity through which the ultimate artistic values can be determined, and to which all other values are incidental. Much of the valid art of the past, certainly, has been produced within a framework of strict and apparently very limiting convention; and in fact one of the striking and characteristic phenomena of the present day is the necessity which artists feel to discover limitations for themselves, in order to give their work the coherence that traditional styles can no longer in any real sense furnish them. Contrary to a whole set of popular misconceptions, it is not uniqueness that contemporary artists are seeking, but principles of organization. What I am saying in effect, in insisting on the crucial importance of individuality, is that a painter's artistic vision comes to him only through his own eyes, a musician's only through his own ears; and that it is his responsibility as an artist to see, hear, and feel for himself.

There is of course more to be said. When we speak of the "ear" of a creative musician we are not referring only to a sensory organ, even an intensively cultivated one—we are referring to a whole set of faculties which coordinate sensations, discover relationships between them, and in the case of composers build imaginative structures out of these relationships—imaginative structures which not only are motivated by fundamental attitudes, but in their turn profoundly affect these latter. The ear—and I am using the word in no private and esoteric sense—merges into the personality as a whole, and is inseparable from it. If individuality be understood in terms of the above considerations, it should be clear that such questions as tradition and convention have very little to do with this matter. An artist's relationship to these becomes comparable to his relation to a specific medium. The composer, for instance, writes for voices or instruments, each one of which has its limitations. He knows that he cannot make the same demands on a soprano voice which he makes on a violin; he knows that a pianist has only ten fingers, which can stretch only just so far, and that once the latter has sounded a tone he has no further control over it except the means to shut it off.

He knows that the tone itself is strongest at the moment of impact, and for that reason it is impossible to bind tones together in the same sense as with the voice, the violin, or the various wind instruments, in which there is continuous and delicately controllable energy behind every note as long as it is sounding. The latter media, however, have limitations and sometimes subtle irregularities of their own; and all of these factors become, as it were, a part of the composer's palette. He must reckon with other factors also. If he writes for orchestra, he must be aware of the conditions under which orchestras work, and decide whether a given detail is worth the proportionate amount of rehearsal time which will be required in order effectively to bring it off. My point is that an artist is accustomed to working under limitations of many and varied kinds, and learns easily to think in terms of these limitations as long as the latter are not of the kind which constitute a fundamental threat to his artistic integrity.

The danger inherent in the tendencies which I have described lies precisely in the fact that on the one hand they by implication do threaten his integrity, and on the other hand tend to drive him into attitudes of his own which, without robbing his art of any degree of refinement or sensitivity or insight, may in the long run deprive it of some degree of essential human content. The point is a very delicate one and I express myself purposely with caution. What I am saying now has been said before, and at other moments than ours, and misapplied to works of art that have not only survived but become in the most authentic sense of the word popular. It even suggests to some extent the kind of objection that has been made virtually from time immemorial to all that is new in art—even the greatest; and such is of course as far as possible from my intention.

There is, however, a difference, and I think a very fundamental one. The tendency toward what we may call dehumanization is very far-flung both in its causes and its effects; many and varied influences from many and varied sources contribute to it, and these influences have made their impacts not only on the arts but on everything else. Nor has their impact been unrelievedly deleterious. For instance: the prevailing scientific, or analytical, attitude of the past half century or so has certainly tended to de-emphasize and even to deflate humanity; but it has at the same time, and even more obviously, provided us with new areas of insight and new vistas of experience, which have added fresh dimensions to our inner life, and hence to contemporary art. It has likewise contributed to a process of purification— to the cleansing of artistic attitudes of much that had become superfluous and therefore vulgar and in any case no longer valid. But at the same time it has tended to support such attitudes as I have described—attitudes which articulate a conception of art as a totally sufficient end in itself, hermetically sealed away from human destinies and human experience except in the narrowest sense of art as such. The difference from such former attitudes as that of "l'art pour l'art" is that while those were at worst defensive in intent and at best assertions of the autonomy of art as a product of the human imagination, certain slogans of today imply or even affirm, as not only a goal but often as the only valid one, the call to strip music, and presumably the other arts as well, of all human connections.

Lest I seem to be lending aid and comfort at this point to the very forces which I have already sharply attacked, let me emphasize the fact that I am speaking only of rather peripheral symptoms, and not of basic conditions. I regard all such slogans, however brilliantly formulated, as froth, and such goals as thoroughly unrealizable in any conceivable human society. As symptoms, however, they are worth noting, since they are undoubtedly, at least in part, reflex actions produced by a state of affairs in which purely quantitative standards play the predominant role that they tend to do in our society today. The real danger to the arts, and to a great deal else, lies in the increasingly rapid infiltration of these quantitative standards, and possibly still more in the rationalizations under which they are camouflaged, at least in our Western society.

It should be clear in any case that a fundamental threat to individuality, as I have defined it, is also, even if in an apparently remote sense, a threat to the freedoms which we cherish most deeply. It should also be clear that such a fundamental challenge as I have described can be met only by an alert understanding and a determined self-confidence on the part of all those who care for the arts, just as on a somewhat different level it makes similar demands on all those who love truth. As far as the arts are concerned, we must perhaps learn to regard them no longer as satisfactions which we buy, but rather as experiences in which we participate. This means that we will cease to look in the first instance for masterpieces (a habit to which we are all too prone) but look rather for vital experiences which call out our resources of vital curiosity and lively response. We must be prepared to be confronted with bad art as well as good, since art is in this respect notoriously wasteful; as someone has wisely remarked, it takes two thousand untalented artists to produce one good one. We will be confronted, too, with the fact that in the total artistic economy, especially in our time, there are many artistic roles to be filled if the arts are to flourish in a really healthy manner, and that none of the types of art which result are intrinsically devoid of interest. It takes all sorts to make a world, in art as in everything else. If we are wise, we will have to be fundamentally tolerant of these types as such, recognizing them for what they are regardless of praise or blame, and regardless of whatever exaggerated claims they may make for themselves. It might be helpful, too, to remember that artistic problems are not to be solved in terms of "styles" or fashions, and that these become significant through the works that embody them, not the converse.

In case I should have been at all misunderstood, let me make it clear that in no sense is it criticism—of contemporary artists, or art, or anything else—which I consider a menace. Nor has anyone any valid reason to complain of honest observation—provided it is concrete and straightforward—however wrong-headed it may seem. The artists of today are not the first, nor will they be the last, in history, to face attacks from their contemporaries. The danger of which I have been speaking lies in what amounts to a generalized frontal assault on the autonomy of the individual, hence on individuality as such, and its implied danger is incalculable. Nothing is drearier than the letters of recantation written by some of the most distinguished Russian composers in 1948, after they had been cited for deviationism in music. These are documents, as it seems to us, of an abjectness beyond which it would be difficult to go. This is not to pass judgment on their authors, who were subjected to pressures of a kind scarcely conceivable to most of us, including that of their own political faith; I cite them rather to suggest that the ultimate evil lies perhaps less in the agony which such recantation seems to imply, than in the violation of the principle of human integrity, which is implicit in the mere circumstance that such recantation was demanded and given. The integrity of the artist, however peripheral it may seem when viewed in the light of the total body politic, is nevertheless an important outpost of truth itself. But we are assailing the artist's integrity just as surely, if less drastically and more insidiously, if we make it a matter of principle that he attenuate his artistic vision in the interest of conformity of any kind, under any kind of pressure from any source, or under the standard of any one of a number of high-sounding slogans.

Perhaps, although a confessed layman everywhere outside my own artistic sphere, I may be allowed in conclusion a few reflections, in an empirical rather than philosophical spirit, on freedom itself. First, freedom is concrete, not abstract—one freedom necessarily limits another, as any page of any newspaper may be cited to prove. Then again, freedom is always either freedom *from* something or freedom *for* something, and in either case it entails responsibilities.

Freedom *from* anything whatever entails, at the very least, eternal vigilance. Freedom *for* anything whatever, entails the clearest responsibilities toward the objectives. Certainly the end does not, in the usual sense, justify the means; but on the other hand it is only ends which can give means whatever justification they can have.

The artist too, therefore, has obligations. But his obligations—and precisely his obligations to society—coincide exactly with the very qualities for which, in the terms cited at the beginning of this paper, he is so frequently attacked. He is obliged, in other words, to seek and to follow his own vision, and no other, and to follow it with no deviation, whatever the demand. Otherwise he can produce exactly nothing of consequence.

It is possible that I have, at least by implication, raised more questions here than I have attempted to answer. It is in any case true, I believe, that the eventual answers are not primarily in the hands of artists. In the broadest sense the obligations of the latter are first and always the same— to do their best: to make to the fullest extent the contributions which they have to make, in the terms which these various contributions allow. They cannot do otherwise than speak out of the fullest conviction, the most mature craft, and the most acute insight which they are able to bring to their task. There are obviously also more primary obligations which they share in common with all men, for they too are human beings. Like other men, they meet these with varying degrees of success—no doubt, by and large, as well as other men.

It seems to me that the real question of today is a quite other one. I tried to formulate it some months ago in an article which I wrote in homage to a great colleague, Igor Stravinsky, who celebrated his seventy-fifth birthday last year. I am going to ask your indulgence in allowing me to quote what I wrote there. In doing so I do not mean to imply that it cannot be expressed better than I have expressed it, but rather to confess my own inability to do so, at any rate at this time. Here is what I wrote, and I believe it with all my heart:

> Every age is unique, and ours, with its universal mass media of communication, its highly organized material life, its vast population, and its unprecedented and infinitely far-reaching historical cataclysms—in the midst of which we are still living—has few points of resemblance to any other except in the continuity of man himself. In such a period defeatism in cultural matters is easy, and unfortunately it is rife in ours. This defeatism is engendered even by the very richness and variety of our cultural manifestations; it is easy to assume that these manifestations cancel each other out, and that they are of little importance anyway, since they apparently involve a mere handful of people in comparison with the great mass of listeners to music, let alone the population as a whole. In a world in which quantitative measurement has become a factor of vital importance, these matters loom large. . . .
>
> A certain pessimism is therefore understandable; but whether it is justified from the long-range point of view is quite a different question. The answer will not be given in terms of music alone, or of the arts, or even of culture itself. It is a question of ultimate human resourcefulness; whether human beings can extricate themselves from the most complex and menacing situation that has ever faced them, and learn to live together in a manner which focuses their spiritual energies instead of scattering them, enabling the voices not only of artists but of all men of intelligence and genius and goodwill to be listened to by all, instead of by the few who possess the patience, the energy, and the dedicated interest to discover what they have to say.[1]

[1] See "Thoughts on Stravinsky," pp. 384-385.

Composer and Critic
[1934]

*Written in response to an article by Olin
Downes, music critic of the* New York Times,
*who in his leading column for Sunday, March
4, 1934, had addressed the question of the
proper attitude of the American critic toward
recent American music. "Should the American
composer be given a handicap over his European colleagues?" Downes asked, and came to
the conclusion that he should not: the best
encouragement would be "unprejudiced criticism." Admitting that in Europe the critic's
role often seems that of an advocate of, or
even a propagandist for, new works, Downes
insisted that the American critic, after doing
what he could to help bring American music
before the public, should then discuss it "in
detail and with unsparing frankness." Downes
later solicited comments on his views from
Roger Sessions and Virgil Thomson, who responded with letters printed in the* Times
the following week.

I THINK it a mistake to regard the critic as having any direct artistic relation to the composer. Mr. Downes will pardon me for pointing out, as he does himself, that musical criticism is essentially journalistic and hence can be of very little help to the composer in respect to his own work. If the composer wants advice in technical matters he presumably has experts at his disposal who, as players or composers, are working directly with musical material, and whose advice is therefore of the most immediate and practical kind.

Letter to the Music Editor of the *New York Times*, Mar. 11,
1934. © 1934 by The New York Times Company. Reprinted by
permission.

The Composer and His Audience

Of course, the composer like every one else develops partly through contact with other personalities. But criticism written inevitably for the public and not for the composer belongs in a different sphere and demands a different set of standards. For this reason I am convinced that every mature or really talented composer, however much he may be momentarily pleased by a "good" criticism or irritated by a "bad" one, will and must remain—through the strength of his creative impulse and for the good of his art—fundamentally indifferent to it.

In other words, criticism is in essence none of the composer's business. He must know that even the most perfect critical judgment is subject to personal conditions, to conditions of time and place, and that the destiny of a work of art is inherent in itself and not in individual opinions regarding it. Its momentary success or failure means precisely nothing. Therefore, a composer needs, and if really gifted, will attain, a degree of self-confidence which precludes any "blighting effect" in harsh criticism.

Concerning the specific question of American music, I wholeheartedly agree with Mr. Downes that music by Americans must be judged on the same basis as any other music and that sincere American musicians would wish this to be so. Only such a policy, obviously, is in accordance with the real interests of American music. Firstly, the "coddling" of American music would tend to put a premium on complacence and self-deception, to lower artistic standards, and to create a completely false set of criteria based on nationalistic dogma. Secondly, a public coaxed into supporting any type of music for reasons other than spontaneous enjoyment is certain to approach that music in a correspondingly unreceptive state of mind, to accept this duty with resignation or enthusiasm, but to fail to listen to the music in any real sense at all. Under such conditions a piece of American music is simply a piece of American music; one is as good as another, and the public interest in it naturally will not last.

Finally, an American music "nurtured" by special treatment would be only a racket, fundamentally dishonest, dealing in goods confessedly incapable of holding their own in an open market. Hence not only "native" music but also music "imported from abroad" would suffer a decline in quality, performing artists like soloists and conductors being more and more chosen for their willingness to play American works as such rather than for the quality of their performances.

Everything should be done to further our music's development. The critic who fails to consider very seriously the problems and, when real, the achievements of native musicians is not only failing in his duty toward the public but in proving himself incompletely aware of some of the conditions of his own effective existence. A community with negligible creative achievement is musically deficient, undeveloped and hence incapable of producing really first-rate critics—except occasionally by accident. While much that Mr. Downes says in regard to comparative critical tendencies in Europe and America is true, it seems to me also true that especially in regard to new works, American critics tend to be unsure of themselves and often to cloak their unsureness in exaggerated assumption of authority. One can observe at times both a somewhat indolent open-mindedness and a rather nervous dogmatism.

In regard to direct propaganda for American compositions, nothing more can be asked of the critic than that he be as active as possible in furthering works in which he believes, and abstain in principle from discouraging the performance of American works as such. For while conditions are rapidly becoming more favorable for the American composer, nevertheless our concert world, so far as new music is concerned, is largely dominated by a mania for "first performances"; and contemporary works of even recognized excellence seldom achieve a sufficient number of performances.

America Moves to the Avant-Scene
[1937]

Read at the annual meeting of the American Musicological
Society in Pittsburgh, Pa., in December, 1937.

L ET me confess at the outset that, in undertaking to write
a paper on this subject, I was intrigued by various ways
in which the latter could be taken. I am sure that those who
planned the program will forgive me if I point out certain
possible implications which were clearly not in their minds.
It might, for instance, imply a nationalistic affirmation of
our country's present or approaching supremacy in the various fields which constitute contemporary musical life, and
to call in some sense for the quasi-historical justification of
that supremacy; it might likewise seem to imply an enu-
meration and a generally laudatory appraisal of the achievements of American musicians, scholars, and acoustical tech-
nicians. Again, it might be taken to imply the emergence of
a specifically American school of composition and a discussion of what constitutes so-called "national" character in
American music.

Of all these things we have heard much; we have heard
much, too, of a "crisis" in western music, which has, according to temperament and special interest been interpreted as
indicating either the great historical moment of the United
States, or on the other hand is a sign that genuine music
belongs irrevocably to the past and that no further masterpieces are to be expected.

To be sure, the music of Europe has for centuries, according to many of the ablest observers, been in a periodic state
of crisis and decay. Yet in spite of the pessimistic observa-

From *American Musicological Society Papers*, 1937, pp. 108-119.
Reprinted by permission of The American Musicological Society.

tions of the Artusis, the Hanslicks, and on a quite different plane, the Philipp Emanuel Bachs and the Brahmses, music has continued to exist and to embody in ever-changing but still vital forms the impulses of the various periods which have produced it. If I may be allowed a quite personal observation, I myself have in moments of pessimism experienced the joy of having my mood contradicted on specific occasions by such works as Hindemith's *Mathis der Maler*, Stravinsky's *Symphonie de psaumes*, Béla Bartók's *Music for Strings, Celesta, and Percussion*, and Berg's Violin Concerto —works which certainly, and with due respect to the difficulty of ultimate evaluation, represent a high level of musical intention and achievement, and which have a genuine and deep significance for all those of our generation who are willing and able to hear and respond. However later generations may "place" these works, it cannot be seriously questioned that they are definitive achievements, among the highest that our time has produced, and that our contemporaries may justly be proud of belonging to the generation which produced them. Furthermore, the most generous possible view of contemporary American music would be hard pressed to find four works, by four different composers, capable of standing honest comparison with these.

But however much we may be inclined to question a popular opinion that the European creative vein is exhausted, we cannot ignore the various signs which place on America's shoulders a heavy responsibility for the future of music. It is not so much the specifically musical situation, as the political and social situation out of which it has grown, which has produced this. It is hardly necessary to rehearse the plight in which the European musician finds himself today as a result not only of the constantly wider encroachment of the political concept of the "totalitarian state," but of the increasing tension—political, economic, and social— which is today the most striking characteristic of European life. In such a case culture, above all in its higher reaches, is the first to suffer; the perpetual lack of inner as well as outer security tends constantly to undermine and inhibit that freedom of imagination which is necessarily the basis of artistic production.

That this is taking place must be a commonplace observation to anyone who has the future of music at heart. I recently questioned one of the keenest and most understanding observers of contemporary European music concerning new compositions which interested him. His reply was to enumerate names as familiar and established as the ones above mentioned. When I pointed this out to him and asked him regarding younger composers, he confessed himself at a loss and spoke of the uncertainty and opportunism of a generation that seemed to have lost its bearings to the point of having no longer anything genuine to say. Yet the musician of whom I speak is a distinguished interpretative artist who has identified himself throughout his career, with admirable and catholic discrimination, with the discovery and championship of new talent. Nor is his testimony an isolated one; it is on the contrary only one among an increasing number of voices, all of which bring substantially the same indictment, not so much against individuals as against the tainted soil upon which they are obliged to depend for nourishment.

Still more conspicuous is the extent to which European musicians of all types have begun to look to America as their main source of hope for the future. It is not only from Hitler's Germany that musicians have arrived at our shores to establish themselves; every musician of fairly wide European acquaintance must have received inquiries from musicians of the various countries regarding the possibility of establishing themselves in the United States, and our musical life has, constantly since the Great War, but especially in very recent years, received an increment of incalculable value from this source. Foreign musicians of distinction have begun to come to us in large numbers for the first time with the genuine ambition, not merely to achieve a successful concert tour or a temporary conductorial position, but to participate actively in our musical life and to find for themselves a permanent place in it. Many of these openly avow their pessimism in regard to the future of European music and their conviction that if the art of music is to be saved, it is for America to save it.

America's growing position in the musical world is therefore not so much one of privilege as one of responsibility. The following remarks represent an attempt to define certain aspects of that responsibility and to discuss some of the conditions which I consider necessary for its fulfillment. I propose, in other words, to take America's position and opportunity for granted and to make certain observations which seem to me vital regarding the problems which it creates for us as American musicians.

America, then, is faced with the task of building on her soil a musical tradition—a task which cannot be accomplished either overnight or through the simple process of willing it or taking thought. It is, of course, a gradual—a very gradual—process and one may easily doubt to what extent any sort of conscious action can achieve genuine contribution to it. No sudden development, moreover, can take place without years of preparation, in which the foundation is laid through the gradual accumulation of the raw materials of artistic and human experience; and in the United States there is no question but this has for a long time been taking place. The very presence of all of us here in this room is an indication of the fact that some of the elements of a musical tradition, at least in its early stages, are already here in the making. If I speak of musical tradition, therefore, in a more static sense, and project its development somewhat into the future, I do so entirely in order to simplify the problem and to bring it within the scope of possible discussion. I wish, in other words, to speak of necessities and possibilities, regardless of the extent to which these are actually being realized.

At the center of any musical tradition is the composer and his work. This will scarcely be denied; the work of the interpretative artist, the critic, and the musicologist, depends on creation, without which it can consist only in gathering up the loose threads which remain over from the past. At the center of the American musical problem, therefore, lies the problem of the American composer. By this I do not of course mean the fate of the individual, but the question of musical production and what must be done to further its healthy development. If I speak today, therefore, mainly of the composer, it is because it seems to me clear that his activities constitute not only the decisive element which determines the vitality of musical culture, but quite clearly the goal which alone gives sense to all the rest. We cannot continue indefinitely to live on the past; the latter, indeed, must lose its meaning for us precisely in the measure in which it fails to respond to aspirations which are still genuine and vigorous. And if such aspirations are present they will inevitably embody themselves in the actual creation of works of art.

What, then, does the American composer of genuinely serious aims most need? Speaking as one who comes as a teacher frequently in contact with young aspirants, I cannot help being impressed and touched by the genuineness of impulse on the part of our younger men; nor, even aside from the achievements of a few outstanding individuals, do I find it possible to agree with the oft-heard complaint that American composers have nothing to say. On the contrary, American music is assuredly lacking neither in ideas nor in the spontaneous impulse to give them utterance. What one observes all too often is rather that these ideas fail to attain full and convincing expression. Their effect is too frequently embryonic and half-baked, uncertain in direction and inadequate in fulfillment. In individual cases we see the results of bewilderment and disenchantment, in sterile opportunism or in the frank and generally futile pursuit of "success"; in others we can observe all too frequently the search for a point of support in the espousal of this or that musical cause; either one chosen, so to speak, at random from among specific contemporary tendencies, or, what is on the whole more healthy, one gained by a frank incursion into the field of "popular music." In the latter case, no doubt, the individual often finds a real fulfillment. The musician who does so is neither "slumming" nor waving the American flag but obeying a genuine musical and artistic conscience. Let us, after all, accept American popular music for precisely what it is. To recognize the freshness of many of its rhythms and melodies and the real technical distinction which it often attains is not for a moment, however, to admit that it is either a final or an adequate embodiment of America's musical potentialities. But it is admirably sure of itself, and definitive in a sense which is much less often true of American so-called "serious music."

What is the reason for this?

The answer seems to me roughly twofold. First of all, in spite of some individual achievements of a high order, no leader has as yet established himself to the point of giving American music a sure and inevitable direction. It may perhaps be questioned whether such a direction is ever achieved in precisely this manner. But whether such a leader is the result of forces tending in a certain direction or the actual creator of the direction is, however, quite beside the point. The fact is that such a direction is non-existent until actually embodied in works of commanding character which serve in some sense as a point of departure for the future. Until this occurs—and who can confidently speak regarding its likelihood?—all attempts, necessarily selfconscious and arbitrary, to find such a point of departure are doomed to failure. We have witnessed many such, and we shall certainly witness more until the direction is given, almost automatically, by the mature and compelling force of one or more truly evolved personalities.

Until this happens, however, the individual must shift for himself and find his way as best he can, knowing at the very least that his effort, if genuine, will contribute in some measure to the ultimate development of American music.

The Composer and His Audience

One thing above all he needs—a mastery of the musical language and a knowledge of its possibilities sufficient to allow him true freedom in its use. To my mind the real nature of musical technique, or "craftsmanship" as it is sometimes called, is too often misunderstood. First of all, it is frequently regarded as a form of knowledge or even science; its essentially practical nature is minimized in favor of this or that historical or theoretical point of departure. The very term "theory" applied to those branches of musical training which contribute to the composer's development is an indication of this, and the content of such training often corresponds all too exactly to the faulty conception at its basis. Instead of being conceived as the systematic presentation of, and the thorough-going practical experience in, the basic materials of music, the studies of harmony and counterpoint are conceived far too often either as vaguely motivated abstract disciplines, or increasingly often as exercises in this or that "style." A study, more or less penetrating or desultory as the case may be, of classic "forms," combined with a certain amount of general criticism, too often completes the entire technical training of our composers. Small wonder that many of them find themselves bewildered by their own not fully understood lack of mastery which they so often mistake for some far more mysterious problem—perhaps not musical or individual at all, but attributable to "our time," the social and economic system, a false relation between the artist and his public, etc. While I have no intention of denying the existence of such very obvious maladjustments in the cultural life of today, it seems quite clear to me that very often they become scapegoats for shortcomings which lie much nearer home, just as inadequate mastery may so easily be mistaken for essential lack of ideas. It is unfortunately too true that a work of art consists not in intention or impulse but in concrete performance, and the necessary equipment of the composer consists in a real command of his language, not in the mere understanding of the principles of correct or effective writing.

The Composer and His Audience

The truth is in fact that real technique, far from being in any sense an abstraction, is manifestly inseparable from the musical ideas which it embodies and is ultimately as much the composer's personal possession as any individual trait of his style. Yet the degree of mastery which this involves is attained only by a very few of our composers, though as a result of painfully and gradually accumulated tradition, it has been, and still is, the rule rather than the exception in Europe.

This, I would like to suggest, is at least one of the basic as well as one of the most clearly remediable problems of our musical life. And yet the remedy hitherto in vogue—European study—seems to me one beset with real dangers. The value of European experience to the composer as a part of his development, seems to me incontestable; but it is equally important that the formative years of a composer's career be spent in the environment which he best understands and in which he will be ultimately obliged to live. Above all, there is nothing to be gained, any longer, by study in Europe: if the aspiring composer still chooses to reject the native teacher, however competent to supply his needs, there are plenty of distinguished Europeans available on American soil.

The legitimate artistic problems of the American composer do not, however, rest there. Certain basic attitudes in our musical life are, I believe, hostile not only to the composer but to the development of musical culture in the wider sense. In enumerating and dwelling on some of these, I am quite conscious still of stressing negative, rather than positive, elements in our musical life. An outsider, however, might be expected to dwell more fully on the undeniable and even remarkable development of American musical life in nearly all of its directions during more than a century: the growth of public taste, the progress of education, the development of a heartening number of native composers, performers, teachers, and musicologists of unquestioned worth and standing. Within the family, so to speak, it is perhaps more fitting to pass over these things and to examine the points at which the fulfillment of America's above-mentioned responsibility demands a revision of current and even dearly cherished values.

First of all, the American composer has, until he has passed definitely beyond the formative period of his career, far too little opportunity to function in the musical life of the country in his specific capacity of composer. It is not so true as was formerly the case that he has not sufficient opportunity to hear his works performed. What is true, however, is that such performances generally take place under rather special circumstances before a carefully selected public, and that as far as a larger public is concerned it is generally works of definitely unexacting character— of however little intrinsic merit—which arrive at performance. It is true that certain outstanding figures among interpretative artists have challenged, at times successfully, this state of affairs, and have preserved intact the fine tradition of artistic conscience which insist on a hearing for new works of interest, quite in the spirit of the earlier Philharmonic conductor who, told that "the people do not like Wagner," replied, *"Den dey must hear 'im 'til dey do."* But such figures are subjected to constant pressure from the outside to an extent which is discouraging not only to themselves but necessarily also to all those who have the development of American music at heart. We are told that the reason for this is that the public is unwilling to listen to music by new and untried composers. But the time was comparatively recent when the performance of new works of interest and calibre was considered an artistic duty of the performing artist; indeed, the overwhelming absorption in the music of the past, so characteristic of our times, is a comparatively recent development dating back certainly not more than a hundred years and coinciding with the development of what we may call the virtuoso spirit.

The truth of the matter is that, by and large, the American public of today still thinks of music overwhelmingly in terms of its performance instead of its intrinsic qualities. It is hardly necessary to adduce evidences of this; it is quite familiar to us all and its symptoms constitute an outstanding feature of our musical life. One is frequently tempted to question the depth and the seriousness of a musical culture which is so preoccupied with this or that detail in the interpretation of works which every musician knows by heart, or which regards as matters of essential musical importance the differences in the "reading" of a symphony by Tchaikovsky or Sibelius by reigning conductorial stars of the moment. I do not wish, of course, to imply that interpretation is a matter of indifference, least of all to the composer; it is the tendency—not new, to be sure, but all too characteristic of our times—to regard it as an important end in itself which leads one sometimes to question the extent to which our public is genuinely interested in music. One can legitimately draw the same conclusions from the type of reception accorded new works, even by composers of established reputation. It is not the specific reaction of public and critics which one would question, or even the length to which such and such an event is discussed in the press; it is, rather, the attitude of a public which seems to regard the performance of a new work as essentially of lesser importance than the tempo at which Mr. So-and-so conducts the *Andante* of Beethoven's Fifth Symphony.

All this is distinctly unfavorable to the development of native music, not so much because it deprives the composer of the stimulus of contact with a large public and of hearing his work presented under the most favorable conditions; but because the frequent hearing of his work in rehearsal and the practical association with those who perform it is so essential a part of his musical training and development. It cannot be too much emphasized that a composer is developed not primarily through study but through long and varied experience of everything connected with his art. Surely one of the primary preoccupations of all those connected with the performance of music in this country should be to provide for our native composers the opportunities for this experience. It is true that from many sources these needs are being supplied—notably by government music projects and by various private agencies which have the interests of native music at heart. This, however, is not sufficient any more than is the granting of prizes or commissions to those fortunate enough to receive them. Much remains to be done, and even a great deal of second-rate contemporary European music might profitably be omitted from our programs in favor of American works which are certainly of no less intrinsic value and of incomparably greater importance to the public to which they rightfully belong.

It is not only more frequent performance, however, which American music needs, but a more intelligent and informed interest on the part of those capable of understanding it. One hears it frequently said that the American composer needs criticism. I think this is to a certain extent true; but if criticism is to be of any use to him, it must be the type of criticism which starts from a recognition of the paramount importance of his work, not so much in the specific as in the general sense I have indicated above, in the whole musical development of America, and accords it the serious interest and study which it deserves for this reason alone. It is a common experience of American composers who have spent some time in Europe to note, with sincere surprise, that this type of response is accorded him to a far greater extent abroad than it is at home. It is not that critical standards are more lenient in Europe than they are here; on the contrary they are in general far more clearly defined and hence in the long run more exacting. But the composer of serious intention in Europe can be far more sure of a degree of intelligent interest and responsive effort than is generally accorded him at home. One can understand that the enormous pressure of daily routine makes it difficult for the newspaper reviewer to accord extensive study to each new work as it appears; what is a legitimate cause for surprise is the lack of information regarding the works and activities of our composers which these critics so often reveal. It is not, however, the attitude of the journalist to which I refer so much as to that of the serious professional student. It is noteworthy that extremely few really searching studies have thus far appeared, of the work of American composers.

The above are but a few of the considerations which have occurred to me in regard to the problems which confront us in our new position in the musical world. The deepest problem of all is perhaps the extent to which we are willing, as a people, to lay aside the glamour of cultural promise, and assume the very real burdens of maturity. We are still shy, perhaps, in that regard; the glittering possibilities of a brilliant future are so much more alluring than the actual hardships of fulfillment. Our composers themselves still tend to hesitate before these hardships. But is that not too, finally, in large part because so little beyond "promise" is expected of them and because we still tend a little to associate vitality with precisely the unfulfilled quality characteristic of those whose definitive proving and achievement lies still in the future?

Finally, let us ask what we may expect and toward what we must strive in American music, in the creation of the American tradition. Are we to heed those who wait for the emergence of a so-called "indigenous" or specifically local American style, and to demand that our composers make a conscious effort to create such a style? It cannot be too clearly pointed out, first of all, that an artistic tradition is not built afresh but rather carried from one time and place to another. Quite aside from the fact that this is what has happened, time after time, in the course of history, it cannot but be true in a world like our own where communication is so swift and the commonest elements of our daily life—the intangible as well as the material ones—are drawn from sources distant as well as close in space. To be sure, the Christian doctrine that man cannot love God, whom he hath not seen, unless he love his neighbor, whom he hath seen, remains eternally true, for the artist as well as for other men. But the truly modern man, and precisely at his strongest, not his weakest, must inevitably be aware of a world in which specific locality becomes constantly less important. Cultural isolationism is bound to be more and more relegated to the sphere of anthropological or sociological confectionery—folk-dancing, local color, etc.,—simply because it no longer corresponds to the serious and imperative preoccupations of today. In somewhat overworked but still useful contemporary jargon, it represents a flight from the actualities and responsibilities of modern life, rather than a resolute acceptance of it.

American leadership in music, therefore, can only grow on the basis of an attitude not dissimilar to that of the "good European" of a century ago. It is a little strange that our cultural isolationists should not have thought their position through to the point of seeing that it is precisely cultural isolationism—the loss of the universal principle and the over-glorification of, so to speak, the accident of locality— that has destroyed the good European and come very near to destroying Europe itself.

It is, above all, for this reason that the American composer must learn to renounce the facile exploitation of specifically and all too definably "American" traits in his work; and that the American critics and musicologists must cease to expect this of him. This certainly does not mean, for him, the equally facile adherence to this or that "school" of contemporary music, or the equally suspect eclecticism of a so-called "modern" or selfconsciously universal style.

His task is far simpler, far more exacting, and certainly more unpopular—that of discovering his genuine musical impulses and following them assiduously into whatever paths they may lead him. This means not only the abjuring of the pursuit of what is generally called "success," but also the renunciation of all preconceived ideas regarding what our music, or any music, should or should not be; it involves the attainment of a fresh and unspoiled vision and the constant effort to give this vision adequate embodiment.

Only in this way can he become truly himself—and, as a consequence, truly American. Being American involves, after all, first being human; and what Americanism can have any ultimate value except as the specific and inescapably inherent coloring of this humanity?

To Revitalize Opera
[1938]

IT is fairly evident that, during the last three centuries at any rate, the theatre has been the channel through which the "great public" has become most immediately aware of the music of its own time. The popularity of Handel was at its height while the music of Bach was unknown and rejected by his contemporaries; and while this is the most spectacular example, others readily occur to anyone fairly well versed in musical history. In general it may be said that purely instrumental music of the highest quality, however accessible to the elite of its period, wins recognition far more slowly than the theatre music which in the most general way corresponds to it; there is even some ground for believing that in certain cases the public has been prepared for the understanding of "pure" music by means of successful stage works. The fact for instance that the later works of Beethoven were first made popular by Wagner and his disciples should not be forgotten, even though this led to distortions which later generations have at least begun to correct.

There are obvious reasons for the process above described; they have to do not only with the appeal of the stage itself, but with the type of music best adapted to the theatre, and the concurrence of poetic and visual conceptions with musical ones, by which means is contributed an emotional illumination of much that may at first be aurally difficult. The theatre—as ballet, opera, or incidental music—binds the music in the clearest possible manner to its time and place, and thus at least to its contemporaries gives it

From *Modern Music*, vol. 15, no. 3, pp. 145-152. Reprinted by permission of the League of Composers—International Society for Contemporary Music, U.S. Section, Inc.

an actuality which they are slower to feel in the concert hall.

If dramatic music is, in this concrete though somewhat restricted sense, the most "actual" form which music can take, so is it undoubtedly also the most perishable form. While other types of music have often won recognition only after decades of neglect, it is scarcely possible to name a single opera which has survived without having achieved notable success at least within its own generation. The case of *Boris Godounov* may perhaps occur to one as an exception, until one remembers the peculiar history of this work; it is conceivable also that a work like *Falstaff* may still seem to await its true success at some future period. But *Falstaff* too is an exception by reason of the fact that it is the maturest fruit of a long, triumphant, and varied experience of the theatre; a work which embodies the ultimate perfection of that experience, thus transcending in a measure the purely temporal demands of which Verdi was certainly as keenly aware as anyone ever has been. Though "success" does not, certainly, insure vitality, the fact remains that if an opera or ballet is not successful within a few years of its creation, it almost certainly never will be. Likewise it is the earliest of musical forms to grow old, depending as it does on so many complex factors which are strictly subject to the taste of the period.

With such considerations in mind we can honestly examine some of the aspects of the "operatic crisis" of the present day. To be sure, we hear far too much today about cultural "crises" and "problems," since the very use of these words suggests that a solution is possible through thought and effort—possible, that is to say, in terms of technique, or of this or that aesthetic formula. Ever so often it becomes necessary to reiterate the most obvious of truisms, that the solution of any artistic problem depends first and last upon the genius of the artist; that genius is subject to its own laws, and these alone; and that the gulf between genius and non-genius is not to be bridged by formula or otherwise. The "operatic crisis" in other words can be overcome only by music of real power and dramatic intensity; and it is safe to say that whenever such music appears, the "problem" of opera will find one of its many possible solutions.

We may, however, enumerate certain of the basic characteristics of successful opera, and form a reasonably clear idea of certain conditions which the truly successful opera of the future must fulfill, if it is indeed to take shape.

First of all opera is drama; drama in the real sense means vividness of character, situation, motive. It is obvious therefore that the libretto chosen must be one in which these qualities can be achieved. Though such considerations seem axiomatic enough, recent operatic history—especially in the United States—proves that they are by no means always understood. It is difficult to establish any very definite criteria in this respect, since genius has so often shown itself able to breathe life and relevance into the most unpromising material—witness *Die Zauberflöte*, or *Così fan tutte*. But the very artificiality of the operatic form has at various periods led to the degeneration of opera into "concert in costume" —why the costumes and why the concert?—or a pleasant masquerade in which, say, an anemic exoticism or a faded romanticism supplies a dubious motive for the varied enticements of the opera house. Hence the periodic appearance, too, of operatic reformers who revive an apparently decadent form by replacing the old conventions with new ones.

For in opera the question of convention is paramount. The problem of opera from this point of view consists in establishing a set of conventions which will bear the burden of dramatic truth to such an extent that the hearer is able to accept them without undue effort. The same may of course be said of poetic drama or, indeed, of stage drama in any form. In opera, however, there is not only the added artificiality of words sung instead of spoken, but the perennial conflict between the demands of music and of dramatic action—a conflict which can be solved only through a wholehearted acceptance of the artificiality of the form, and the establishment of a consistent and convincing framework for this artificiality. The more successful the effort to abolish it, the less effective the result. To be sure, the composer of instinct generally arrives at some kind of solution, though too often the result is not in any final sense satisfactory. Wagner of course demands, in this respect at least, a special chapter; but everyone certainly knows his moments in the Wagnerian maze where he wishes that those people on the stage would keep quiet, in order that he might listen to the music in peace.

This brings us to what is perhaps the central point of all —the fact that opera is first and above all vocal music, and that the determining character of any operatic convention lies in the vocal style which it embodies. Again a truism; the voice is the medium through which the characters reveal themselves, and the vocal line ultimately the basis on which the opera must stand or fall. The "problem" of opera is therefore also the problem of vocal music and all that this implies, in regard not only to specifically vocal style, but to diction, prosody, vocal technique, and accompaniment as well. If any proof of this were needed, consider the immense extent to which the style and form of opera is conditioned by the language in which it is written. For example: "secco recitativo," which is so extremely effective when properly sung, is adapted above all else to the Italian language of which it is a perfect embodiment, just as the German composers of the late eighteenth century found the "Singspiel," with its spoken words, more adapted to the more ponderous accents of their native tongue.

With these criteria it is possible to estimate more closely the present operatic situation, and to reach a certain precision in regard to abuses which might well be corrected.

Some of these abuses are, indeed, peculiar to the American situation, others more general. Specifically though not exclusively American is the "star system" under which our operatic public has been educated. The "star system" can of course hardly be called new, since it has been, in one or another form, for at least two centuries, the target of operatic reforms. Whether the cause, or only the main element in a tendency, apparently inherent in opera, to lose at intervals its dramatic vitality, it is obviously destructive of the most essential element in adequate operatic production-ensemble, and thus fosters miscomprehensions on the part of the public regarding the essential demands of operatic production. Opera becomes completely unreal and operatic conventions lose their vitality and relevance under such conditions. It is very clear that if there is to be any general revitalization of opera, the star system will have to be eschewed and an ideal of ensemble substituted for that of highly paid and spectacular voices.

Closely allied to this is the question of language. Once more let it be reiterated that opera is drama, and can only be fully understood as such. This writer is as fully aware as anyone of the advantages of presenting opera in its original language, and has writhed under *Die Macht des Schicksals* in Berlin. *La Flute enchantée* in Paris, and *Sigfrido* in Italy. Nevertheless, and in spite of all that has been said above, close observation has convinced him that the vitality of opera on the European continent is due at least in part to the fact that the listener participates not only in music and the "story" but in the actual text of the opera, and thus apprehends the work as a complete whole, and not as presented to him from a distorted side view. Good and singable translations of opera into English are indeed rare; but one reason for this lies undoubtedly in the fact that thus far there has been no serious demand for them. Occasional exceptions such as Professor Dent's translation of *Figaro*, prove that the question is by no means insoluble. The objection of purists, that English is not a suitable language for singing, is controverted by too many concrete examples, of which our popular music furnishes by no means the least, to be worthy of serious consideration. The task of translation is one which requires imagination and tact; it is however undoubtedly a possible, and, one must hope ultimately a necessary one. For it is fundamentally as incongruous to present opera at the Metropolitan in German or Italian as it would be to present works of Ibsen in Norwegian on Broadway. Should the change ever be made, two results would undoubtedly occur; first, a more rational attitude, on the part of many singers, toward English diction, and secondly, more careful listening on the part of the public. To hear and understand a singer's words is an acquired aptitude; but it is one which is readily gained with practice, provided the diction be adequate.

It is obvious that the above considerations apply more specifically to the production than to the creation of opera, though in the last analysis they have important repercussions also on the latter; since operatic conventions, like those of other dramatic forms, depend for their effectiveness largely on the manner in which the taste of the public has been formed. Opera, in other words, is not only the most "actual" form of music, but in a real sense the most traditional, the most closely bound to the cultural tradition which produced it. Hence the well known "types" of opera—opera "seria" or "buffa," "romantic opera," "verismo" etc.; hence the immense strength of specifically "national" characteristics in the development of operatic convention, since the characteristics of opera are so largely the result of the language in which it is written. Hence, too, it may be seen that the choice of subject is not without a certain significance, since the opera is even more conventional in this respect than drama of other types. It is of course quite impossible to define what the poetic content of contemporary opera should be—this definition will, let us hope, be given eventually by

The Composer and His Audience

works and not by theories constructed, so to speak, as advance criteria. What is necessary is of course drama—drama which is real for the composer and which he can communicate as such to his public. It is inevitable that in a period such as ours, so sharply defined by clear historical and social forces, the truly relevant dramatic material should nearly always in some way reflect those forces, either directly, or by analogy or implication. It would be absurd to limit operatic material to our own time and place; but if vital opera is to be produced the dramatic motives will of necessity be relevant—sufficiently real and sufficiently important to both composer and public to stir their imaginations—and not, as is so frequently the case, a merely fortuitous evening's distraction. It is only very rarely and perhaps as the result of extreme maturity both in a culture and an individual that vital drama can be created out of materials which entirely transcend the present and its vital preoccupations. American opera therefore will in some sense be an interpretation of present-day America even when the scene is laid in some distant or purely legendary landscape.

If American opera should ever to any extent really develop, it would certainly be in large part the result of a revival of the instinct for idiomatic and musically expressive vocal writing, based on English diction. The reasons for this are obvious; since no tradition is present a new one must gradually be created, and unless sterility is to be the result it must be created with first principles as a point of departure. Signs are not entirely wanting that such a revival may take place—our popular music, a very few more pretentious works by American composers, and a couple of stage works, may be taken as evidence of this. The same problem exists in Europe as a result of the havoc wrought by the Wagnerian tradition; and there are still more numerous evidences of a vocal renascence there. In any case this is the indispensable condition of solution of the "operatic problem." Inadequate vocal writing cannot be vitalized by the most elaborate and expressive accompaniment: and dramatic music in which the voice does not take part is too essentially dehumanized to carry very far the weight of real drama. A really revived opera will in fact inevitably be mainly vocal, with a vigorous and expressive vocal line furnishing the real motive power of the music, the orchestra once more playing a secondary role, and the whole constituting a really vivid and moving dramatic whole.

There remains the question of specific operatic form, or operatic convention; the external problem, in other words, of the relationship between drama and music and the respective rights of each. It is clear that the solution must depend on many factors which cannot certainly be specified in advance. Quite possibly, for instance, opera will gradually move, bag and baggage, to Hollywood and take up permanent residence there. This is not likely to happen immediately or suddenly and can take place only very sporadically until the taste of the public has evolved to the point of creating a definite demand for pictures of a more evolved type than all except a very few yet produced. If it does take place it may very easily prove to be the healthiest possible state of affairs. If one wishes, one can find plenty of excellent reasons for believing that perhaps the ground is already being prepared for this. The presence in Hollywood of musicians of real authority may easily exert a gradual but decisive influence on moving picture production; the extent and nature of such influence will undoubtedly prove to be a factor of serious importance in determining the future of dramatic music. Such a state of affairs will impose upon the composer and his collaborators an entirely new set of problems. It is unlikely, so far as we can see for the present, to entirely supersede operatic production on the stage; it is at all events too early to see clearly what its role will be—there are far too many factors involved.

Meanwhile composers have the task, or opportunity, of creating a revivified opera. There is no reason whatever for believing this to be impossible provided they have the real impulse to accomplish it. Opera, if properly understood, possesses many advantages over spoken drama; its greater emotional precision, greater powers of evocation and suggestion, and even its inevitable conventions, which at best create a framework for an imaginary world, different from the world of reality but definitely a portrait of it. It is this world that composers may rediscover, if they wish, under new and freshly experienced forms—in a rediscovery of the voice and its potentialities, a fresh experience of whatever is dramatic in the actual world, a new vision of the roles which music and words, music and drama, can play in collaboration with each other. And if composers seek a model, a point of departure, what better one could they find than the work which perhaps more than any other of the last hundred years embodies all these qualities, a work which, though nearly half a century old, still remains mysterious in its vitality and wisdom and perfection—the old Verdi's *Falstaff*?

The Scope of Music Criticism
[1947]

*Read at a Symposium on Music Criticism
held at Harvard University in May, 1947.*

In preparing this paper I have been reminded of a luncheon which I attended some twenty years ago, at the Tavern Club in Boston. The guest of honor and speaker of the occasion was Mr. Ernest Newman, the well-known English music critic. His remarks were devoted to the thesis that it is more difficult to criticize a piece of music than to compose it. It was a serious discussion; and I regret to say I do not remember his arguments. But I remember very well my momentary indignation at what seemed to me a professional slight, an implied belittling of the work of the composer.

On more mature thought, however, I felt less and less inclined to quarrel with Mr. Newman, or at least with this particular thesis. The question of relative difficulty is of course eminently irrelevant as well as quite incalculable; and one may also very well recall the saying which I have heard ascribed to Victor Hugo who when asked if it were difficult to write an epic poem is said to have replied, "Madame, it is either easy or impossible." The same saying may perhaps in the deepest sense be applied to all works of art. The composer, for instance, may well encounter difficult problems of execution, even quite aside from the question of his mastery of his technique—which, after all, is expected of him. But if he finds the conception difficult—if he is ever in real doubt as to what he wants, his plight is a very serious one. His conception may either develop slowly, or be with

From *Music and Criticism: A Symposium*, ed. Richard F. French, Cambridge, Mass.: Harvard University Press. Copyright © 1948 by the President and Fellows of Harvard College; 1976 by Richard Frederic French. Reprinted by permission of the publishers.

him in essence from the start—most artists have, I fancy, had both experiences; but if it ever assumes the aspect, for him, of a problem to be solved, his work is in that measure almost surely predestined to failure. With the embodiment of his conception, his work is finished, and the success of a later revision of his work will depend precisely on the extent to which he is able to recapture both his conception and his relationship to it.

With the critic it is perhaps different; his work is never finished and, exactly when it is most worth while—when the objects of his criticism are works or questions in which he is most passionately interested—it will consist in a constant process of revision which, at best, will go on in other hands even after the critic himself has disappeared. His work is, indeed, by its very nature problematical and inconclusive; and though he doubtless strives for finality, he can achieve it only in relation to works which have lost their vitality, and in regard to which criticism has become irrelevant.

In all this I have of course been exaggerating differences and ignoring similarities. In a subtler and deeper sense the composer's work, too, is a continuous effort—his inner development reflects the development of his personality and his experience as surely as do the critic's; just as the critic's successive judgments even of the same work may well have their independent value. Both, however, have a still deeper bond in common: that both, when they are contemporaries, are in a very real and inescapable sense products of a common cultural situation and, in however varying manners, parts of a whole.

This is of course obvious enough; but I think it is worth emphasizing here. When we speak of "contemporary music" we are generally referring to the work of contemporary composers and more specifically to that part of it which differentiates itself most sharply from the work of previous generations, and in particular of the generation immediately preceding. I think it is not often enough pointed out that the musical spirit of any given period is exemplified not only in the work of its composers, but also in the prevailing modes of interpretation and the prevailing tastes. It is very easy, for example, to note the wide differences between the tastes and the interpretative modes of today and those of thirty-five years ago, and it is no way fantastic to discover that these differences in aesthetic attitude find quite exact parallels in the differences between the actual creative productions of the two periods. Our contemporary emphasis on the punctilious following of the composer's directions in the interpretation of, say, the Beethoven Symphonies; the revival of half or even wholly forgotten symphonies of Haydn; the resurgence of Verdi and Berlioz; the relative eclipse of Liszt —all these are a few symptoms of a changed musical attitude, of which other and more striking symptoms are to be found in the music of Bartók and Stravinsky and Hindemith.

I emphasize this point because I believe very strongly that the critic's primary function and his deepest obligation are to be found in his relationship to the musical community of which he is a part, and his recognition, first of all, of the fact that he is inescapably a part of it. I call to mind the remark which I read some years ago in one of our more important organs of musical comment, to the effect that while the level of creative work in the United States was vastly lower than that of Europe, the level of criticism was by so much higher. The observation seemed to me naïve and meaningless precisely because it implied a detachment of the critic from the primary object of his criticism. It seemed to me an implied admission of the justice of an estimate of American musical affairs which I had so often heard voiced abroad— that American musical achievement consisted in an overwhelming measure of the ability to pay for what were, in their relationship to our scene, essentially luxury products from Europe. The observation seemed also to relegate musical criticism to the status of an appraisal of these goods in relation to their value in the luxury market; for if a living culture, as I believe, consists primarily in the production and not merely the consumption of cultural goods, and consequently of values, the experience and the work of the composer stands at its very center, and the critic finds his point of departure in the common musical experience which is at its most intense in the most important productions of its composers.

If this be true, the critic is essentially the composer's collaborator. I do not of course mean that his judgment must be always favorable, or indeed, necessarily ever wholly so, either toward the artists who are his contemporaries or to the so-called "tendencies" which they represent; but that his first and most serious objective should be the understanding of his own musical time and place, and that without this understanding of what is most immediate he almost certainly lacks a vital portion of that which is necessary to a living relationship with the products of other times and places. His contacts are likely to be secondary contacts, his knowledge book-knowledge rather than that primarily derived from experience.

I would therefore ask of the critic, first, an understanding and conscientious judgment of his own musical time and place, the time and place of which he is unavoidably but one part and one voice. Of what elements should this judgment consist, and how is he to arrive at it?

It is scarcely original to point out that we live in a period in which our intellectual life is dominated by science, and that our habits of thought tend to approach the methods of the sciences. In criticism of the arts a familiar cry is for "objectivity," and an overwhelmingly prevalent tendency is the search for objective criteria. Thus music is held up for measurement to any number of frames of reference —aesthetic or technical systems, national "styles," and even political ideologies. No doubt such frames of reference can have their value, but I would like to suggest that they are at best secondary, and at worst evasions of the first and far more difficult consideration, which is the inherent quality of the music itself. I would like to suggest first of all that there is no possibility whatever of an objective method of determining this issue. This inherent quality is precisely the quality in the music which must be felt and experienced; the capacity for feeling it is developed through experience and through that aptitude for musical experience which is generally called musical instinct. In order to distinguish the reality from the appearance of musical imagination or invention the attitude of the critic must be anything but "objective"; he must first of all be ready to enjoy the music or, if you prefer, to feel it and to receive its impact or its message. If he feels nothing, the music has not yet begun to exist for him—it has not yet begun to be music, but remains at best "style" or "tendency," generalized and without real identity. The same is essentially true if the music arouses his response through its associations, its context, the circumstances of its production or performance, or through any other means than the direct impact of its melodies, harmonies, sonorities, or rhythms. By experience the critic will have learned in one degree or another to evaluate his impressions in terms of their intensity, their directness, their coherence and their durability. He will know, for example, whether he is tempted to hear the work again, and to explore it further; if he is conscientious he will do so if the work gives him the smallest encouragement, since he will have learned that music is essentially designed not simply to be heard, but to be experienced to its fullest extent. He will perhaps have reflected that it is not primarily for listeners at all, but for performers, and especially singers, that the composer fashions his works, and that any musical work is understood only when it is inwardly reproduced—much as the reader of poetry grasps the rhythm and sound of a poem through reproducing them in his imagination.

The critic's primary concern, then, must be the work itself: whether it really possesses the quality of direct communication; whether the composer has really felt, or, as I would prefer to say—for the term seems to me simpler and less misleading—whether he has felt, or *inwardly heard*, something which he has been able to communicate—that is, to make his listener inwardly hear. He will know from many experiences that composers possess this quality in very varying degrees, and he will, if he is gifted and at the same time untroubled by preconceived ideas, have developed a more or less reliable power of discrimination between what is genuine and what is false. I stress a lack of preconceived idea precisely because strained efforts toward objectivity seem so often, through emphasis on so-called objective criteria, to produce a kind of sectarianism and a lack of receptivity. The true critic must be able to distinguish varying degrees of quality in types of music which are unsympathetic to him as well as in those which are sympathetic, and even to admit that a good work of an unsympathetic *tendency* is preferable to a bad one of sympathetic tendency —he is no true critic if he does not do this.

It is at this point that the creative artist often fails. This failure is not universal. Indeed, one of the wisest and most genuinely educated men I have known—a critic of one of the other arts—once said to me, "The creative artist is the best critic of all, provided he takes the trouble." The proviso is of course a very considerable one—he seldom takes the trouble, and in fact generally has no desire or incentive to do so. He is by his very nature absorbed in his own conceptions; sometimes, and especially in our own day, afraid to open himself to other influences lest they disturb his serenity; and sometimes jealous. The fact remains, however, that some of the greatest critics of the past have been creative artists whose generosity or whose vital curiosity have enabled them to bring their best powers to the task of criticism, and who could see their individual predilections or personal destinies at times in the perspective of their love for music as such. Far more frequently, no doubt, even the greatest composers have failed to make the effort which this type of criticism demands, and have remained poor or indifferent critics. It should be noted, however, that not composers alone, but professional critics as well, often become the victims of similar bias.

I have stressed this question of immediate and primary contact with music, not because I imagine that it is ever entirely absent from a critic's appraisal of a musical work, but rather because one hears it so seldom given as the reason for a critical judgment, while I believe it is in reality the primary one—the court of final appeal, to which others are necessarily subordinate. Technical questions, for example, have no meaning whatever except in relation to this primary contact. We speak so often, for example, of "craftsmanship"—so-called—in terms which relegate the mature composer to the same level as a first-class student. It is as idle to praise a composer for his craftsmanship as to praise an engineer because his bridge does not collapse. On any other basis, after all, technique becomes superfluous and even obtrusive; one may even say that it is not genuine technique unless it is quite inseparable from the musical content, and in fact identical with it. The value of Bach's *Die Kunst der Fuge* or such a contemporary work as Hindemith's *Ludus Tonalis* is neither enhanced nor diminished by the technical complexities which these works embody— these complexities belong to the essence, the conception, of the works, and would otherwise be meaningless and tasteless. Similarly, technical devices which do not come to life in the perceptible shape of the work must be considered as at best the purely private affair of the composer, introduced for his own purposes but irrelevant apart from his own psychology—not, in any case, relevant to either the character or the value of the work.

Similarly, technical flaws in a work—if they are genuine —are most often flaws not of execution but of conception. The composer's impulse has faltered, or his attention has wavered, his ideas have not been clear, or he has surrendered momentarily to convention. I am referring of course to the kinds of flaws which arise in the center and under the sign of the composition itself, not to practical miscalculations, such as mistakes in instrumentation, or departures from conventional procedure such as Rimsky-Korsakov found in *Boris Godounov*. But judgment based primarily on technical criticism I believe to be irrelevant unless the critic has the power to make clear the technical facts in terms of a faulty —that is to say, unrealized—conception, or, on the other hand, a successful one.

Having established his initial contact with the musical work, and gained in this way an essential insight into its nature, the critic is bound to fit it into larger patterns. He will inevitably judge it, for instance, according to his own aesthetic predilections. He will pass, in other words, from the phase of a critic of works to that of a critic of tendencies and of aesthetic aims. If I have stressed the necessity of the first phase, it is not because I wish in any sense to belittle the importance of this second one, but rather to make clear that no judgment of aesthetic tendency is possible except on the basis of a real understanding of, and insight into, what the composer communicates. For a vital aesthetic movement is embodied not in programs or intentions but in works, and can be appraised only in terms of those works. To take two examples from recent musical history: neoclassicism, or the twelve-tone technique, are to be judged, not as such, but only in terms of their successful embodiment in more or less convincing works—they can prevail only as the works prevail, and then the victory will be for the works and not the systems and principles. Need one quote musical history in proof of this? Each generation is obliged to solve its problems afresh and a tendency or system can be nothing more than a point of departure.

The critic of tendencies must therefore beware of the easy criteria which systems afford. This, however, is not the whole story. For aesthetic tendencies are, insofar as they are vital, the embodiment of deeper attitudes—not so much strictly artistic attitudes as basically human ones; and a thoughtful critic will eventually find himself, perhaps, regarding them in that light. I am not referring to what is sometimes called "social significance," which is to an overwhelming extent a matter of association, not of the essence of the work itself. Thus, for good or ill, Beethoven's *Eroica* Symphony is loved to all appearances equally well by those who see in it a glorification of Napoleon, the standard-bearer of Revolutionary France, and by those who prefer to see in it the glorification of the head of the French state. Thus I was told in Germany by a German radical that young and revolutionary-minded people there were stirred by Stravinsky's *Symphonie de Psaumes*, regardless of its religious associations, because it constituted for them a new and exciting experience. We must therefore seek deeper than mere association if we are to arrive at the final questions which a critic will find himself asking—and to which he is least likely to find a satisfactory answer. Instead of "social significance" he will of course seek "significance," and he will try, perhaps never wholly successfully, to define it. But he may well find himself thinking not only of aesthetic creeds but of personalities and of works in terms of basic human attitudes. I hesitate to use the much-abused word "moral"; it suggests not only certain primitive misconceptions regarding the nature and function of art, but calls up visions of censorship and other highly dangerous practices. Yet I think we cannot possibly evade the fact that, for instance, those of us who find Wagner's music distasteful, do so not on the ground that he was in any sense an artist of secondary stature, which he certainly was not—nor primarily because Wotan and Siegfried and Parsifal were unpleasant characters beloved by Hitler and his followers (we can ignore them by treating them as we do story-book characters who are often even more unpleasant)—but because the music, even apart from its dramatic associations, embodies basic human attitudes and gestures which we find in the last analysis repulsive: either because the passage of time has robbed them of a large part of their magic and made them seem stilted and mechanical, or because we see in them the grandiose and essentially cruel gestures of the magician whom Nietzsche described so well, and instinctively recoil from an art in which the aesthetic shudder or caress has become an end in itself, a tool in the hands of a supreme egoist whose art, so genuinely expressive at times, consisted so much of calculated effect at others.

I have given this one example, partly because it seems to me so obvious and so clear, in order to hint at the critic's ultimate and most difficult problem. For the question of the relation of art to society as a whole, however much we may dismiss some of the more naïve and more tendentious forms in which it is raised, has inevitably arisen in a period like our own in which vast changes are everywhere in progress, and in which even human survival has become problematical. In such a world the basic human attitudes become decisive, superficiality becomes an encumbrance, and in the last analysis intolerable, and the responsibility of not only artists and critics but of every thinking human being a decisive one.

I have tried to deal with what seem to me the essentials of musical criticism rather than with certain of its specific details—the question of performance and interpretation, for instance, the separate question of musical journalism and its relation to criticism as such, or the relation of the critic to the economic colossus which determines to such a great extent the course of our musical life today. I should like to close with the observation, once more, that the work of the critic is never complete, and his judgment never definitive. Any one who has observed, over a period of years, the changing musical climate, the rise and fall of reputations, the fluctuations of prevailing style and tendency, the shifting concepts of interpretation, and the varying reactions of critics to them, must come to realize that decisive judgments are made, not by critics or other individuals, but by numerous forces which frequently—even constantly —work in ways which are surprising to all concerned.

It is easy to be pessimistic about the fate of mankind, and

The Composer and His Audience

I would be the last to minimize the dangers with which the human species is confronted. These dangers come, in fact, not from outside, but from within the heart and mind of man himself. The illness is a deep-seated one—chronic and possibly inherent in man's nature. The recovery of the patient is problematical and the danger both mortal and immediate.

These are of course near platitudes, and must form the greater part of the premises of every adult man today. It is not only culture or civilization that stands in imminent danger of destruction.

But assuming the survival of culture we must assume also that cultural values will survive, that genuine quality in art will always prevail in any moderately long-range view, and that the qualities which we value—richness of imagination and invention, intensity and lucidity of expression, the basic equilibrium which is the ultimate sign of both inner and outer mastery—will always in the end prevail, and that, with all fluctuations of critical climate, and whatever the destiny of the individual artist or aesthetic tendency or epoch, art itself will go on; and that whatever qualities are genuine will make their contribution, either directly or indirectly, to its growth and its survival. There is no more destructive belief in the world than pessimism in this regard, and no more dangerous symptom of mankind's various and complicated ills than the widespread and visible belief in propaganda, and tendency to rely on it, which such pessimism engenders. As a final word I would simply point out that for the musical critic in particular such pessimism is fatal. His undiminished love for music, his sensitiveness to tones and rhythms and harmonies, to timbres and sonorities, his fundamental responsiveness to music and his belief in its reality, are the very essence of his task and the condition of his validity.

Music in a Business Economy
[1948]

No fact regarding music in America is more obvious, more pertinent, or more all-embracing in its implications than the fact that music here is in all of its public aspects a business, and a big one. There is no doubt that this is an inevitable state of affairs. I do not regard it as a favorable one for art or for culture, however we may define the latter term; but it is a condition which is wholly characteristic of our society, and one which exists and flourishes as a part of that society, entirely independently of the will or the intentions of individuals. I am not therefore deploring it —it raises problems, to be sure, and great ones; but unless and until our economic system is changed we must treat it as a condition and not a temporary accident. The music *business* is here to stay; it is as many-sided as music itself, including as it does, everything from publishing to concert management, and it is run—as every successful business must be—by strictly business methods.

If I speak of the music business I am referring, not to a monopolistic structure, which as far as I know does not exist, but to a set of effects which in all of the smaller units which go to make up the whole of public musical enterprise —effects which are due simply to the adoption of business methods and to the dynamics of business enterprise—work together in the same general direction. These same effects are visible throughout other phases of American life and are in fact taken for granted; and their connection with the musical fare which the public receives is clear enough. But its ultimate consequences and implications are just beginning to be clear to a large section of the public.

One of these consequences is, of course, an enormous

From *Berkeley: A Journal of Modern Culture*, July 1948, pp. 1-2, 7-8.

centralization of musical enterprise in New York. This centralization is not entirely due to the workings of the music business, not visibly so, at any rate. New York is the largest center of population, and the tendency of the last eighty years has been towards a greater concentration, not only of economic activity, but of talent of all kinds there. For years the countryside of the East flocked there, and such cultural centers as Boston and Philadelphia tended to lose their earlier position of preeminence through the attraction which the larger center held for so many of their gifted younger people. Today that particular tendency is not perhaps so strongly pronounced. Other parts of the country have proven capable of attracting talent in very considerable quantity, and have grown capable, too, of nurturing this talent and providing it with soil in which to create and to be fruitful.

But what I have in mind is the tendency of purely business enterprise to grow large and to expand. The number of communities which have independent musical resources to any degree whatever is really very small indeed; and it is only inevitable that the music business—with good effects which at least in any short range view certainly far outweigh the bad—should move into such regions, furnish their musical fare, and control their musical taste.

At the same time this has resulted in the growth of a gigantic business empire; its expression has tended to accentuate its purely economic problems and to promote solutions of these which are not always in the best interests of art. A good business, for instance, will certainly try first to produce its goods as cheaply as possible. Secondly, it will try to get the largest possible return on those goods, partly by doing everything possible to enhance their value, partly by catering to the demands of the largest possible number of customers. Third, it will try—as far as possible, though it will have to contend here with a number of imponderables such as a demand for luxury products or the prestige of sheer quality—it will try to encourage in its customers a demand for those products which are cheapest and most convenient to produce.

Let me try briefly to apply these points to the actualities of our musical situation. It is true that the musical fare of the American public has become much more varied, by and large, than it was twenty years ago. This is partly the result of business expansion—especially of the radio business, which, still in its infancy, has tried many experiments, and which, with the possibility of providing programs at every hour of the day, has brought about immense changes in the musical taste of the American public. In the average concert program, however, opposite tendencies are visible. The so-called "standard repertoire" has tended to shrink, for the reason that a small and familiar repertoire is safe—being familiar, it is less forbidding than an even moderately adventurous one would be. In the case of orchestral music, familiar music requires less rehearsal, and is therefore cheaper to produce.

I am not talking idly, or in mere generalities, but could back up these statements with any number of instances. A young pianist of my acquaintance once landed in a Western city and was greeted by expressions of disappointment that no Beethoven sonata had been included on her program because, as they had been told, she played none. She was quite able to change her program and did so, and upon investigation found that no Beethoven sonata had been included on her program simply because it was cheaper to print a single program, in New York, for all of the concerts of her tour, than to print more than one, and that in order to make this economy acceptable her public had been deliberately misled as to the repertoire at her disposal. In another connection, many talks with conductors of major orchestras have convinced me that the infrequency of performance of Mahler's symphonies—to pick a concrete example—is, in spite of palpable popular enthusiasm, due in very large part to the need for extra instruments, extra rehearsal, and therefore extra cost. These are, I am convinced, the finally determining factors, and it could be shown, I think, that other factors are subordinate to these.

The most obvious example of all is, of course, the status of contemporary music. Contemporary music of the most significant type—I mean, the contemporary music that has palpably exerted a major influence—is relatively seldom heard on major programs. In judging the significance of this fact it is unnecessary to refer to the work of young and relatively unknown composers, or to those whose reputations may be considered in any obvious way problematical. Musicians know, if the general public does not, that the music of Schoenberg, of Stravinsky, of Béla Bartók has influenced that of every younger composer, of whatever tendency. Yet a striking fact of today's musical life is the discrepancy between these composers' acknowledged reputations and the frequency with which their mature music is performed. Nor is this state of affairs to be laid primarily at the door of performers, who are frequently found to be willing and interested enough to perform new works on the proper occasion. The result is that while these composers are known by name, and, especially in the case of Stravinsky, by a few early works easily performed and easily accessible—since, like all early works, they are still largely derivative—in spite of their reputations their mature work is comparatively little known except to a few people who are equipped to investigate it for themselves. A still more striking case is that of Berg's opera *Wozzeck* which for years before Hitler was successfully performed even in the smallest opera houses of Europe, yet had but two performances in the United States—one performance each, in New York and Philadelphia—both under the direction of Stokowski. The crux of this matter is not the hostility of critics, which plays a very small role indeed in determining the destiny of creative works, but the fact that new music—especially new music which is original and exacting and,

aggressive self-assertion added themselves to the original brew; the original, all-inclusive American ideal, which welcomed foreigners to our shores and took richly of what they had to offer, for the common welfare, was forgotten, in a competitive fear which at least for a time poisoned the musical atmosphere and made it one of exclusiveness. We were far indeed not only from the healthy spirit of old Bach, who tirelessly copied the Italian masterpieces of his day, in the hope of learning something, or even from the fiery patriot Chopin who allowed himself to be influenced by the works of the Irishman John Field or the Italian Bellini, and developed his own individuality not through a valetudinarian diet but through his healthy powers of digestion. The fundamental objection to the American musical nationalism is that it became dogmatic precisely at the moment when it became nervous and exclusive, a symptom of impoverishment and not of strength.

Granted—wholeheartedly granted: music betrays the characteristics of its creator—the national characteristic as well as the others. But what is a nation, in the real and profound sense, other than the localization of a human aspiration which is essentially universal? Is this not true above all of America, "conceived in liberty and dedicated to the proposition that all men are created equal?" Are we to conceive our art in terms of "blood and soil" or rather in terms of music—music springing from the impulse felt by us as, first of all, human beings, and colored by the thousands of intangible influences to which we, as human beings living in a real world and a vital environment, are inevitably subject? Do we really want the decisive or the final characteristic of our music to be its local color, its tricks of so-called "native" style—or are we not rather to strive first of all for genuine expression and let our musical culture develop naturally out of the impulses of gifted men who feel within themselves the strength to be really free, and to build their music out of the elements that best suit them? Are we, in other words, to trust in an economy of abundance in the cultural world, or to seek refuge in a shrewdly calculated economy of scarcity? I cannot believe that in the long run we shall choose the latter.

The second tendency which I have described—the glorification of "accessibility" or "mass appeal"—seems to me dangerous because, again, it would put music in a strait-jacket, and would cut it off from some of its most vital arteries. On the highest level we might consider it symbolically as a glorification of Beethoven's Fifth Symphony at the expense of his A minor quartet or his *Grosse Fuge*—to mention two works which were still widely considered esoteric and obscure even within my own memory. To be sure, we live in an age of specialization; today, so to speak, one man tends to compose the Fifth Symphony (if any), another "The Battle of Vittoria," another the contredanses, another the *Grosse Fuge* and the A minor Quartet, another composer, let's say, the operas of Rossini. Moreover the differences between the various categories which these works suggest—even, if you prefer, the gulf between them—seems, at least, greater than in Beethoven's time, though it is hard to determine this, and the readiness with which "popular" music adopts the technical devices of the "serious" music of day before yesterday, would seem in some degree to belie it.

But are we not, once more, impoverishing our conception of music, and even demanding too little of it, when we make of "accessibility" a goal to be striven for? What we ask of music, first and last, is that it communicate experience—experience of all kinds, vital and profound at its greatest, amusing or entertaining at another level. But communication is two-sided—vital and profound communication makes demands also on those who are to receive it—not, in the last analysis, purely technical demands, but demands in the sense of concentration, of genuine effort to receive what is being communicated. This is, as every one of us knows, as finally true, even today, in the case of Beethoven's A minor Quartet or *Grosse Fuge* as it is in the case of a quartet of Béla Bartók or a concerto by Schoenberg.

Or, to look at it from the other end—how can the composer communicate anything whatever unless he does so in full conviction; how is he to create music which others will love unless he creates what he loves to the full himself? At what point is he to avoid writing the chord or the interval which alone fully expresses what he is to convey, in the fear that Mr. X or Mrs. Y will find it difficult to understand? Shall he not rather write exactly as he feels—with his practiced composer's ear, inevitably in advance of less experienced musical ears, in the faith and even the certainty that his musical message will reach those who are ready for it, and that, if it is genuinely vital, it will ultimately reach everyone who is willing to listen?

Certainly, the musician must be a member of society. That, indeed, is his duty as a human being and not primarily as an artist. Certainly, if he is a vital and sensitive artist, he will be instinctively drawn to real issues instead of to false ones. That must be taken for granted. But it must be taken for granted also that he will have the power to see connections where others do not see them, and to reveal significances where they are not obvious.

I see that I have arrived far from my starting point, which was the impact of our business economy on our musical life. I should like in closing to refer to that condition once more—a condition which, as I said, I regard as inevitable, precisely because it is in the nature of modern economy. None of the existing proposals for changing that economy seem to me in any way likely to change that state of affairs in any very essential respect—nor have I any others to offer. A state-controlled economy would certainly bring new elements into the situation and might easily make the problems still more complicated—in any case, the political arguments have to do with quite other phases of the total modern problem.

The Composer and His Audience

It seems to me rather that the real solution of the artistic dilemma must take place along quite other lines. We must place our hope rather in the increasing undertow which I believe I feel on every side—the growth of musical awareness among the people, quite independently of the commercialized musical fare which is purveyed to us through the great business agencies which furnish our public music. This is a prerequisite not only of any living musical culture, but of any real future for the music business itself—since, I believe, it will eventually become clear that the latter also cannot continue indefinitely to flourish without constant injections of new ideas. The most hopeful sign—and at times for me a very hopeful one indeed—for the development of a really rich musical culture in the United States is to be found, certainly, not in the public musical life at all, but in the development of local musical activity in so many parts of the country.

Musical culture begins in one's own locality with the musicians who are contributing their best efforts to the community in which they live and to those music-lovers who, independently of organized publicity, seek genuine musical experience, wherever it can be found, with active curiosity and with the only genuine discrimination—that born of varied and deep experience. If such local developments as have sprung up all over the country continue to flourish and to enjoy abundant local support, we may see the growth of a real musical tradition, one which will find more vital nourishment than that offered at present by our over-centralized, standardized musical economy, and which will in its creative achievements aspire to something more than, on the one hand, the gentility which masquerades as high traditionalism, or, on the other, the slick marketability concealing itself behind slogans such as "Americanism" and "mass appeal."

How a "Difficult" Composer Gets That Way
[1950]

I HAVE sometimes been told that my music is "difficult" for the listener. There are those who consider this as praise, those who consider it a reproach. For my part I cannot regard it as, in itself, either the one or the other. But so far as it is so, it is the way the music comes, the way it has to come.

I once asked Alfredo Casella, who had pointed out the technical difficulties in my violin concerto, what could be done to make it easier. He answered that nothing could be done: for you see, he said, "è nato difficile"—it is born difficult.

I also remember a remark of Albert Einstein, which certainly applies to music. He said, in effect, that everything should be as simple as it can be, but not simpler.

I would prefer by far to write music which has something fresh to reveal at each new hearing than music which is completely self-evident the first time, and though it may remain pleasing makes no essential contribution thereafter. Naturally I do not try to write either kind—how can one? I try only to put into each work as much of myself as possible. It is very hard to put into words what this means. One is fully identified with the work, possessed by it, living in the world which the work makes for one, and trying to bring it into being. When one is finished, one loses this particular sense of identity. One's work becomes, as it were, an objective fact.

Experience, however, has shown me over and over again that the "difficulty" of my music is anything but insuperable. This is, of course, true of all new music if it is genuine, if it really has something to say. Last year in San Francisco I was present at a rehearsal of Alban Berg's Violin Concerto, superbly performed by Szigeti and Mitropoulos. In the intermission half a dozen musicians of the orchestra came up to me, expressing bewilderment that they could have found the music suddenly so clear and simple, after having found it very problematical and difficult on earlier occasions. The enthusiastic and unequivocal reception of the work proved that the public, too, had caught up with the work and had been deeply stirred by it. The idiom and the language of Berg had seeped through, over many channels, and was no longer so unfamiliar as to seem forbidding.

I have had ample occasion to observe that a work which was "difficult," say, ten or twelve years ago, is no longer so. Both for performer and listener, these difficulties have meanwhile cleared up, with results that have been surprising to all concerned. This really is the key to the understanding of contemporary music. What the listener needs is familiarity with the language—sufficient familiarity to be able to respond to tones, melodies, harmonicas and rhythms it contains.

Once, with a class of fifty students, all relatively unprepared and some quite innocent of contact with contemporary music, I tried the experiment of familiarizing them, at the beginning of the course, with Schoenberg's Fourth Quartet, one of the composer's most "difficult" works. My whole effort was to bring them into contact with the music, and I deferred speaking of the problem of tonality, or the twelve-tone system, until the students knew the music thoroughly. By that time—believe it or not—one could hear the opening theme of the quartet, or other passages, being whistled by students on the campus. At the end of several weeks I spoke only briefly about the technical questions involved and they fell, it seemed to me, in their proper place. My students had learned to know—some to love— the music; their ears had been conquered.

A great deal of harm has been done by giving too much

emphasis to the technical aspects and even to matters of so-called "aesthetic." Certainly, we live in a period of transition, of upheaval; we all know that and it is hardly necessary to dwell on it. But contact with the music—and all the art of our time—is to be made through the works themselves and through the experience which these works communicate; it cannot to any degree whatever come through the concepts, technical or otherwise, of the composers or of their self-appointed spokesmen.

One cannot insist too strongly on this fact. The technique is the affair primarily of composers themselves and is simply the vehicle of their expression, as it always has been for all composers of all time. As Arnold Schoenberg once wrote in a letter which I particularly treasure, "A Chinese philosopher, of course, speaks Chinese, but the important thing is what does he say?"

III

Education and Training

Music and the Crisis of the Arts
[1954]

Delivered at a symposium on "New Frontiers
of Knowledge" celebrating the inauguration
of the Graduate School of Arts and Sciences
at Brandeis University, Waltham, Mass., in
January 1954.

WHEN I was invited, as a representative of the creative
arts, to address a symposium entitled "New Frontiers
of Knowledge," the first question which I asked myself was
regarding the meaning of the word "knowledge" in connection with the arts. Clearly it was in the minds of those who
invited me that I should contribute to the discussion some
thoughts regarding the place of the arts in the curriculum
of a great university, and hence it seemed clear to me that
this word "knowledge" must be taken, in such a context,
to have implications somewhat wider than those which the
word is often supposed to possess, for I need hardly recall
that the arts, at least in their essentials, are not in any way
bound up with facts to be acquired, arguments to be pursued, or hypotheses to be tested. If we are, in other words,
to include them under the heading of "knowledge," and
thus, by implication, within the scope of the university,
not only are we obliged to extend the meaning of the word
"knowledge," but to face very clearly the issues involved
in this extension of meaning.

Perhaps one valid approach to this question may be found
by looking at it from a specifically contemporary point of
view. Very few words are needed in order to draw attention to the state of the various arts today; and it is even
immaterial whether we deplore that state, as is widely done,
or whether, on the contrary, we regard this as one of the
most exciting and—to say the least—one of the most chal-

lenging moments of history. As a creative artist, it is only to be expected that I myself should incline very strongly to the latter view. But perhaps no one can know better than a person who is actually working in one of the arts that their very existence today is to all appearances problematical, if not actually precarious, and their future uncertain.

Let me make this point a little more clear, for, of course, there can be hardly any doubt that books of all kinds will continue to be written, pictures to be painted, sculpture to be chiseled and music to be composed and performed. It is quite possible, in fact, that there is today more activity in every one of the arts—and certainly some new ones, like the cinema, have been added to the traditional list of these— than at any previous time in history. And if—as we still can not wholly allow ourselves to assume—civilization itself endures, there is every reason to believe that these activities will go on, in one form or another. The problems of which I speak, however, are rather of another order. It is not a question of existence, but of life and growth.

The problems exist, in other words, only on the most serious level; at every level short of this the arts might even be said to flourish more luxuriantly today, and especially here in the United States, than at any other time or place. For better or for worse, art is no longer the exclusive property of an elite. The largest of possible publics is served, and served on the whole better than one might easily expect, through a formidable and even closely woven mass of channels which are devoted not only to satisfying but also to whetting its appetite for whatever the past and, let us gladly admit, also the present, have to offer in the way of artistic experience. The picture is on the whole a very complicated one, and any summary account of it is subject to a thousand qualifications. But the qualifications are voiced freely, and often lead to conflicts in which the more vital and progressive forces have thus far generally prevailed in the end. The result is, without any question, that the large public is far more versed in, and far more receptive to, not only what is greatest in the literature, visual art, and music of the past, but also what is boldest, freshest, and most serious in that of the present, than it was thirty, twenty, or even ten years ago.

Let me therefore repeat once more that I do not consider that it is on this level that the real problems occur. I am well aware that one of the most oft heard complaints against contemporary art, and perhaps especially against that which I myself represent—contemporary music—is that it does not reach the heart of the common man. As in all such cases, this complaint is not entirely without its basis in fact. It is quite true that, by and large, contemporary art has not yet become "popular." And yet one should ask, far more frequently than is actually asked, when, except in fairly rare cases, what has been most contemporary in art has *ever* been "popular" in the sense that this word is assumed to have today. No doubt, the Italian operatic public of the eighteen fifties left the house after the premiere of *Rigoletto* humming or whistling "La donna è mobile" just as we are told it did. But, though this fact certainly does not lower our estimate of *Rigoletto* or of Verdi's genius, neither do we think of "La donna è mobile," or for that matter any of the other similarly popular tunes which Verdi wrote, as constituting more than one of very many ingredients in a truly vital musical personality whose span was enormous. Other composers of comparable stature were less fortunate than Verdi, and others comparable in fortune failed to approach his stature.

The truth is that, at least since the revolutionary period of the eighteenth century, the gap—or, to put it more accurately, the "time-lag"—between the publc and the contemporary artist has been always apparent; and if it has seemed to become wider, this is very largely explicable in terms that have little to do with specific modes of art. Before that time, the public in our modern sense cannot be said to have existed, and since that time it has grown from an elite of a few thousands to a mass public of many millions. What we call the public today is, in fact, of the most recent origin; it dates from the period of the development of mass communication. In particular, it dates from the stage in that development in which the wide diffusion of cultural goods began to be a real concern of the radio, the press, and the book publishing world. It is hardly surprising, therefore, that in a period of immense cultural ferment and activity, this rapidly expanding public should have developed problems of its own in regard to cultural products which, in each generation, have offered to it new sensations and new experiences—which have introduced it to new landscapes in the world of the senses, the feelings, and the mind, and which have therefore confronted it with new and unfamiliar challenges and demands.

I do not wish to suggest, of course, that the problem does not exist, or even that it is not a serious one. I wish to suggest merely that it is not in itself new and also that, even in our own time, the public has met the challenges which contemporary art has offered it about as well as one could expect. It has not met them, in our own time or formerly, promptly enough to satisfy those of us who care deeply about art and its fate; and it would be easy to point to cases where years of neglect and opposition have led to great bitterness and even to personal tragedy of the most poignant and the most disturbing kind. The point I wish to make, however, is that the distance between artist and public is a problem not so much of contemporary art as of contemporary society, and that where it is related to the problem of contemporary art, it is as in a very partial sense a by-product, rather than as a genuine symptom, of the artistic situation of today. For we still have ample evidence that the public—even the great public—eventually catches up with genuine artistic expression, however unpromising its initial response may be, and however confusing the din of voices, sometimes intelligent, often ignorant or ill-informed, arguing, explaining, interpreting, proselytizing, demolishing, analyzing, theorizing, registering love or hatred, surrender or disdain, interest or boredom, voices which form such a characteristic and possibly (let us admit) such a vital—but in any case such an unavoidable—aspect of our cultural life today.

As I have said, all this has very little to do with the central problem of contemporary art, which is that of developing an artistic vocabulary in terms of which the sensations, feelings, impulses and attitudes of contemporary human beings can be given articulate organization. You will easily perceive, of course, that I have chosen my words with great care, and that the result is a rather formidable sentence; I must confess in fact that it is far more formidable than I like. In some respects, too, it may easily seem to be merely a statement of the artistic problems which any generation faces. And indeed, the artist of today often finds himself in the position of having to explain that his aims are in no essential respect different from those of any other time or place, that he is, to be sure, localized historically and geographically, but that he is nevertheless aiming to use both his inner and outer resources to create artistic objects which have real meaning for him, in terms of the world in which he lives, just as artists have done in other times and places.

In speaking of "developing a vocabulary," however, I meant to imply a problem which is apt to our time as to few others of which I know. In the first place, I have wished the word "vocabulary" to denote not only meanings but symbols, not merely relationships but basic concepts of organization, in the artistic sphere. And I have wished to imply that, where the arts in Western civilization have for at least a number of centuries past developed a relatively continuous tradition, embodied in a traditional vocabulary which steadily accumulated fresh modes and nuances of expression within its own terms; our time—and who shall set its limits with exactitude?—has seen that tradition called into question and challenged in a way that can only mean

179

one of two things—either a major cultural catastrophe or a major turning point. A vast revaluation is taking place, a revaluation which is not in any sense confined to the arts, but which embraces the whole of conscious human activity —a revaluation on the basis of all of the human experiences, discoveries, and solutions of at least the last century and a half. It is quite clear, at least to all those to whom the arts are a matter of serious concern, that this revaluation was bound to take place there too, and in a most radical manner, for the experiences of which I have spoken have placed human beings in a radically transformed world, not only of thought and action, but of sensation and feeling as well. And they have obliged each individual to cope with this transformed world and to bring his consciousness somehow to terms with it.

Let me try to give some kind of concrete indication of this process as it affects the arts, and let me do so in terms of the art of music which I myself serve. Our time has often been compared, and not without some justification, to the period of musical history which began roughly at some time during the sixteenth century, when—along with other and similarly radical developments—what we call the "tonal system" began to emerge as a principle of musical organization.

This is not the place, and there is not the time, to attempt to describe this system in any adequate detail. What musicians discovered at that time, however, was the possibility of orienting the ear of the listener in such a way that, first of all, fixed relationships between tones could be established by the composer and perceived by the listener, so that one tone became the ultimate point of reference, or, in somewhat more technical terms, the key tone or tonic. Thus, when we speak of the "key" of, for instance, E, we mean that the music is so organized that the tone E becomes the constant point of reference. Secondly, and perhaps of even greater significance, musicians discovered that this point of reference could be shifted in the course of a single musical movement, through the process known as modulation, thus not only yielding new resources of contrast and of movement, but, through this means, achieving a greater span and making possible music of genuinely large design, in which far-flung contrasts could be brought into play as organic elements of a vast but clearly conceived whole.

But as this musical vocabulary developed, and more and more subtle relationships between tones were brought into play, the center of musical interest gradually shifted—especially after the death of Beethoven and Schubert—from the larger line to the detail itself; and, in the music of Wagner and those who followed him, it was centered to a preponderant extent on the single striking phrase, the characteristic sequence of harmonies, or the sharp contrast, often driven home by sheer repetition. And though the music was by no means devoid of design, the design tended to become the means by which the smaller but nevertheless intensely expressive features were held together and given significance, rather than the cumulative and sweeping deployment of a sustained musical impulse. And gradually, as contrasts in detail became sharper and nuances of expression ever more subtle, the tonal organization itself became weakened. A vast quantity of new expressive resources had been introduced into music, but these new resources, consisting as they did very largely of hitherto unused combinations of or relationships between sounds, burst the bonds of the older tonal system, and, though the ear of the composer undoubtedly conceived them in terms of the tonal system, the musical impulse which they embodied led to something more like the effect of constant modulation. Thus the resources and impulses inherent in the tonal system from the beginning led first to the filling out of that system, but later to its disintegration, till at length the very early years of this century found musicians already speaking of this system as a thing of the past and regarding themselves as emancipated from the restrictions which it placed on them. They had not at this time left it sufficiently far behind to search systematically for principles to take its place, as did Arnold Schoenberg at a somewhat later date, or to seek fresh contacts with tradition, as did Igor Stravinsky.

The two names which I have just mentioned have become in a sense symbols, as did Wagner and Brahms in the latter part of the nineteenth century, for opposing tendencies in the music of today; and like those former symbols, they represent widely different responses to the common situation. It is not part of my thesis here to discuss them or to attempt to formulate the implications or consequences to which their contrasting attitudes are commonly supposed to lead. It is sufficient to note that both have—for good or ill— left their indelible mark on music. No composer lives who has not felt their influence, and all composers outside very narrow circles indeed have felt the influence of both. This is equally true of those who have been drawn to their music by sympathy and those who have consistently opposed it; and it is true also of those who have not consciously come within the orbit of either, for influences of this kind are all-pervasive; they affect not only the work of individuals, but what I have called the musical vocabulary in general. And since this is so, I have no hesitation whatever in predicting that, possibly fifty years hence, they will appear to be far closer together in both aim and spirit than seems generally conceivable at the present time, for the central fact regarding them is that they have devoted the greater part of their creative lives to the solution of the same major musical problem.

The problem is one which involves music as a whole, and the very sketchy account which I have given above by way of illustration attempts to deal with only one phase of it. It is indeed this fact, at which I have been able barely to hint, which makes it possible to compare our present musical situation with but two others of which I know—the period in the early middle ages, when musicians first began to explore the effect of two or more simultaneous but different melodic voices, and the period of the sixteenth and seventeenth centuries, when not only was the tonal system evolved, but when so many other major developments—the sudden florescence of instrumental music, the emergence of "square" rhythm as a kind of norm, the development of accompanied monodic song, the attempt to revive the spirit of Greek drama in the modern form of opera—all coincided to effect a comparably profound transformation of the art of music.

I have spoken, of course, of a crisis in only one of the arts, and that in which I feel able to speak with some degree of competence. Though I am extremely chary of analogies—however learned—between the various arts, I have every reason to believe that anyone competent in contemporary literature or visual art would give an account, somehow similar in general intent if not in detail, of the actual situation in these respective spheres, for what I have been discussing is very clearly but one phase of an enormous cultural transformation which confronts us with tremendous challenges and of which no one can yet foresee the outcome. As I have already intimated, such a situation spells either death or renewal, and the eventual artistic issue is whether the imagination of artists is to prove equal to developing the vocabulary of which I have spoken, or, in other terms, whether this imagination is powerful enough to bring its vision of order and coherence to bear on the chaotic inner life of today, and more specifically in terms of our Western civilization. The answer which time will eventually furnish does not, of course, depend solely or perhaps even primarily on artists; but it is certainly much more fateful, in all of its far-flung implications, than appears on superficial consideration to be the case.

Let me point out too that, even should we shift our con-

sideration of art from the most serious and problematical
level to that of pure entertainment, we would not thereby
avoid the basic challenges; for entertainment, if it is real,
if it is something more than nostalgia, or mechanical distraction, or the reshuffling or reflavoring—neither very vital
nor very enduring—of familiar devices, must eventually
grow out of the same roots as what is most serious in art.
It is hardly necessary to labor this point; we see it exemplified all around us in our every-day visual experience, our
popular literature, our popular music. If on this level we
no longer speak of problems, it is because it is not on this
level that solutions are, or should be, expected to occur.
The basic vocabulary of entertainment, simply because of
its nature as entertainment, is inevitably taken over from
that of art on its most intense and, in the generally accepted
sense, serious level, which is in this manner adapted to purposes which present few challenges and make no demands.
Thus in listening to the popular music of today, we often
recognize the musical language of the Ravel, Stravinsky, or
Bartók of twenty-five years ago. The so-called "serious"
art of any period furnishes, in other words, the very life
blood of the whole artistic manifestation to which that period gives rise. Its problems belong, in other words, not
only to the relatively few persons actively engaged in grap-
pling with them, but eventually to the whole artistic community, and ultimately seep down to the human community
in the largest possible sense.

If what I have said is even partially true, the fostering of
the arts, in a period such as our own, should certainly be
a major concern of the University, for the matters of which
I have spoken lie pre-eminently within the realm of the
humanistic idea—they lie in fact at the very heart of it,
if the humanities be conceived as concerning themselves
primarily and above all with the spirit of man, in its living
essence, and not simply in those documentations which time
has passed on to us. It is therefore in the highest degree
heartening that, in the course of the last twenty odd years,

so many American universities have taken the drastic and undoubtedly difficult step, so much at variance with the older University tradition and so shocking to many cherished academic prejudices, of embodying this concern in the university curriculum, and making of our universities major centers not only of scholarly but also of creative, and as an eventually necessary corollary, reproductive activity in the arts. It has been an act of rare courage, of which the consequences have already borne incalculable fruit in the development of the arts in the United States. Speaking, once more, strictly as a musician, one cannot say less than that the level of musical achievement in the United States has completely transformed itself in these years and that a major share of this transformation must be credited to standards which universities have established and maintained, by confronting students with genuine artistic issues, and not merely with those incidental to pursuing a profitable career or satisfying a volatile public. No doubt, some of the credit belongs also to the professional schools, which in their own provinces have made some indispensable and even distinguished contributions. Yet I believe that it is above all the universities that have taken the lead; it is among university students above all that one finds the sense that art is an exciting and significant adventure in its own right, and regardless of, or at least over and above, the considerations inherent in the pursuit of a career in the musical world of today. This is not only because nearly all of the distinguished composers of today are teaching in universities, but because it is in universities that students are confronted with the challenges which only the most serious and even esoteric approach can furnish. It is in the emergence of such an attitude, among countless young musicians, that we can see the greatest hope for a transformation of that musical world, for signs are already visible, here and there, that this vitality and enthusiasm is communicable, and that it is gradually exerting its effect upon a small but growing portion of the public.

So we finally arrive once more at the question concerning "knowledge" at which I hinted at the beginning of this paper, for what is it that the university as such has to offer, first of all, to the prospective artist, if not knowledge of a kind? Undoubtedly it has nothing whatever to offer him unless it can provide him with training on the most serious and exacting level, in the essentials of his art, and unless it provides him with conditions which enable him to make the most of this training. But what I have tried to show is that such training, if it is to be genuinely serious, must entail much more than strictly technical exercise. It must cultivate in him also knowledge in the sense of awareness—awareness of himself, of the inner world in which he lives, both as an individual and as a member of a cultural community, awareness of the real demands, problems, and standards of his art, and possibly also of the real insights and challenges which its history can offer him. And, above all, through the presence of serious artistic activity, the university has a similar awareness to offer the layman. It can offer him a first-hand insight into the nature of art itself, of what it means both in terms of human effort towards genuinely creative ends, and in the minds and hearts of those whose vocation it is to serve it.

It is, first of all, because I believe so ardently in this role of the university that I have welcomed this opportunity to speak today on an occasion so auspicious for Brandeis University, which has in the short years of its existence succeeded in building up a truly distinguished Music Department. To the university I wish to extend my hearty congratulations and to its Music Department my heartiest good wishes, in the conviction that it is destined to become one of the outstanding centers of creative musical achievement in the country.

New Vistas in Musical Education
[1934]

IT is hardly necessary any longer to point out the unmistakable symptoms of unsureness which are becoming more and more characteristic of contemporary musical life. They may be seen in the already advanced confusion of critical standards: the tendency to replace standards based on a sound and self-confident musical instinct, with others culled almost at random from external sources, such as musical history, aesthetic theory, up-to-the-minute fashion, nationalistic, racial, or sociological dogma. As far as composers are concerned, even if we leave out of consideration the extremely poor quality of so much contemporary music, we may observe the feverish attempts of certain ones to "explain" their works, the increase of cliques and self-protective, self-adulatory, or self-consoling groups, and the tendency to enroll under banners of various colors—often with the purpose of hiding some half-suspected nakedness. One may even observe a certain tendency, especially in the United States, to formulate principles of criticism in advance of the works to which they are to be applied; one sees composers discussing "style" before any musical ideas have presented themselves, or elaborating external and often complicated formal patterns which have no essential relationship to the specific musical material which is forced into them.

All of these symptoms, along with others less obvious, betoken in unsureness of instinct which, no doubt, has its manifold causes. One of the principal causes, however, is undoubtedly a disharmony in the relation of the composer to his materials—detachment of his musical consciousness

From *Modern Music*, vol. 11, no. 2, pp. 115-120. Reprinted by permission of the League of Composers—International Society for Contemporary Music, U.S. Section, Inc.

from the facts, both "musical," in the strictest material sense, and psychological, which form the basis of the musical impulse.

It should be the task of musical education to correct this disharmony; but when we look at the educational methods which have been evolved in the past two hundred years, we can see that they have in many respects contributed to its gradual emergence. It is already many years since Brahms made the remark that he had learned nothing essential from his early music studies, but was obliged to discover his guiding principles for himself; and since Brahms' day the gulf between theory and practice has become even wider.

It is hardly necessary to point out the extent to which this gulf exists. The study of harmony has evolved, out of the science of thoroughbass, into what is fundamentally a set of rules for voice-leading, formulas of chord-connection, and modulatory schemes, in which the actual relationships, the structural implications, and the manifold musical embodiments (figuration, melody, musical texture and elaboration) are at best scarcely hinted at; that of counterpoint into a set of rules of ostensibly universal validity, rules which no composer has ever regarded in his actual composition and of which neither the psychological basis nor the pedagogical purpose is very often made clear—with the result that there is a hopeless diversity of principle, of method and conception. "Fugue" is conceived as an abstract discipline instead of as a living musical form; and what passes for "form" is generally conceived as a set of abstract patterns into which the student is asked to fit his "ideas" as best he can.

There can be no doubt that the result is profoundly bewildering to the student, and more especially to the student who has something to say, and who only asks to be taught the essentials of living musical speech. When he finds that precisely this is not forthcoming, he is likely to turn away in disgust, and to seek substitutes for what he has failed to find, either in auto-didacticism—inevitably of a specious kind —or in an attitude of equally specious and sterile revolt.

Since musical instruction has been presented to him in the form of abstract theory, he is as likely as not, to try to formulate other theories, unlike the original models but having dogmatism, superficiality, and academic abstractness, even though of a "radical" kind, in common with them. That he remains completely uneducated in every real sense is demonstrated by the very fact of such theorizing, which is a familiar form of over-compensation in those whose contact with the realities involved has been imperfect and incomplete.

This is not the place to discuss the processes through which the above described conceptions have developed, nor the precise reasons why their effect has become so much more acute in our day. But the time is obviously more than ripe for a complete reexamination of educational principles in the whole field of so-called "musical theory," and the fact that this reexamination is taking place, in several centers, is one of the really hopeful signs of our times.

The main problem, then, is to reestablish, first of all, a coordination between the teaching of music and its actual practice, and, on a still profounder level, the primordial feeling of the composer for his materials and the sense of their ineradicable nature. Education is, in any real sense, nothing more nor less than experience, and teaching, purely and simply the directing of experience with the object of saving the student from as many waste motions and as many blind alleys as possible. The teacher of music, therefore, has the unique function, not of retailing abstractions, but of *bringing the student into contact with facts*—facts of a demonstrable and fundamentally inexorable nature. First of all, the elemental sonorous and rhythmic facts on which music is based, and to which it is subject. Such a fact is the overtone series, of which the properties are inevitably at the basis of our whole perception of musical tone, and from which the human ear has deduced a whole hierarchy of relationships between tones—relations which are in Nature itself and hence quite independent of human will or convention. Similar facts are the principles of rhythmic expression, which have their psychological basis in the most profound and vital movements of the human organism. The composer must learn to think in terms of these facts as inevitably as the architect must learn to think in terms of the fundamental laws of balance and symmetry, otherwise his sonorous and rhythmic structure will crumble as completely as would the material structure of a rickety building.

Such elementary facts as these are the subject-matter at the basis of harmony and of counterpoint, the "rules" of which are purely devices for limiting the student, for pedagogical purposes, to the simplest modes of procedure and teaching him to make sharp distinctions of a type which would become necessarily modified by the use of more complex material. Needless to say, the purpose and the scope of such studies must never for a moment be lost sight of by either the teacher or the pupil, and the "rules" adopted must be only such as contribute to this purpose. And the student will gain his mastery, as in all branches of art, through constant and manifold practice, not by the mere achievement of correct writing.

The study of "form" in music is not, in any profound sense, a study of abstract patterns, but of living materials— of psychological entities which have their anatomy and physiology in as true a sense as any physical organism. The Fugue, the Sonata, the Variation forms arose because the ideas of composers inevitably took certain shapes, and not because of any abstract or conventional pattern which the composer concocted independently of his musical ideas. In other words, these forms, so far as they really exist as such, are general terms used conventionally to classify the inevitable results of certain types of development or of contrast; they are infinitely varied in musical content and can be truly studied only in relation to living musical matter. A Fugue or a Sonata is not an abstraction but a living organism, and

must be studied as such, in relation to the *musical content*
which it embodies and not to any abstract scheme. It will be
found that the Fugues of Bach, all quite different in form,
are dependent for their form on the nature of their themes,
as are the Sonatas, Quartets, and Symphonies of Beethoven.

The student of musical "form" must, then, learn above
all, to hear and to grasp the inner relationships and necessities which form the basis of a living musical organism or
train of thought; first of all the organization of the musical
idea itself, and then the chain of acoustic and psychological
necessities to which it gives rise. Eventually, through this
means, he will learn to appreciate in a completely new way
the indissoluble connection between form and expression,
and gain a new insight into the so often misconceived problems of technique and style.

For technique, in any really profound sense, is the ability
to sustain and develop an organic musical train of thought.
Today it is too often confused with métier, which is the
acquired knack of manipulating formulas. The former is
the attribute of an active and creatively sensitized ear, the
latter that of mere practice and knowledge.

Style, on the other hand, is the individual inflection which
an individual, a nation, or an epoch, spontaneously and unconsciously gives to its music, and has, fundamentally, nothing to do with the conscious and carefully circumscribed
choice of materials. A real style will include and find a place
for the simplest means as well as the most complex. But
style in our day is too often confused with mannerism, a
product of ultra-refinement and fundamental lack of creative force; and there is the very wide-spread tendency, as
a result, to resort to "stylization," or conscious mannerism,
in the search for a personal, national, or, let us say, "modern" idiom. The demand is even sometimes made that musical education should concern itself with such things.

Such a conception is manifestly false, since it would substitute formulas and devices for the living substance of musi-cal thought. The only way American music—or any other music—can arise is through composers writing *music* first of all. That is to say, by writing what is natural and spon-taneous to them; or, in other words, seeking truth of ex-pression, which means keeping faith with themselves and with the materials through which they are working. Let us by all means seek truth (or, if you prefer, reality) in our own way; but let it be above all truth, and not some facile or vague abstraction or idiom, which we are seeking.

Composers cannot, certainly, be taught to keep faith with themselves. The impulse must be there, the courage, and even the intelligence. But they can be helped by teaching to understand their materials and to come to real terms with them. Musical education must make this, above all, its ob-jective, basing itself first on the acoustic fact, of exactly what we hear; secondly on the psychological facts, of how and why we hear as we do, and exactly what effect such and such a musical procedure produces.

In other words, the primary task of the teacher is to help his pupil to *hear* straight, and then, as a consequence, to *think* straight and *feel* straight, in musical terms.

The Composer in the University
[1949]

A contribution to a symposium on the graduate study of music, designed as the program of a joint session of the American Musicological Society and the Society for Music in the Liberal Arts College, held in New York City, December 1949.

O NE of the advantages—or disadvantages—of reading a paper on any subject lies in the fact that, when the paper is finally prepared, one is by no means as sure as one was when one began that one has settled the question at issue, even to one's own private satisfaction. One learns, first of all, the extent to which conclusions that one had considered to be based on matters of fundamental principle have been conditioned by the circumstances under which one has personally lived and worked; and secondly, one is faced with the necessity of accurately formulating, then questioning, one's basic assumptions, in the light of concrete facts. Very often one may find, when one is through, that, instead of a neatly arranged set of positive conclusions one has achieved, actually, a chain of conditional sentences which in the final analysis depend for their resolution on facts and conditions of a very concrete and specific nature.

I make these observations, not by way of apology for any or all of what I have to say, but in order to draw full attention to the presence of imponderables, both in American education as such, and American musical education in particular. In speaking of "imponderables" I am not of course referring to the conflicts of philosophy or objective which trouble us.

It is rather two other points which I have in mind. First of all, American education, in nearly all fields, is constantly

193

subject to a variety of pressures, which in their practical effects show great differences both in form and intensity, and therefore present educators with a wide diversity of problems. Secondly, music in the United States has in an incredibly short period of time experienced a growth, in quantity but also in quality, which can be considered as little less than phenomenal, and American musical education has in its turn found itself subject to the demands which that growth makes inevitable. It is hardly surprising, in these circumstances, that we should find ourselves confronted by a bewildering multiplicity of conditions, a bewildering multiplicity of tendencies, a bewildering diversity of material and of quality, leading to an inevitable difference of standards.

It is for this reason that my remarks on the present topic are of necessity abstract. I find myself obliged to speak mainly of principles; and in doing so I find myself acutely aware that principles often prove disconcertingly inefficient in application by reason of the specific means available for carrying them out.

Let me start my discussion by asking the obvious fundamental questions: Should composers go to universities for their training? Can they get adequate training at universities? On the other hand, should universities offer training to composers, and if so, for what, specifically, should they train them? The first of these questions, whether the university is a good place for the composer, depends for its answer upon the answer to the second—whether the university can offer him adequate preparation. The advantages of a university background for the composer, in the United States at least, seem to me clear. My feeling in this respect rests basically on the fact that, first of all, we do not in the United States possess a millennial cultural tradition within the framework of which the serious composer, whatever his personal inclinations and tendencies, can place himself. Rather the composer must find his way among a maze of conflicting tendencies, opinions, and influences of all kinds, many of which seem more apt to confuse than to help him. He must do this in a society whose public cultural enterprises are supported in very large measure, not by disinterested private patronage nor yet by a governmental department of cultural affairs, but by a competitive commercialism, which, while certainly beneficent in many of its effects, is necessarily compelled by its very nature to be mindful of its own aims, aims which are neither inherently nor inevitably those most calculated to foster healthy creative development. The young composer of serious aspirations needs, among other things, to find for himself and his gifts a means of orientation in the cultural world; he needs contact with the world of non-commercial, non-competitive experience, the world of feelings and ideas not subject to commercial pressure or control. He needs, in other words, to spend at least a few of his formative years in an environment which is not dominated by the pressures which are attendant on the problem, the idea, and the necessity of "getting ahead" in a competitive world, and by the standards which that competitive world imposes. He needs the experience and knowledge of other standards—not for the purpose of shielding him from contact with competitive standards, but of showing him that he is, as a serious artist, subject to far more difficult ones, and most grapple finally with problems for which there are no easy solutions. I believe that in our society, as it is developing in the greatest crisis civilization has yet encountered, the university is the only place where such standards are to a certain extent still upheld; and that its importance and its obligations are growing rather than decreasing as a result of that fact.

I have spoken of "serious" and not of "professional" composers: this distinction is, in my mind, closely connected with what I have said, as well as with the next point which I wish to make. For composing is not, in itself, a "profession" in the United States at the present time. It is not—that is, at all events not yet—an occupation that fulfills a function in our society that is recognized in any dependable fashion, which receives rewards that can in any sense be counted upon, however inadequate, or in which any recognizable standards exist, however low these may be. I am of course speaking of composing as such, without qualifications; for it is certainly true that there exist fields of composition—such as popular music or music for the movies— which may be considered as "professional" in all of these respects, where the function is obvious, the rewards tangible, and the demands definite. The demands, however, are in these cases primarily and even narrowly functional, and above all derive from the exigencies of a mass market; they have little to do with artistic expression except in a purely incidental sense and to a purely incidental degree.

I stress this point in order to make clear certain vital respects in which, for the present at least, the training of composers is not "professional" training in quite the same sense as is the training of instrumentalists; and thus the university can, if it so wishes, assume a very important role in creating and maintaining standards of a very different sort. It can, in other words, set itself the task of providing composers with an adequate preparation for work in composition as such, and can make this preparation the basis of its curriculum of so-called "theory" courses.

But first let me devote a little time to my third question, which has to do with the interests of music departments in universities. Bluntly stated, it may be phrased thus: Does the University—as represented by its music department—really want to have composers around, and if so, why? It would be easy to give a facile answer, somewhat in these terms: "Yes, the university is certainly glad to have composers around, and even to encourage a certain amount of composition among the students. But its practice must be subordinate to the pursuit of scholarship, to the study of musical literature and history; it can be in fact a valuable adjunct to such study, which is the true purpose of the university music department. The creative aim must never be a primary one; and while naturally the development of a genuine composer is always to be welcomed, it is not the true business of the university and cannot be allowed in any respect to become a major aim of the department."

Such an answer, I believe, is quite inadequate from the point of view of both the composer and the university. It is inadequate first of all because composition in which the creative aim—the aim to produce music that has independent artistic value, and that engages the full energies of its composer—is supplanted by a lesser one, is not, properly speaking, composing at all. It is not composing because in a very real sense it never fully comes to grips with the real problems of composing—the problems, that is, of independent musical thought, and of the adequate embodiment of that thought. The student who tries to compose with any other end in view—I am speaking of aims, of course, and not of results—never learns what composing actually is, nor is he likely to acquire the tools with which actual composing is possible.

Once more, let me emphasize, I am speaking of aims, not of results, which as we all know are in no way to be guaranteed. Independent thought does not imply original or distinguished thought, in music or elsewhere; it does not imply power or charm or even wit. It does however imply the assumption of means that are adequate to the end, to any end toward which the imagination of the student, no matter how gifted, may lead. It implies, in terms of the university, instruction on the highest level available.

So, the question remains to be answered, why should a university have composers around? Can a case be made for the training of composers which is really satisfactory from the university's point of view? I believe it can, and would put the matter somewhat as follows: music, or what we may call musical *society*—by which I mean the structure of our musical life—does not rest, here in the United States, upon an established tradition, but is very much *in the making*, as is not the case anywhere else in the world. Musical scholarship—and I use the term to include the study of musical literature as well as the stricter musicological disciplines—must, if it is to be vital, be a part of that musical society. It cannot ignore any of the issues which confront the composer today without running the grave risk of isolating and essentially impoverishing itself. It must in other words find some relationship with the musical sensibilities, the musical impulse, of the time and place in which it exists, unless it is to become static in aim, dogmatic in spirit, and ultimately without vital content. I believe the aim of the university music department, in other words, must be that of fostering what I have called a musical *society*, in which creative activity, as the expression par excellence of the musical impulse of a given time and place, must play its part. On a more specifically scholarly level, also, I believe the composer has his contribution to make. For musical *theory* is, I believe, in a transitional stage: that of catching up with developments in music which in their origins date back for more than a century (who can say precisely how old any artistic development actually is?) and of systematizing the musical syntax, or musical syntaxes, of the present day. The composer, if he is mature and articulate, can make valuable and even decisive contributions in this respect, by his first-hand experience—by the type of understanding that can come only from first-hand experience—of creative musical thought. He knows from constant practice what the experience of composing is like; he knows as well as can be known what processes go into that experience, and, in fortunate cases, on the basis of that knowledge is in a position to make illuminating contributions to musical theory and even in some cases to music history.

I believe, therefore, that the teaching of composition, and on the most serious level, is one of the vital functions of the university music department. How shall this function, then, be incorporated into the curriculum of the department, and what can be offered to the composer in the form of credits and degrees? In the first place, it seems to me that the study of composition as I have tried to describe it is definitely a graduate-level discipline and should be recognized as such. It presupposes a degree of preparation for which a full undergraduate course—that is to say, four years of seriously studied harmony and counterpoint, and the practical application of these disciplines to elementary studies in form—is not by any means too much. This in itself raises serious questions, for the discussion of which I have no time in the present paper. I wish only to reiterate what I have so often said in the past, that in the course of seventeen years of teaching composition, the chief problem I have encountered was inadequate training on the elementary level. At the beginning of this experience, such inadequacy was almost universal. I believe the situation is far better today; the quality of teaching has obviously improved, as has the quantity of study demanded. But the problem remains nevertheless as a very serious one, perhaps the most serious and the most difficult one to be solved by any university music department which has as one of its aims the training of composers. I would offer as comment only my firm belief that essentially harmony and counterpoint cannot mean one thing for the composer, and something else for others; but that if a student is to become a serious composer, a far greater technical mastery is required of him, and therefore a considerably greater amount of practical work, than is required of the average student of music. Moreover, if a student is to use his technical knowledge for serious analytical or theoretical work, he, too, requires more than can be expected of the average student—his needs are far closer to those of the composer, and his preparatory work will begin to deviate from that of the latter only at the point where actual studies in musical form begin.

In any case, the study and teaching of composition is essentially graduate work, and graduate work of the most advanced type. Its nature, however, makes exceptional cases inevitable—students of a generally undergraduate status who through private study have achieved adequate preparation and for whom special provision must be made if the student is not to be forced into a wasteful repetition of ground already covered.

What shall we say, then, about graduate degrees?

The answer to this is difficult mainly for reasons of a practical nature. I personally find myself in agreement with both of the principal universities—Princeton and California —with which I have been connected in favoring the degree of Master of Arts in Composition.[1] It seems to me wholly sound both to require of the student of composition a degree of knowledge of musical history and especially of musical literature, and at the same time to allow his achievement of a certain grade of technical mastery in composition to count in an essential way toward his Magisterium.

The question of the Doctorate, however, is more problematical; in certain respects it is difficult and even poignant. The difficulty rests not in the nature of the degree as such. It rests first of all in what I hope I am not too indiscreet in calling the widespread corruption of the doctoral concept, throughout many sections of the country. I need hardly enlarge on this rather unpleasant state of affairs; in fact, I find that I have not retained in my memory any accurate list of the weird Doctorates which have at various times come to my attention. A doctorate in Musical Composition seems by comparison with many of these an eminently sound concept.

At the same time we are confronted by the fact that for an overwhelming number of colleges, even some renowned ones, the doctorate is a *sine qua non* for admission to the faculty, or at least to its higher ranks. In the absence of a doctorate in composition as such, the young composer is often faced with a dilemma, of which neither the poignancy nor the serious consequences should be ignored. Either he is virtually to abandon his composition, at a formative and

[1] In addition to the Master's degree (at Princeton, a Master of Fine Arts), both universities now offer a Ph.D. to students of composition.

possibly crucial stage of his career—a stage at which he should be, and if he is genuinely gifted will be, intent on production above all; he is to devote himself to research; to matters, that is, which might possibly be of secondary interest to him if he had the opportunity to pursue them under more favorable circumstances, but whose relevance to his real work is at best secondary, and under the circumstances grotesquely out of proportion to the sacrifice which it demands. Or else he is to find himself seriously and possibly handicapped if he wishes to achieve any significant place in the academic world. The question has a real and vital bearing on those discussed earlier, and it is one which cannot fail to preoccupy anyone who has the interests of American composition at heart.

Nevertheless, I have come to feel that the arguments against the Doctorate in composition are unanswerable. I have reached this conclusion not in the interests of scholarship or research—for which I possess no qualifications—but of composition. To whom, and for what, should such degrees be awarded, and how could we establish standards which should be reliable? Surely not on a purely technical basis. To do so would be, it seems to me, to misconceive the whole nature of art. Yet any other basis of judgment would, and should, involve matters of personal predilection which would rob the degree of precisely whatever serious content one wished to give it—it would become not a degree, but a *prize* of incalculable value and of fateful effect. It would in all probability have the effect of generally lowering the standards which university music departments wish to maintain, by tending, or at least attempting, to standardize—which means, actually, to injure and perhaps destroy—what is by its very nature impervious to standardization.

We should, then, I believe, adopt a strong stand, not only against the Doctorate in composition but, what is even far more important, against the requirement of the Doctorate as a condition of the admission of composers to academic status. I can see no other satisfactory solution of a genuinely vexing and difficult problem.

This brings me to my final question—that of the university teacher of composition. I need hardly say that I believe he should be a composer, and by that I mean not simply one who composes, but one for whom composing constitutes his main interest and his main source of distinction. I should like in fact to recall the term "scholar-teacher," which appeared in one of the earlier statements of the Society for Music in the Liberal Arts College, and adopt the term "composer-teacher." What will be the nature of his influence in the Music Department, and what can we expect of him?

First of all we must be prepared for the fact that the teaching of composition is essentially personal in character. The composer-teacher will exert a strong personal influence upon his students, who cannot fail to be to a degree impressed with his point of view. The greater his gifts, and the stronger his personality, the truer this will be. The same is of course true, or should be, to a degree, of the scholar-teacher; I need hardly tell a group of distinguished scholars that scholarship, too, is personal. But personality is, we may perhaps put it, the vehicle of scholarship—it determines its liveliness and its gait but not its content or its aim; whereas it is in a very real sense the essence of artistic creation. We would do well to recognize this fact, and take its inevitability and its implications into account.

And yet if the composer is really a teacher he will learn above all to respect the personalities of his pupils, and will seek to develop those personalities and not to mold them. He will take pride not in their likeness to himself but rather in the diversities which result from their maturing development. He will find it not entirely unwelcome when they differ with him; he will of course defend his own point of view with the utmost energy but if, after having done so, the students remain unconvinced he will accept the fact gracefully. He must, naturally, be sufficiently sure of himself as a composer to be able to do this, and even be strong enough to let himself be influenced by his students on occasion.

The composer-teacher and the scholar-teacher will find, almost certainly, that their points of view diverge at times. If they allow themselves to become too involved in such divergences, a tug-of-war will result. Up to a point this may be stimulating for the students, but if it becomes serious it is almost certain to be destructive. The two—scholar and composer—must therefore remain in genuine communication, and recognize clearly the nature of the work done by each, and the different roles which they each play in the total picture. If they can do this they may easily find that they cannot only live in peace but actually enjoy each other's society. Seriously, I would go further than this. I have already hinted at not only the value of the university to the composer, but at specific contributions the latter can make in furtherance of the work of the scholar. I therefore believe that, provided they listen seriously to each other, and then examine their respective points of view with an open mind, contacts between them can be only of benefit to the development of both.

What Can Be Taught?
[1967]

THE question of the education—or, as I would prefer to put it, training—of the composer is, in my opinion, to-day much cluttered up with a quantity of extraneous matter which tends to confuse or even to obliterate the central issue. A good part of this confusion may certainly be traced back to a traditional system of teaching which had not only become frozen in its essentially cut-and-dried treatment of materials, but had also and with still graver consequences, taken its basic assumptions so much for granted that they had finally become desiccated to the point of sheer abstraction, devoid of relevant content.

Consider, for example, the word "form" as it is often still used, both in theory and in practice. Fortunately the practice has remained in many cases superior to the theory. Nevertheless, "form" is still much too often conceived in terms of "forms," either frozen from the distant or immediate past, or postulated for the (strictly speaking, non-existent!) "present," or "future," as a *Ding an sich*; all too seldom is it conceived as an outgrowth of musical ideas themselves, in their immediate and dynamic aspects, and the growth of these ideas in the mind and will of the composer.

Many times, for instance, I have been asked by young and inexperienced composers whether a given formal scheme, thought out and planned in advance of its eventual musical content, will "work." But such a question can only be answered by the composer himself, in terms of specific musical material and the way he treats it—it makes no sense whatever in any other terms at all. If it is really a musical

"To the Editor," in *Perspectives of New Music*, vol. 5, no. 2, Spring-Summer, 1967, pp. 81-97.

idea—one which has its origin in tones and rhythms concretely imagined and "heard"—it may have some value to him, and in that case it is up to him to realize it in such a manner that it does "work"; otherwise the scheme itself is, to say the least, premature.

This brings us already to what I have elsewhere referred to as the central issue,[1] which is that of craftsmanship. This is a better word than "technique," in my opinion; the latter, through many associations, is too easily confused with the idea of gadgetry, which is precisely the opposite of genuine craftsmanship. In any case, craftsmanship is nothing more nor less than the ability to cope, successfully and with assurance, with any problem with which a composer may be confronted. This would seem so obvious as to be hardly worth saying. While no analogy is perfect, the analogy with the knowledge of a language in which one aspires to be a writer is as nearly apt as an analogy can well be. One cannot expect to achieve "style" on any level whatever unless one can speak as well as write easily and fluently, and above all with precision at all levels; and no amount of rationalization can possibly gainsay this necessity. A composer, like a writer or anyone who makes, constructs, discovers or creates in any field whatever, needs to acquire precision, fluency, and resourcefulness in the highest degree. Only on that basis can he move with assurance in any direction he may choose, and recognize—through experience—the technical problems he will have to face, and discover the means of solving them.

All this is, or should be, obvious enough; but we are today surrounded by such a tropical luxuriance of verbiage that it is sometimes difficult to see through the foliage to the bare facts of life. The point is that an art is, first of all, and to an overwhelming degree, a craft; and that a craft is mastered through prolonged practice—not through theory or "learning" in the usual sense.

[1] See, for example, "Conversation with Roger Sessions," in *Perspectives on American Composers*, B. Boretz and E. T. Cone, eds., New York, 1971, pp. 98-99.

So, what can be taught, and to what elements do the above remarks apply?

Obviously, the aptitudes on which ultimate quality depends—imagination, invention, vitality, daring, temperament —cannot be taught; and while a teacher can and should certainly communicate attitudes toward music, and no doubt will communicate enthusiasms which he himself feels, his primary function is not that of teaching his pupil to write "great" or even "good" or "interesting" music. This of course cannot be taught, and such an aim could easily, and often does, interfere with the primary task of the teacher, which is purely and simply that of teaching him to write: that is, to use the materials at hand with precision and assurance. He is teaching *composition*, not literature or aesthetics or, in any real sense, theory; and in my opinion he can teach effectively only to the extent that he keeps the goal of craftsmanship, and the practice by which this is developed, constantly before his own mind and that of his pupils. This has to be emphasized for a number of reasons, of which one important one is an all too prevalent tendency of today to crowd a number of disparate objects into one pedagogical package. If it is kept in mind that the single goal of instruction is the pupil's resourcefulness and independence (which can only be achieved through mastery) in the actual *handling of materials*, not that of learning rules or theories or imitating "styles," one need not concern oneself unduly about methods. The teacher's function is above all that of keeping before his pupil's mind the real demands of his craft, pointing out to him, as far as possible, the most efficient means by which he may learn to meet these demands; and then, following with helpfully critical attention his actual progress in meeting them. When, and to the extent that, the pupil begins to possess real security with his medium and the assurance that this brings, his teacher will become less and less a "teacher" in the full sense of the word, and more and more a (let us hope) understanding and sympathetic adviser.

Education and Training

To pass on to more specific matters: an aspiring composer must understand, from the beginning and always thereafter, that nothing he does or "learns" can be of any real value except insofar as he has formed the habit of complete accuracy of both outer and inner hearing. This applies, of course, not only to tones, but to note values, rests, articulation, rhythmic pattern, tone color, dynamic nuance—everything, in fact, that reaches the ear of the listener, and in terms of actual media, not of abstract ones. One of the most persistent problems, and certainly the most crucial one, that one encounters in teaching composition is sloppiness and lack of precision in this respect—a lack of what I have sometimes called "musical realism." No doubt this situation is today complicated by elements peculiar to the present period; but the problem itself is not at all a complicated one, and one would not even think of mentioning it if one were not quite frequently confronted with instances—sometimes neatly rationalized, but nevertheless patent—in which the composer's intentions, as indicated on paper, do not correspond to what one actually hears, or to anything that even an ideal performance could "bring out."

In regard to this point, careful meticulous training, beginning as early as possible, can certainly be helpful. But vital above all, in this as in many other areas, are the habits which the student must himself form. He must learn, that is, to reach the point where he will imagine, or in other words, "inwardly hear," musical sounds, rhythms, and the rest, with the utmost immediacy, precision, and vividness; where he will envisage musical symbols and musical concepts in these terms just as automatically as he translates a written word into the sound of that word as pronounced. Only insofar as he does this, do the symbols have any meaning.

To be sure, what we call the "musical ear" embraces a number of related but clearly distinguishable abilities, which may be unequally present in the same individual. A "good ear," in terms of musicianship, is not simply the ability to identify sounds, rhythms, and musical patterns accurately. It is not simply the ability to read music and inwardly hear it. It includes also the ability to coordinate sounds and patterns of sound, even on a very far-flung scale; and, of course, for the composer, to conceive and construct them, with precision and clarity. This "inner ear" is of course the composer's principal domain, and eventually it can become almost or even in a sense wholly independent of the outer ear, as the obvious example of the late Beethoven demonstrates. A composer who is also a performer should understand very well what this implies. He knows that, as well as learning and knowing his own and other music from the inside, he has to study it as a performer, which means, in terms of precise hearing from the *outside*, as it were, as well. This means, in simpler terms, not only knowing exactly what he wants, but how to achieve it in terms of performance, which—and this is my real point—is not quite the same thing. The composer needs some experience in dealing with the actual process of projecting music, as well as hearing it inwardly. Certainly, for composers, the inner ear is, and must be, paramount; and the stories of composers—even very eminent, even great ones—who in conducting their own works fail to notice that the clarinet is playing in B♭ rather than the prescribed A, or that the cello in a given passage is playing in the bass instead of the tenor clef—such anecdotes are quite believable if not necessarily always true. They mean exactly nothing in terms of the aural capacities of the composers in question; they indicate only that at the precise moment involved the composer's attention is focused inwardly rather than outwardly, most likely perhaps on some other moment or phase of the performance itself. In a similar sense composers frequently develop the ability to remain quite oblivious of the sounds around them (even at less rewarding moments in the concert hall or the opera house!) and pursue their own musical trains of thought, inwardly listening to tones, rhythms, phrases, which have no conceivable connection with the live sounds being emitted all around them. There is nothing very mysterious about this, after all; most people are able to carry on a connected and even very serious conversation in a noisy restaurant or waiting-room provided their attention is not compellingly demanded elsewhere. In any case, I find it important for the composer to have at least some experience as a performer. This is simply a part of his training in artistic realism, of which I have already spoken.

There is little that a teacher can do in regard to the training of a composer's ear, beyond making clear the demands involved and stressing the fact that the necessary faculties are to be acquired only by practice and experience. No doubt certain "innate" qualities are in some degree necessary, or at least helpful. But the possession of these "innate" qualities does not in any sense presuppose or guarantee musical ability—nor can either the former or the latter be measured in terms of the other. All of the faculties I have described must be acquired by the composer, for they are the elementary "tools of his trade." They are still only "tools"; we must really grow out of the superstition that "genius" or "talent" can be determined or measured in terms of anything short of real achievement. But the composer cannot get along without the possession of these abilities, in the highest possible degree; and he needs to cultivate them to the point where they become, as it were, second nature.

The earliest stage in the composer's specific training must obviously consist in a thorough mastery of the elementary materials of which music is made, and a resulting awareness of the effects which can be produced by those materials. By "thorough mastery" is meant the ability to use them not only with precision but with ease and assurance; to be able to do with them whatever one chooses, and not to be limited in one's choice either by lack of fluency, or by imperfect awareness of every element involved, or by imprecision at any level whatever. Obviously I am talking about counterpoint and harmony, or in other words elementary practice in the "horizontal" and "vertical" dimensions, respectively.

Let us not labor here the terms "vertical," "horizontal," or even "elementary"—they are quite sufficient for our present purposes. One begins with harmony and counterpoint as distinct disciplines because they represent—on the elementary level—distinguishable aspects of musical movement, and present, on the same level, distinguishable problems. They are more easily grasped at this stage if the problems proper to the one are for the time being eliminated as far as possible from the study of the other. These are exercises in ultimate precision. Not only is the habit of precision most easily formed in the early stages of any craft, but it is most easily and efficiently attained if one has only one problem to worry about at a time.

One might strongly emphasize, however, that the disciplines of counterpoint and harmony, for the composer or for any other practical musician, are not a matter of "learning the rules" or of studying "styles." It is a question of mastering a craft in the only way that a craft can be mastered—that is to say, through *practice*. Obviously, and not only for our time but for centuries past, the "rules" have been neither binding nor, as such, relevant, outside the elementary discipline itself. But within the discipline, they serve a twofold pedagogical purpose. First of all, they provide logical limitations to the materials involved, reducing to a minimum the exigencies of context, thereby confronting the student only with problems which he can handle easily and on a quasi-objective basis. Secondly, they accustom him to awareness of some of the most common pitfalls; at the same time they furnish him with ready means of avoiding these, and eventually, therefore, the means of recognizing the contexts in which they are no longer to be considered as pitfalls, and therefore not to be avoided. In other words, counterpoint and harmony are practical disciplines and can be mastered only through practice, both intense and prolonged. In no real sense can or should they be considered as "theory," to be "learned" in the usual sense.

Undoubtedly, however, they are today almost always

begun at a much later age than they should be. The fact that there is no ready means in sight by which this situation can be improved is no excuse for ignoring the problem. By the time a young musician's tastes and predilections begin to take on a definite shape, he should have all of this behind him. As things are today, a very large number of our young composers begin this elementary training at a time when they have already gained—as indeed they should have done by the age of eighteen or twenty—a certain degree of sophistication regarding music and the musical world; but in all except the rarest cases they have acquired little or no awareness of what the composer's craft entails. In some cases they may have attempted composition of a more or less ambitious kind. They may quite possibly have worked seriously at an instrument and learned that real mastery demands years of practice and even drudgery for several hours a day, in order to gain an indispensable degree of precision and coordination. If a serious student of composition has gone through this experience, he should be able to grasp more readily the need for a comparable effort on the part of one who aspires to compose. After all, at least as much is demanded of one who makes music as of one who performs it.

Obviously, this parallel is not quite exact; it is quite true that the element of physical coordination is not in a direct sense a part of a composer's problem. But the latter on the other hand has plenty of other things to think about, if only because it is for him to discover and imagine, in the clearest terms, what the performer is later to reproduce. In terms of his own elementary training—his harmony and counterpoint—he is obliged to acquire the same degree of precision and ease that his performing colleague acquires with his scales, arpeggios, and other basic exercises.

The logical and the most effective time for all of these disciplines is as soon as possible after a young person begins to show any inclination toward music—which should mean, in childhood. A child has the time to take them slowly and absorb them gradually and will be induced by his budding interest in music to value the sense of achievement which they can give him. It is, on the other hand, very difficult for the eighteen- or twenty-year-old to understand why all this is necessary—and one can certainly sympathize, even while thoroughly disagreeing. If he has not already acquired the assurance and precision that only a real mastery of the elements can give him, he is in the position of one whose immediate aspirations have outstripped his equipment; and he may easily tend to shy away from, and to undervalue, all of those problems and situations—unfortunately often the most fundamental and ultimately the most difficult—which he is not equipped to cope with effectively. He is quite likely to resist both inwardly and outwardly the drudgery, the boredom, and above all the time, involved in acquiring what he needs. If it is brought to his attention that virtually every composer of significance has gone through this training as a matter of course, he is still quite likely to remain unimpressed. He may easily waste a good deal of energy looking for short cuts which, since this is a matter of craft and not of theory or information or "style," simply do not exist. His understanding is not encouraged or facilitated by the persistence, in our country, of certain vestiges of a cultural colonialism, which lags in recognizing the composer fully as a man of potential achievement "here and now," romanticizes the nature of his gifts and therefore undervalues both his real gifts and his craft, and consequently ignores what is required of him. I am not implying that these attitudes themselves persist, but rather various preconceptions derived from them. The fact that "success" of a temporary nature is sometimes achieved by works in which the craft is imprecise and uncertain, compounds the situation. The problem, however, remains. If the composer is to avoid becoming—and remaining, at least to some degree—the slave of his own technical limitations, he has to learn to overcome them; and he can do this most efficiently by beginning at the beginning.

Education and Training

I suppose it is fairly clear from the above that when I speak of "counterpoint and harmony," I am referring primarily to "strict counterpoint" and what is known as "functional" or "traditional" harmony; for it is only the materials generally understood under these terms which fully satisfy the requirements that I have postulated. The usual arguments against such study may be summarized in a general way under two headings: they are considered either a waste of time or part of a hidden conspiracy to tie the student to the past. To the former of these objections I have already given my basic answers; the latter deserves some further comment. Obviously one of the main purposes of an artist's education, and even in a broad sense the whole purpose, is to liberate the student—assuming that he wishes to be liberated—from "the past": not only his own past, but that of the craft of the composer in general. The purpose is, once more, to help him to be the master of his musical materials, not the victim of his own helplessness regarding them.

Like many of the words in common and unfortunately careless usage today, the word "tradition" has come to embrace offshoots of very varied and often contradictory character, and a great deal of loose thinking results. There is no inherent reason why "tradition" should be an unmitigatedly dirty word; one can counter Mahler's dictum *Tradition ist Schlamperei*, which was eminently true in its original context, with Picasso's "Well, you see, everyone has to have a father." One might even in this connection recall that the Oedipus legend is just as "traditional" as that of Orestes! In any case, the "present" is ineluctably the consequence of the "past"; and if a craft is to be learned at all, the beginnings will inevitably be found somewhere in the "past," whether that of yesterday, last month, or at any point previously. That is why I do not find the cited objection a serious one, even if it had not always proven wrong in fact. The crux of the matter is a structural, not a "historical" matter. It is quite true, for instance, that "strict counterpoint" corresponds, though very roughly indeed, with "sixteenth-century" or "Palestrina" counterpoint, and was invented, presumably by Fux in the early eighteenth century, as an introduction to the "learned" style. But its utility to the young composer of today, and to those of many years past, has nothing to do with any "style," learned or otherwise. It is simply a convenient and practical way of introducing a young musician to a set of problems with which he will be confronted, in increasingly refined form, throughout his career as a composer; and of presenting these problems to him at the outset in their simplest form. If it is preferable to so-called "Bach counterpoint," it is simply because the latter is founded on thorough-bass, on harmonic structure, which itself presupposed, in Bach's day, a mastery of voice-leading, as it were, in the abstract. The same is true, in even greater measure, of polyphony as actually practiced by any composer since Bach's time.

It is for this reason that some intensive work in what is generally known as "strict composition" and "fugue" is important to the developing composer. Of course, it is not really "composition" at all; and whatever we choose to call it, it should not be considered as essentially creative activity. The point is that what the student is doing in harmonizing chorales, writing "minuets," "rondos," "sonata movements," "fugues," "inventions," etc., is simply combining the results he has gained by systematic practice with elementary materials, into some kind of organic shape; he is not working in the "style" of Bach or of any composer, but simply, as it were, putting sentences, paragraphs, and topics together coherently and bringing his acquired craft into working order. "Composition," then, if you like, and even "style" of a kind; but of a category quite different from the styles of composers who were working with the total range of materials available to them, and pushing those materials, without inhibition, as far as the impulse toward real musical expression demanded. Style, in the real sense of the word, is after all predicated on this state of affairs; the composer is free to do anything he wishes and to follow his musical impulses wherever they may lead him. The student of "strict composition" is obviously not doing anything of the sort; he is learning to handle materials constructively, and with real fluency. No doubt, a genuinely gifted composer will reveal his gifts in everything he does; experience has abundantly shown me that, even in strict counterpoint exercises, a real composer will somehow produce results of a kind that those written by an ungifted one, however correct, do not. This will be still clearer in the case of exercises in "strict composition." Some compositional element will inevitably be present, certainly, if it is present in the musical nature of the pupil; and a sense of "style," or consistency, already present in the mere choice of materials, is certainly to be cultivated. The work done should be, in other words, presentable in every respect, here as everywhere else. But at this stage the student is first of all solving specific problems; and his energy must, once more, be directed primarily toward gaining fluency and assurance in his craft.

One must, of course, emphasize strongly that, here as everywhere else, it is not a question of what a student has "taken" or "studied," but of what he can do. In this connection one must obviously refer back to the individual teacher, who should be in a position not only to judge the student's prowess, but to adapt his teaching to the latter's real need. I do not at all rule out the possibility of a method of teaching through which a student could learn his craft by means other than those I have indicated. I would still insist, however, that a composer in the fullest sense of the word is one who has the whole range of known musical possibilities within his comparatively easy grasp, and who therefore is free to choose to do whatever he likes, with full assurance. If the student is lucky enough or perspicacious enough to pursue his studies in close contact with a teacher who is both a real master of his craft and genuinely interested in his student's work, the precise means or methods of teaching are of little or no importance. While the principle of apprenticeship, on which the training of young artists and musicians was based for many centuries in the past, has virtually ceased to exist in present-day or even relatively modern times, I think it still represents the most valuable and efficacious kind of training a young composer can have; and I find certain educational tendencies of today a matter of concern in this respect. I shall return to this subject presently, as it seems to me of increasing importance as a student's development progresses.

Subject to the qualifications at which I have just hinted, it seems clear to me, both logically and practically, that the study of counterpoint should precede that of harmony. While "harmony" for me not only means training in the use of "chords," but eventually includes everything which has to do with the relationships between tones, it must presuppose some ability to handle voices; furthermore, it seems to me that, unlike the discipline of strict counterpoint, it can and should be pursued up to the point where the materials involved begin to pose the questions with which our own century has been confronted—which means, up to the point where "harmonic" problems begin to merge with questions of style and composition. Harmony should, even from the beginning, be so taught as to embrace questions of form and movement, as well as to accustom the pupil to clear and precise application of his knowledge of voice-leading to situations more complex and qualified than those he has encountered in his strict contrapuntal studies. Eventually the point will come where the terms "harmony" and "counterpoint"—essentially abstractions, adopted consciously for legitimate pedagogical purposes, but nevertheless quite artificial—no longer serve any useful purpose. They must at this point give way to consideration of a total musical context, and to a large extent one created by the pupil himself. This brings us to a new set of problems, which I shall try to discuss in some kind of order.

It is at this point, for instance, that the question of "atonality" begins to be acute, and a precise critical examination of its implication is in my opinion quite indispensable. The disadvantages of both the term and the concept have been repeatedly pointed out; and it is curious that, in a period like ours which prides itself on its scientific approach to intellectual problems, a term which has the built-in imprecision of any purely negative concept—which originated as a journalistic term of reproach, and was taken over as a slogan—should have persisted as a concept even though the term itself has become obsolete. As I and others have pointed out elsewhere, the fuzziness of the concept is matched by a lack of clear definition in the prevalent usage of the term "tonality."

To be sure, the controversy itself is by this time essentially obsolete. I do not remember whether the term "atonality" was current as long ago as 1911, but the idea most certainly was; and I would not even be discussing it here did I not feel that, for purely pedagogical reasons, it still must be clarified. The essential point is that "atonality" not only came *after* "tonality" but that it was the result of developments inherent in the very nature of tonality itself.

There is in fact a very fundamental point at issue here; and it is, again, not at all a matter of "history" in the usual sense of the word. "Tonality" is not a "closed" system; both its dawn and its twilight were long, drawn-out processes, in which exact lines of demarcation are necessarily arbitrary, and exist, if at all, only in the realm of theory. For theoretical purposes, however, it has often been regarded as a closed system; and in this issue lies both the original motivation of the term "atonality" and whatever rationale it can be logically claimed to possess.

Though this raises both intellectual questions and questions in the realm of criticism, which are far from being always clearly faced, it is not that which is relevant here. The line of development, as far as the musical vocabulary is concerned, is clear enough. The adoption of the tempered system, the proliferation of even sharper harmonic contrasts, the increasingly bold use of "harmonic alteration" and the gradually developing "independence" of the resultant combinations: not only did these and other pertinent developments take place under the sign of tonality, they were the result of impulses inherent in that principle itself. For the crucial aspect of tonality was not simply or perhaps even primarily the discovery and exploitation of functional relationships within the key, but the possibility of shifting these relationships from one locality to another, thus achieving a new dimension of contrast, and thereby a vastly larger area of musical operations than had hitherto been possible. It is in fact the reaching out of the musical ear for this constantly larger area, both in terms of extension and of expressive intensity, that has led to the "technical" developments in question. This is all abundantly documented—as is the massive raising of eyebrows in certain quarters, at each successive stage of the process.

Now, obviously I am not attempting to maintain that "tonality" as hitherto defined is, or should be, still with us. I am emphasizing the *continuum* of which the principle of tonality, as applied rather than as ever formulated, was a phase, as was also the development beyond tonality. The *continuum* is nothing more or less than that of ever-accruing auditory experience; and the problems at issue are to be resolved by the development of the musical ear alone, not by hypothesis and theory, and least of all through sloganizing. In other words, I feel that at this late date nothing but wasted time results from laboring these principles as such. I find it futile and misleading to argue, for instance, whether one is "hearing" "tonally" or "atonally"—still less, whether one *should* "hear" in this or that manner, or to concern oneself with what are sometimes called "tonal references" in manifestly non-tonal contexts, or to identify other than strictly harmonic matters with "tonality" or its absence. Any conceivable succession or combination of tones can be heard as "tonal," in virtually any sense one wishes, if one provides it with the proper context, either in one's imagination or otherwise. The only relevant factor is the actual context of the passage in question and the specific use the composer has made of it. It is of course the task of the composer to make his contexts quite clear, and that of the listener to become aware of the inner logic of the music—in its own terms, and not with reference to something outside the music, unless such reference may clearly impose itself as the result of an evident intent on the composer's part.

To sum up: tonality and "atonality" are not opposing principles in any sense whatever, but successive phases in the evolution of the Western musical ear, the latter being the clear product of the development of the former. But while tonality constituted, over the course of nearly three centuries, the principal basis of musical design, no such claim can be made for "atonality" for the simple reason that, as a purely negative concept, it possesses in itself no constructive implications.

It is quite obvious, however, that strong constructive elements are manifest in the best of the music which we call "atonal." But their clear and adequate theoretical formulation lies still in the future. I am of course not forgetting the possibilities inherent in the serial principle, as well as other developments; but these developments and possibilities, for all the verbiage that is constantly expended on them, remain still in the empirical phase of development. The solution of the problem is, in other words, to be achieved by the composer only on the basis of a sure instinct and a solid background of musical experience—of a total awareness and mastery of the means at his disposal. Of course this has always been true; the composers of the past were not thinking in terms of theoretical dogma any more than are those of today. What they and their contemporaries did possess were general terms in which everything that went on in their music could be more or less adequately discussed. Even this was much more true of certain periods than of others. I doubt whether it was really true, for instance, in the time of Monteverdi. Today we can—and do—discuss procedures, but we have not yet found the terms in which we can adequately generalize about musical effect.

Education and Training

I have dwelt on this subject at considerable length in order to illustrate some of the pitfalls inherent in the present vogue of "analysis" as an independent and self-contained musical discipline. Having as a teacher insisted and even fought for the importance of close and accurate observation of what actually transpires in the course of a piece of music, I cannot, I suppose, be suspected of opposition to analysis as such. In practice today, "analysis" often seems to go far beyond this, not only into the realm of purely speculative dogmatism and even snobbery, but into that of a kind of virtuosistic intoxication with detection for its own sake, often regardless of the relevance or even the actual existence, from a musical standpoint, of what is "discovered," or, in current analytical jargon, "heard" by the analyst. A little experience is quite sufficient to show that one can "hear" anything that one sets out to hear.

Naturally I am calling attention to a problematical aspect of "analysis" as it is sometimes practiced, and not aiming barbed shafts at musical analysts either in general or, so far as I am aware, in particular. I am, however, expressing a strong and fundamental conviction regarding the training of the young composer. He can derive vast benefit from learning to observe how music is put together by a master craftsman, provided he be encouraged to make his own observations—certainly, with some guidance from an experienced teacher: to observe, for instance, contrasts of greater and lesser importance; the articulative elements which throw these into relief; the rhythmic structure in terms of motifs, phrases, and larger sections, or whatever elements go into the making of the music in question—anything, in fact, that the composer has clearly indicated and which seems clearly relevant to the structural flow of the music. Above all, he must learn—once again—to be aware of these things *auditorily*, and to discriminate by auditory absorption, so to speak, between what is most essential and what is less so, or nonessential, irrelevant, or merely problematical. What he has to gain by this, of course, is not only intimate knowledge of the works in question, and a keener sense of what it is really to know music, but a sharpened sense of musical consequence, movement, and structure.

"Analysis" which goes beyond this may certainly be of interest to him, as to anyone who cares for music. However, it is of the utmost importance that he never become confused in regard to the basic difference between the creative and the analytical process. This unfortunately has to be emphasized today because of a very prevalent tendency to seek a kind of pseudo-security in a process of constant "rational" justification and to dismiss, under the term "intuitive," whatever is not immediately explicable in such terms. Thus I have known instances in which young composers have wasted considerable energy in trying to produce an *Urlinie* according to prescriptions derived from the theories of Schenker; or who have been seriously disturbed to find themselves writing music which seemed right to them according to their own musical instincts, but which they could not check according to what they had been led to regard as criteria. It cannot be too much emphasized that the only genuine security an artist can find is in the knowledge of what he wants, in terms of his art, and in getting it, by whatever means he has at his disposal. It follows that first of all he has to learn to trust his own ear, his musical instinct, and his musical imagination, as developed by experience, as the court of final appeal. By no other means can he discover his own criteria, or can he develop the boldness which is a *sine qua non* of significant artistic achievement. The basically analytical, rationalized approach to composition is the essence of academicism, whether of the "left" or of the "right," and the result can scarcely be other than academic, timid, and sterile.

Of course I am talking here about basic attitudes, not passing a priori judgments; and basic attitudes in art are often very elusive, sometimes even to those who hold them. My point is, I hope, clear; it is simply that a student of composition should not be allowed to forget that his primary task is to discover his own musical identity, to discover the music which he, in the most direct and immediate sense, wants to bring into existence. He should therefore not be encouraged to make demands on himself which are essentially dogmatic, premature, or otherwise irrelevant to that process.

I cannot in fact refrain from reiterating here that the ultimate goal of a composer's musical training is to liberate his talents and his creative personality, not to indoctrinate him to or from any specific point of view. His craft must be such as to allow him the freedom to pursue with assurance any direction he himself may choose to take; and his teacher should be neither surprised nor disturbed if, in the process of self-discovery, the pupil seems sometimes or even frequently to shift his direction. This does not happen in all cases, of course; but it can be a normal sequence in any process of growth. The teacher's role then becomes one which challenges his powers of tact, discretion, and sympathetic imagination to the utmost; for there is little he can do other than to make available to his younger or less experienced colleague whatever he himself has learned, keeping the exigencies of fully adequate craftsmanship before the latter, while exerting no pressure whatever on him to go the same way, or to prevent him, as the case may be, from going in a directly opposite one. The crux of the matter is that music, first and above all, must have a *face*, and unless it is going to remain at best in the category of the merely "typical" or "generic" its face can be none other than that of its creator. I am deliberately avoiding the word "style" which is very frequently misused to apply precisely to the "typical," and often in the most superficial sense— *Die Zauberflöte*, we are sometimes told, is a "hopeless" mixture of "styles"! Needless to point out, it possesses at every moment the unmistakable features of Mozart. While I would willingly concede that to cite the mature masterpiece of a Mozart in the midst of a discussion of the composer's process of self-discovery has its problematical aspects, I can think of no clearer illustration of my meaning at this point. What I have called the "face" which music should possess is the result of imagination, craft, experience, and above all involvement (obviously in Mozart's case, all in a supreme degree). It is not at all a matter of "techniques" or "genres," or the like. Neither is it a matter of "avoiding influences," which cannot in any case be avoided, or even of striving for "novelty" or "originality" as such. These, if they become major preoccupations, are essentially desperate measures which at the very best can never work except in the most temporary sense. What constitutes a "face," "personality," "character," or originality in any sense whatever derives from positive elements, qualities that are present in the music, and not from negative ones. It is a question of fully digesting everything—including "influences," which are always present—and making it wholly one's own.

The application of all of this to the teacher is obvious. In my opinion, no one can possibly be a good teacher of composition if he attempts or wishes to mold the style of his pupils in any way further than that of helping them to envisage and become aware of the problems in their own work, and if necessary suggesting lines along which the solutions might possibly be found. In such cases it is indispensable that the ultimate solution be at least as satisfactory to the pupil as to the teacher. Otherwise, the problem has not been really solved, nor has the pupil really learned anything.

At the same time, I still believe that the best training a composer can have, certainly at the "advanced" but quite possibly at every level, will be that derived from close association with a single teacher. This mode of study is not particularly in vogue today, for a number of reasons too involved to discuss here. But a young composer who is in the early stages of his development is almost certain to derive more benefit from association with an older colleague who takes a real interest in him, and with whom he can talk freely and informally about his own problems, about music and musical questions in general, and about many other matters not so obviously connected with music, than from almost any other single source. Experience of this sort is likely to teach him far more about the actual process of composing than anything he can learn in a classroom; for obviously this kind of contact between teacher and pupil is so much more immediate and so much less constrained by the inevitable limitations of classroom work. This is no doubt also true of other subjects than music; but once again the analogy of instrumental or vocal study occurs to one. The more individual and fruitful dialogue, and even to some extent collaboration, that a young artist can have with an experienced older musician, the better. I believe also that in general it is better that the greater and more important part of a young musician's study should be done with one rather than with several teachers. For one thing, less time will be wasted in "adjustment"; for another, I believe more is learned, in the early stages of a composer's development, by reacting strongly and profoundly to one personality— whether *for* or *against*, and generally a mixture of both— than by the ultimately much less challenging process of dealing with advice—often conflicting—from various sources, and most likely coping in depth with none of them. However, this last observation, like most generalities, is subject to obvious qualification, and at any point in a discussion of this kind it is plausible to stop and demand whether a real musical gift will not instinctively seek and find the soil that offers it the most nourishment. I am sure that many a musician who has acquired a reputation as a teacher finds himself frequently asking himself what his teaching really consists in, and questioning whether it has not been simply his good fortune to have had gifted and stimulating young musicians around him.

It may have been noticed that I have said nothing regarding systematic instruction in the serial technique or in other methods or techniques in present vogue. My omission has been intentional; I don't feel that this is a part of a composition teacher's business. In this I am in full agreement with the point of view of Arnold Schoenberg, who always insisted that such methods are for the composer, young or old, to discover for himself. Since the time during which Schoenberg was teaching, years have passed, and many arguments have been heard, both pro and con. The key word on the subject seems to me to have been said by Schoenberg himself. On being told by Darius Milhaud, just after the Second World War, that the dodecaphonic technique was much in vogue among the younger French composers, he replied with the question "Do they succeed in writing some *music* with it?" In other words, I believe that, as a matter of course, a teacher should encourage his students to familiarize themselves with the works of composers who have used the dodecaphonic method, as with all music of the last half-century, and adopt it themselves as they see fit. But they will find their own ways best if they do this as the result of their own inclinations toward music and the urge—call it curiosity, or involvement, or what you like—to gain from music whatever experiences it has to offer. Naturally the teacher should be ready to help them in any direction they desire; but his overriding preoccupation should be with musically convincing *results*, not with methods. Perhaps the essence of the matter is that by the time the young composer has arrived at the point where he can think of using the materials and methods of today, he has gotten well beyond the stage of exercises in "strict composition," and must be encouraged to make his own explorations and his own decisions.

I have also said nothing thus far about the necessity for a knowledge of "musical literature." Certainly such knowledge is an essential part of the equipment of every composer, young or old, and, in fact, of every full-fledged musician. But I might just as well add that every musician —and composers above all—of real distinction whom I have ever known has been a man or woman of outstanding general culture. Such knowledge is not the result of training, but of profound inclination. As someone once remarked, "one does not *memorize* a work like the Eroica Symphony, one *knows* it." A knowledge of musical literature should be a matter of course, "not," as has also been said, "of courses." Knowledge in depth, moreover, is what really counts; one does not know a work simply by hearing it a few times, or even by having "analyzed" it; one must have taken it into one's inner life, experienced it, and reacted vitally to it, strongly and repeatedly, to the point where it has become, as it were, a part of oneself. If a would-be composer has not had this experience with quite a considerable amount of music, it is difficult to imagine that he will accomplish much. But this is something that no kind or degree of instruction can give him; it is an inherent habit which he must have acquired spontaneously and as a by-product of the kind of musical involvement he needs to have if he is eventually to create anything of significance. To be sure, this to some degree presupposes opportunities, economic and otherwise; but the strong inclination must be there.

What I have outlined indicates the requirements, as I see them, for a composer who has set no limits on what he wishes to achieve. Obviously, many composers have achieved considerable "success" and reputation on palpably less than what I have outlined as minimum requirements. In a very few cases I would certainly be among the first to acclaim these achievements as significant in the most real sense. I suppose the case of Moussorgsky is the most striking of these. The stories one sometimes hears about Schubert (and some of his well-intentioned friends!) and Wagner, for instance, are quite baseless; neither of them was at any moment helpless in any sense of the word. But the whole history of *Boris Godounov* and the various revisions it has undergone, as well as the specific type of weakness one frequently finds in Moussorgsky's other work, is as good an illustration as I could ask—above all because of his enormous gift—of what I have tried to convey here. Obviously there have been many musicians of far greater "competence" than Moussorgsky whose contribution to music can in no way be said to match his. But it is of no value whatever to point out, for instance, that Rimsky-Korsakov's version of *Boris* robs the work of much of its character and its musical force. This seems to me quite evident, and I cannot imagine disagreement from anyone who has witnessed the opera in a version closer to the original. But this would be true even if Rimsky's musical invention had been the equal of Moussorgsky's. Only Moussorgsky himself could have really "improved" his work. What is relevant here is that one finds Moussorgsky at certain points helpless; if he had not been, there would at no time have been any question of "revising" his work. It would have been completely realized, totally "itself," as are at least a number of his smaller works, and not to be tinkered with by any musician in his senses. The point is that Moussorgsky's craft *was* defective, and the only relevant, if unanswerable, question, is what he might have achieved if this had not been the case.

IV

The Limits of Theory

Heinrich Schenker's Contribution
[1935]

Heinrich Schenker, the renowned musical the-orist and pedagogue, died January 14, 1935.

THE recent death of Heinrich Schenker has brought re-newed attention to the name and achievement of one of the remarkable figures of the contemporary musical world. It furnishes the occasion for a consideration of his contributions to musical theory, both in their intrinsic aspect, and their significance as symptoms of the musical temper of the present time. For although Schenker remained bitterly hostile to all that is contemporary in music, his work and his ideas nevertheless embody very clearly certain aspects of contemporary musicality which here surely find one of their most striking expressions.

The very fact that this work takes the form of musical theory is in itself symptomatic, as Schenker would have been the first to admit. For at its cornerstone lies the thesis that, owing to the hopeless desuetude into which the art and technique of composition have fallen, nothing but a body of fresh and sound theory, based on the actual prac-tice of the masters, can save it or, indeed, since it is appar-ently beyond salvation, permit hopes of its renewal. It is this fresh and sound theory which Schenker has attempted to furnish, both as a writer and as a teacher; and however much one may dispute certain implications in his thesis as stated above, there is no question that to a very real extent he has succeeded in contributing to it, even if one must reject some of his doctrines, and precisely some of the most

From *Modern Music*, vol. 12, no. 4, p. 170-178. Reprinted by per-mission of the League of Composers—International Society for Con-temporary Music, U.S. Section, Inc.

important and striking among them, as forced, untenable, and essentially sterile in tendency.

It is of course impossible, in the space of a short article, adequately to treat such a vast and complex mass of theoretical material in the detail which it deserves and indeed demands. The following remarks are intended therefore only to give an indication of the general character of his work and to come to some conclusions regarding it.

At the basis of Schenker's teaching lies the most important possible goal—that of effecting some kind of *rapprochement* between musical theory and the actual musical thought of the composer. It should be hardly necessary to point out, at this late date, the vital necessity of some such *rapprochement*. The older theory of harmony, virtually a compilation and standardization of the purely practical teachings of earlier days, consisted little more than a systematic catalog of "chords"—and what was a chord but the simultaneous sounding of any two or more notes, regardless of their syntactical significance? That the harmony books catalogued only the simplest of such phenomena does not in the slightest alter the fact that fundamentally the conception went no farther. While distinctions were made between "harmonic" and "nonharmonic" tones, and the number of possible chords limited by professorial fiat, such distinctions and limitations were patently arbitrary and often contrary to actual usage, and in any case no substitute for the real task of discovering the true order beneath what was assumed to be merely conventional, and therefore sanctified by tradition. There even exist harmony books which dogmatically assert the inferiority of certain cadence formulas, on the ground that the masters used them *less frequently* than others of different structure!

For the "chord" as fundamental harmonic entity Schenker substitutes the *Stufe*, literally translated as "degree," but perhaps best rendered in English by the simple word "harmony." According to this conception a harmony becomes a far more real and sometimes a very complex affair, governed in its definition and its boundaries by what is actually heard in listening to a piece of music. It may be roughly defined as a complete unit, formed as often of many "chords" as of a single one, or frequently consisting not of chords at all but of single notes, or traits of melodic character. This is a far more significant discovery than it seems. Most theoreticians of the older school would presumably analyze the opening measures of *Die Walküre* as a tonic triad in D minor, regardless of the B♭ in the first measure and the fact that the harmony takes the form of a scale figure rather than a "chord." But Schenker's theory carries this same principle much farther and conceives harmonic events in the largest possible sense, grouping them into a hierarchical order of which musicians of instinct have always been aware but which had never before been adequately formulated. They also lay the basis for a more adequate conception of the really guiding principles of musical structure.

The concept of the *Stufe* led Schenker to two others of similar importance. The first of these he calls *Tonikalisierung* or "tonicization"; the second, *Auskomponierung*, which may be translated as "harmonic elaboration" or "development." *Tonikalisierung* defines the processes whereby a harmony is intensified and brought into relief through the introduction of features which give it the significance of a quasi-tonic. The process is quite familiar, but the conventional classification of such intensified harmonies together with true modulations is obviously false, and Schenker's new conception here again contributes immeasurably to the clarification of musical theory by establishing a distinction which corresponds more closely to the true relationship between form and harmony, as they are perceived in the course of listening to a musical work.

The boldest of Schenker's new harmonic conceptions, and one which takes him eventually beyond the limits of harmony as such, is that of *Auskomponierung*—a term which is used to designate the various means by which a harmony or even an interval is elaborated, given extension or development, and above all brought to life by the infusion of musical content. Literally the term means "composing out," and the principle is one which, like those already mentioned, is easily recognizable in its smaller aspects. Schenker himself gives, as a very simple example of this, the opening measures of Chopin's B-minor Prelude, which embody the tonic triad in living material; but in his later and more speculative work he gives the principle infinite extension. It is this extension of the principle of *Auskomponierung* which forms the basis of what is most problematical in his work. We will return to these questions later; suffice it for the moment to stress the interest and importance of the principle itself and to pay homage to the admirably clear thinking which formulated it.

The above principles are expounded in Schenker's *Harmonielehre*, a book which, in spite of some features that still remain problematical, is certainly unsurpassed and perhaps unequalled in its sphere. The second part of his magnum opus, of which the *Harmonielehre* forms the first, is devoted to the problems of counterpoint. Here Schenker offers less, perhaps, that is strikingly new, and there is more material—chiefly in detail—with which this writer is inclined to disagree; but the central conception, at least from a theoretical and in the deepest sense pedagogical standpoint, is admirably clear and just.

What Schenker has done, briefly and crudely stated, is to "clean up" the current conceptions of counterpoint and place them on a more intellectually and pedagogically tenable basis. Counterpoint is here conceived, for almost the first time in two centuries, as the systematic and logically developed study of the fundamental problems of voice leading, considered in themselves and without reference to the other elements of the musical language. In his view this is the only tenable approach to a real understanding of these problems; to consider (as is almost universally the case in current methods of teaching) the study of counterpoint as in any sense a study of composition is as futile as to regard the highly simplified exercises of a beginner in a foreign language as literature. He therefore rejects as superficial both the empirical and the specifically historical approaches to counterpoint, and devotes himself to the consideration of the facts of voice leading in and for themselves, with a result that is very close to the principles of counterpoint originally formulated by Fux in the early eighteenth century. The whole is as masterly an apology for adherence to tradition in this branch of study as one could expect to find. While there is here and there an argument that seems a little sophistical, or a piece of analysis that seems over-refined, the general effect is one of sound and expert reasoning and of successful application.

The most questionable portion of the book is his argument against the attempt to revive the "modes" of the medieval church as a basis of musical syntax. His objections to the erstwhile mania for exoticism, folklorism, and archaism are sound enough. Heaven knows, though the violence and bitterness of his polemic sound rather strange at a moment when this particular tendency has for the most part been left behind. But the essence of this problem lies far deeper than a question, merely, of musical syntax. While recognizing the deeper psychological issues Schenker nevertheless attempts to solve the problem by means of theory alone. With admirable courage and candor he attacks it at its most difficult point, by analyzing examples of quasi-modal usage from the works of the greatest masters. The conclusions are interesting: Beethoven's *Dankgesang* is not in the Lydian mode at all, but gains its quasi-modal effect from the (in Schenker's view) forced and unsatisfying avoidance of the fourth degree of its scale, while Bach's settings of *Gelobet seist Du, Jesus Christ* prove, in spite of certain admirable features, how the instincts of even a great master may be sidetracked at moments by false teachings. It is easy enough to follow the logic of Schenker's argument. But unfortunately he asks us to choose between theories which, for all the clarity, sincerity, and verve with which they are advanced, remain purely speculative, and, on the other hand, the actual deeds of the greatest masters. For the musician of instinct there can of course be only one possible choice, and Schenker's attempt to establish a dogma which shall have the effect of a genuine criterion demonstrates in this case very clearly the oft-proved fact that the essence of great art is something so infinitely delicate that it is likely always to remain an unfathomable mystery. Schenker's harmonization of the chorale in question, which he offers as the correct one, is precisely that which any reasonably competent musician would make. Only Bach's versions, as a comparison shows with devastating clarity, happen to be actual deeds of a man of supreme genius, and as such carry us to a realm of far more profound musical reality. And the history of music, like history of other kinds, consists of deeds and not of theories.

The last twenty odd years of Schenker's life were devoted principally to the study of the more abstruse and speculative problems of musical form, studies which were embodied first of all in a series of analyses or *Erläuterungen* of classic works and which culminated in his treatise on form, entitled *Der freie Satz*. In these works he carries the conception of *Auskomponierung* to its farthest possible conclusions in the principles of the *Ursatz* and its embodiment the *Urlinie*, the principles through which he has become best known. These terms are somewhat misleading since they seem to define as primary conceptions, at the beginning of a composer's musical thought, structures which can be laid bare only after painstaking analysis. It is doubtless far from Schenker's intention to imply that the series of seven notes which he finds ultimately at the basis of the first movement of the *Eroica* Symphony were in Beethoven's mind as the origin of the work; he presumably intends rather to deduce them as its ultimate background.

An adequate definition of the *Urlinie* and an exposition of the means by which Schenker deduces it from a given work would be manifestly impossible within the space of a short article. Sometimes his methods are logical and incontrovertible; too often, however, they seem arbitrary and speculative in the extreme, dictated by the impulse to find confirmation for an a priori assumption, even when one must admit that this assumption was arrived at only after years of painstaking research. Every composer is aware through his own experience of the reality of a "background" in his musical construction that goes beyond the individual traits of melody and harmony which constitute the most immediately perceptible features of his work. He is conscious, that is to say, of a type of movement which takes place gradually and over large stretches, and which embodies itself in the need which he feels, say, at a given moment, for such and such a high note, or for this or that particular harmonic or melodic intensification. This is in a very real sense one of the most essential features of the composer's impulse and is far more than a part of an impulse towards "design" in the usual sense of the word. But the composer, too, will recognize the fact that musical line is, in its full significance, an extremely complicated affair, and that a single note may be fraught with a hundred implications and embody a hundred relationships within a given work. Most intelligent musicians, moreover, will realize that a musical impression is an integral thing, and that the various terms in which it is described and analyzed are, however useful and necessary, abstractions of a decidedly approximative nature. This holds true, ultimately, of Schenker's work just as fatally as of the older systems which formed the basis of the training of the composers themselves and which governed a large part of their speech about music.

There are two fundamental objections, therefore, to such a conception as Schenker's *Urlinie* and *Ursatz*. The first is that it is far too primitive as a description of the actual events which constitute a musical work, or the sensations and apperceptions that constitute the ultimate comprehension of that work. With an arrogance that is all too characteristic he makes the claim, on the title page of his treatise on the *Eroica* Symphony, that the latter is "Zum erstenmal in ihrem wahren Inhalt dargestellt [presented for the first time in its true content]"! The reader may follow him through pages of analysis, some of it brilliant, some of it overingenious, and if he is thoroughly familiar with the text of the symphony he will find it comparatively simple to "hear" it in the manner laid out by Schenker. But if he is musically gifted and really familiar with the work, the chances are that he will already have learned to hear it in its larger features, and that Schenker's analysis can at the very best do no more than illuminate certain points of detail. At worst it presents the music to him at secondhand and interposes a dogmatic and ingeniously conceived scaffolding between the hearer and the work as the composer himself heard it, thus interfering with his direct response which is the only possible basis of real comprehension. In any case there is no possible substitute for a highly evolved musical ear and a robust musical instinct, and if he is possessed of these he will certainly find Schenker's description all too insufficient. He will conclude that the true content of the *Eroica* lies in the text of the work as conceived by Beethoven, and that there can be no adequate approach to such a work except through the accumulation of years of constantly more profound but always direct experience of the music in its entirety, an experience for which there can be no substitute and to which there can be no short cut. And while knowledge is a most essential element in this experience, he will find that the only dependable source of knowledge lies in those elements of which the composer himself was aware.

This brings us to the second objection, and one which is equally vital for the time in which we live. It is perhaps a more fundamental objection than the first, since it concerns, above all, such conceptions of music itself as lie at the basis of Schenker's work. It is in essence the Alexandrian or ex post facto conception which envisages creation as the painstaking and meticulous embodiment of principles that were once vital and in process of development, but whose very definiteness and, so to speak, formulability proclaim either their insufficiency or their exhaustion. A culture which no longer can grow through its own vitality will end by gnawing the bones of its past; for the past can be kept alive only through vital growth into a present, in which the creative impulse is still alive and the ultimate criterion no artificially cultivated set of judgments based on analysis or research, but the living response of sensitive and exacting minds. It is precisely when Schenker's teachings leave the domain of exact description and enter that of dogmatic and speculative analysis that they become essentially sterile.

Nevertheless it remains true that the contemporary composer faces problems of extreme difficulty, in regard to the materials of his art as well as to the spiritual questions which are so vital and so fateful today. The solution however lies exactly where it has always lain—in clear and honest musical thought in addition to creative power. This is more difficult, possibly, to achieve in our day than it has been at various times in the past, when a living tradition came to the aid of the composer and, by setting a tangible standard, put a premium on clear musical thinking and good workmanship. Today the composer is thrown back on his own integrity, and can, so to speak, find artistic salvation only in the dictates of that integrity, clearly understood and religiously followed. In such a manner, under the leadership of really powerful personalities, it is not wholly inconceivable that new values might arise and a new tradition be created. It is certainly hardly conceivable that Schenker's proud boast should be fulfilled and a revival of the older tradition take place in Vienna, under the standard of the *Urlinie* and *Ursatz*. That tradition has already, so to speak, developed away from itself and is not to be revived by an adherence to doctrines derived from esoteric interpretations of the musical Scholiasts. A far more exacting discipline—

that of the directly perceiving and spontaneously co-ordinating musical ear—is demanded of the musicians of today and tomorrow, if they are to be equal to the tasks before them. And they will derive much profit and help from the clear and profound conceptions in Schenker's earlier works, just as they will turn away from the Talmudic subtleties and the febrile dogmatism of his later ones.

Hindemith on Theory
[1937]

The first of a series of four articles discussing three important books in the field of music theory. Although only one of the books (Hindemith's) has appeared in English, all three represent points of view that have been highly influential among musicians in this country.

HINDEMITH's *Unterweisung im Tonsatz* (Vol. I)[1] embodies the results of a rich experience in teaching, in speculation, and in the ex post facto analysis of the composer's own works. It is confessedly an attempt to accomplish for the musicians of Hindemith's day what Fux, two hundred years ago, wished to do for his contemporaries: that is to say, to bring some order and control into the prevailing confusion of the musical language. In an exceptionally fine preface Hindemith discusses, with great sincerity and evident feeling, the problems of the present-day composer when faced by this confusion, and bears witness to the necessity which many contemporary composers—including this reviewer—have felt, and the effort which they have made, to attain for themselves and for their pupils a real perspective in the maze of contemporary musical procedure, as a prerequisite of genuine mastery. Hindemith himself comments on the singular fact that after Bach, and until very recent decades, no great composer distinguished him-

[1] Mainz, 1937. Translated (by Arthur Mendel) as *The Craft of Musical Composition*, New York, 1942.

From *Modern Music*, vol. 15, no. 1, pp. 57-63. Reprinted by permission of the League of Composers—International Society for Contemporary Music, U.S. Section, Inc.

self as a teacher, while recent composers have, once more, begun striving to pass on to their younger colleagues craft and knowledge from their experience, and, what is perhaps even more striking, to formulate this knowledge into a coherent body of musical "theory."

The result is, as might be expected, an extraordinarily interesting and provocative book. It deals with music in its harmonic and, as a consequence, its melodic aspects. In his organization of the material Hindemith seeks a triple objective, consisting of, first, a solid basis in the physics of sound, second, a constant link with tradition, and third, a formula which will include as much as possible of the new material (and this means hitherto unexploited relationships as well as new "chords" or sonorities) which has transformed the musical language of the past eighty years. The book is divided into six sections, the first introductory, the others dealing respectively with elementary materials, the classification of these according to character, harmonic principles, melody, and analysis. Hindemith's observations are always illuminating and vital; they are also clear, shrewd, and, granting his premises, generally consistent. They are, furthermore, often just and definitive, the conclusions of a musician of race and instinct in the finest sense of the word. Time after time this reviewer felt impelled whole-heartedly to applaud not only the unfailing justness of observation and analysis, but the precision and vividness with which they are expressed. Many young composers in the United States would profit, for instance, by reading Hindemith's general remarks on tonality, and above all his searching dismissal of such concepts as "atonality" and "polytonality" not only as outmoded but as demonstrably contrary to acoustic, psychological, and aesthetic fact. These however, are only isolated and striking examples, and the reader will find this justness and precision duplicated whenever Hindemith speaks directly, as a practical musician speaking of concrete musical matters.

The Limits of Theory

Furthermore, the book makes at least one extremely valuable and, as far as this writer knows, quite original contribution to musical theory. It has been customary to distinguish in musical technique two principles, each of them cumulatively mastered by composers over the course of two great historical periods. From the Middle Ages to, say, 1600, musicians devoted themselves to the gradual mastery of counterpoint, the vocal or horizontal principle and, after a tremendous period of experiment, to the creation of masterpieces made possible by this ultimate mastery of language. The seventeenth century, through the emergence of instrumental music and the necessities of its organization, brought about the active development of a new dimension in music —the vertical or harmonic principle—the mastery and elaboration of which characterized and preoccupied the composers of the next two hundred odd years. In the music which resulted, the previously discovered technique was retained, profoundly modified, and inextricably fused with the newer, in a language of infinitely greater range and breadth.

It seems to this writer that since the earlier nineteenth century a similar change has been taking place. The importance of this change it is not yet possible to determine, but its recognition is indispensable to the full understanding of contemporary music; its mastery, to music's future development. This new "dimension" arises from the vastly increasing consciousness manifested by composers of the last hundred years, in respect to sonority or what has been somewhat indefinitely called "color," and to the various factors which contributed to it. The most obvious among many events which favored this was the development of the orchestra as a comparatively standardized, flexible, and finely differentiated unit. As the century progressed composers became more and more conscious of the possibilities of "color" not only in the instrumental sense but in the sense of the individual harmonic sonority; a chord was chosen not only for its structural value—its relation to other chords in a complete tonal scheme—but also, and often almost exclusively, for its absolute sonorous value, as expressed in its instrumental coloring, the grouping of its component parts, and the "expressive," "emotional," or "coloristic" value of its component intervals, considered in and for themselves. Without a keen awareness of this element and its importance in contemporary music, no coherent understanding of that music is possible, any more than the technique of Bach, for example, can be understood in terms of strict counterpoint alone.

This reviewer is convinced that a great part of the confusion in present-day musical theory and teaching is the result of a failure adequately to distinguish this principle and hence to investigate and formulate in clear terms the nature and limits of its possibilities and its relation to the other elements of music. "Harmony" in the theoretical sense has been, in view of these relatively new facts, an essentially vague concept embracing generally the problem of chord structure, certain aspects of the problems of voice leading and the as yet inadequately defined problem of the individual sonority.

It seems to this writer, then, that the significance of Hindemith's book lies precisely in the fact that here, for the first time, an attempt is made to classify all possible harmonic sounds on this basis and, with this as a point of departure, to formulate principles relevant to their usage. This is not the place to reproduce the necessarily involved processes of his thought or to evaluate his conclusions. Since the latter, indeed, aim to establish general principles rather than simply to elucidate concrete instances, an evaluation can only take place slowly and as a result of painstaking observation and experiment; the reviewer has not yet found the leisure nor the time to do this. He feels fully prepared, however, to testify to the importance of Herr Hindemith's investigations and in particular to the observations included in the chapter entitled *Harmonisches Gefälle*—a term for which "harmonic gradation" or "incline" would be a literal rendering but which must wait for its definitive English equivalent until the translation appears.[2] Here, as far as we know, for the first time serious theoretic attention is given to a set of facts of which every contemporary composer must certainly be aware.

When all this—and it seems to the writer a great deal—has been said, the reviewer finds himself in complete disagreement with much in the book. First of all, he feels that Hindemith assigns far too great an importance, in the construction of a musical theory, to the physics of sound. He read the opening chapters of the book with pleasure and profit, recalled much previous but half forgotten knowledge, and gained some that was new to him. Nor would he think of denying the usefulness of such facts, to the musician. It seems to him, however, that such considerations are only relevant when taken in a completely ex post facto sense; that the musician as such is interested not in the objective nature of sound, but in the effects which sound produces and may be made to produce, and that physics can be useful to him primarily as a confirmation of effects observed, never as a point of departure, or as an adequate explanation of effects which are the manifest result of centuries of cumulative musical experience. It seems to him altogether too facile, for instance, to explain the chromatic scale on the basis of highly complicated acoustical calculations, rather than to show clearly how its present-day usage, and the finely differentiated relationships contained within it, have arisen out of this cumulative experience and of the compromises and artistically exploited ambiguities of the tempered scale.

In the writer's opinion, likewise, Hindemith pays too many respects to certain other tendencies in nineteenth-

[2] "Harmonic fluctuation" is the term used in the translation.

century theory—its emphasis (in other connections than the above) on the purely, so to speak, material, at the expense of the psychological or functional aspects of musical sound; its preoccupation with details of chordal structure at the expense of a clarification of their relationship to the musical line as a whole. Hindemith himself points out the tendency of certain recent musicologists to consider too exclusively the purely horizontal or "linear" aspects of counterpoint; but earlier theorists considered harmony in a far too abstractly vertical sense. It seems to the writer that Hindemith himself does this; specifically, that he fails to recognize, or at least adequately to provide for, the fact that the more complex a harmonic combination, the more its specific harmonic significance becomes modified, *for the ear*, by the musical context, and the less definitive, unambiguous, and univalent its sense. This is already clear in the case of such a simple harmonic combination as the "chord of the sixth" which functions often quite literally as the first inversion of a triad, but sometimes likewise, by virtue of the associations set up by the context of the music, as an independent chord in its own right, with its root in the bass. If the conception of a harmonic "root" or fundamental tone has any meaning at all it must be a psychological one; and experience seems to show that only in the case of the triad is this always fixed and apparently unalterable. While in the case of relatively simpler combinations a correspondingly simplified nomenclature is possible without distortion of the acoustic and psychological fact, this ceases to be the case when a higher degree of complexity is reached. It would be absurd to pretend that Hindemith is unaware of these facts, and indeed he pays constant homage to them in the course of the book. But he seems to underestimate the necessity of maintaining always a clear and exact picture of the acoustic and psychological elements involved in a musical impression. The older theory now seems inadequate, not only because it is not inclusive enough, but because it has long since ceased to do this. For reasons of a

similar kind, though different in application, Herr Hindemith's system seems to us in some respects inadequate. This
can be seen clearly in the analysis at the back of the book.
The analysis of a passage from Stravinsky's Piano Sonata
seems to us to lay far too much stress on comparatively
minute detail and to give therefore an unduly complicated
picture of what is after all an extremely simple tonal impression. Hindemith himself recognizes the simplicity; but
aside from the fact that he goes to the trouble of explaining
harmonically the details of a passage that is fundamentally
linear in character, he fails to relate the details to the central
harmonic fact or make clear the binding elements which
knit the whole together into a single basic harmony. The
result is an "analysis" which is scarcely less complicated
than the passage itself.

Similarly in the analysis of the *Tristan* prelude the picture which he gives of the harmonic flow, and the relationships within this flow, seem to us, as they will seem to many,
a distorted one. Taking only the first three measures: it is
impossible for us to hear the first as a chord of F, or the
second as a chord of G♯. As the root of the first measure
we should insist on A; for the second measure it seems clear
that the B is the real root.

This is not the place for what at best must involve a rather
long explanation; but the fact that Wagner in the course of
the work often lifts the "chord" of the first beat of the
second measure (the "*Tristan* chord") out of this context
and subjects it to the most varied possible harmonic treatment does not change our opinion; the very fact that, according to the specific context, any one of the notes of this
chord may become its determining harmonic factor—and
Wagner's technique utilizes such properties to their limit—
only confirms us in our conviction that Herr Hindemith,
in spite of the tremendous interest and force of his observations, has not succeeded in reaching a definitive solution of
the problem. If and when the latter is reached, it will doubtless be the work of many unconscious collaborators, among

whom Herr Hindemith will certainly hold a place of high honor.

Meanwhile, and in spite of certain dogmatic tendencies of today, it should never be forgotten that musical theory is a very different thing from music itself, and one can even plausibly question to what extent the former really influences the latter. Composers who have instincts will invariably learn through practice to follow them, and those who have none are not, in the proper meaning of the term, composers at all. Even a good teacher of music will necessarily lay overwhelmingly greater stress on the practical exercise of his pupil than on the theory which he may adduce in order to illuminate and guide this practice. The real work of the composer lies in the unconscious or, let us say, superconscious activity of his musical impulse; the meager part that calculation plays is entirely subordinate in remaining either purely instrumental—in the process of orientation toward concrete problems—or critical and ex post facto. If we are to have theory, however, it must at least furnish a reasonably complete picture of the musical language and the elements of which it is composed. And while in a musical culture of strong and self-confident tradition, like that of Germany and to a lesser extent the rest of Europe, much may be left to the already formed instinct of the gifted student (the background shaping this instinct is, for good or ill, far more powerful than any musical theory can be), in one like our own, which is still in process of formation and where all but a few exceptionally gifted individuals are still in a phase of groping and uncertainty, it is infinitely more important that the basic realities of music, technically as well as otherwise, be presented in as clear and flawless a manner as possible.

Exposition by Krenek
[1938]

IN the world of contemporary music, the group of composers adhering to the tenets established and followed by Schoenberg and his school exert an almost unique moral and intellectual force. No other group of contemporary composers has—as a group—such lofty and unspoiled artistic ideals; no group has been so tenacious and unswerving in the pursuit of them, or has preserved such an attitude of loyalty and devotion among its members, and no group has at its disposal a more brilliant array of persuasive intellectual force. As far as creative achievement is concerned, at least two of its members—the master himself and his pupil Alban Berg—belong, through their far-flung influence as well as by their actual work, without question among the foremost composers of today.

All of these reasons, together with its own very high merits, combine to make of Ernst Krenek's *Über neue Musik*[1] a book of extraordinary interest and, in many respects, even for the dissident reader an inspiring book. The "twelve-tone system" and all of its implications, both in historical origin and aesthetic, moral and even social implication, constitute—indeed like all genuine art—in the intensity with which they are believed, not merely a system of aesthetics and of technical procedure, but what amounts to an artistic religion. Krenek's book is not only the product of one of the most subtle and profound minds which concern themselves with contemporary music; it is a confession of faith, and has all the compelling force of such.

[1] Vienna, 1937.

From *Modern Music*, vol. 15, no. 2, pp. 123-128. Reprinted by permission of the League of Composers—International Society for Contemporary Music, U.S. Section, Inc.

It is not surprising therefore that in his first chapter he summarily dismisses, by way of definition, from the category of "new music" all music which does not correspond to these tenets. His critique is, of course, general, but always brilliant and often, though in a strictly generalized sense, just. It has, however, the incompleteness that a cursory critique of tendencies rather than works is bound to have, and the keen partiality of a thoroughly convinced, a priori judgment. On this basis Krenek proceeds in the second chapter to a clear and highly interesting discussion of musical elements; he adduces illuminating and original conceptions of the nature of the musical "idea," "language," "articulation," "binding elements," and "form," which he uses as the basis of later chapters. The third section is devoted to "atonality," a term which he boldly if somewhat reluctantly adopts, with, however, the proviso of exact and painstaking definition, both of the term itself and of its antithesis which he confesses himself forced by the occasion to define in its narrowest and most strictly academic sense. The following two chapters, entitled "Twelve-Tone Technique" and "Music and Mathematics" are devoted to an extraordinarily clear, illuminating, and persuasive exposition of the technicalities and specific aesthetic problems of the twelve-tone system; the final one, "Music and Humanity," to a discussion of the relation of the new music and its creators to society. In this chapter, in which one feels more than a trace of profound disillusionment and deep pessimism, he gives voice to the high idealism of the group to which he belongs, a proud and even aggressive affirmation of the isolation of the artist, and a well-merited disdain for the points of view, so popular today, which regard this isolation as deplorable.

There is much in the book that this reviewer can regard not only as penetrating and profound, but as true. This applies not only to Krenek's attitude as an artist but to much of his fundamental technical and aesthetic analysis. Many of his interpretations, both of phenomena and of values, and of the psychology of composition, are so much like the reviewer's own as to cause the latter genuine surprise and pleasure—indeed, insofar as he found himself in disagreement with anything in the first two or even three chapters, it was a disagreement in detail, inevitable in the case of any book dealing with the subject to which he too has devoted his life. Moreover, Herr Krenek's presentation is so masterly and so convincing, his argument so completely evolved, that whatever objections are made to it are only to be made, so to speak, on the highest possible plane. The same may, of course, be said of the music of composers like Schoenberg, Webern, and Berg. To understand and to judge this music requires one's best faculties—to estimate it accurately and fairly puts all the qualities of heart and of intellect, as well as of musical understanding, to the test.

Herr Krenek's book deals, of course, not with specific musical works, but with a musical system. It is always necessary in speaking of any such system, never to lose sight of this distinction; the fact, that is, that systems and works belong to quite different categories, as different as those of grammar and literature. The test of the former is ultimately a purely empirical one—that of its proven adaptation to the ends which it serves. This is certainly as true of the twelve-tone system as of any similar quasi-grammatical basis of art; the ultimate judgment must rest on works and not on theories or points of view.

The first point of difference with this system which this reviewer feels—a difference in no way lessened by Herr Krenek's admirable exposition—lies in the very fact that it is, as has already been pointed out, a system which seems to claim more than empirical validity; a system, that is, in which the works seem to be almost of secondary importance in comparison with the theory behind them. This is never clearly stated, and would no doubt be denied by Herr Krenek and his colleagues. One can well understand that a new impulse in art, by reason of its very novelty, is often forced into a polemical position by the intensity of the attacks upon it, and what begins as a fruitful artistic discovery soon degenerates into a dogma. In this case the bitterness of the attack, though by no means unique in musical history, reflects itself on the other hand, in the form, also not entirely new, of sharp antagonism in principle to whatever is contrary to the tenets attacked. Such opposition tends therefore to force the issue of partisanship.

Mediocrity, Heaven knows, is common enough, as is its tendency to rationalize itself in attitudes of escape which provide refuge from vital issues. But it is hardly possible to evade the realization that mediocrity exists within a movement as well as outside it, and for a certain type of mediocrity there is nothing so comforting as precisely such a movement as this, in which isolation itself provides a comforting feeling of warmth and over-compensation. It is therefore impossible to the outsider, aware as he may be of the prevalence of mediocrity, to accept as valid a distinction based on principles of style or aesthetics; his very awareness of the rarity of what is truly great inevitably must drive him to other criteria. Thus the specific dogma remains, as such, essentially false even if one were to admit that at a given time and place all the outstanding figures were numbered among its adherents.

The second reservation is a more specific one. This writer has already voiced an attitude toward the twelve-tone system which Herr Krenek for all his compelling persuasiveness has not modified but, on the contrary, served to intensify. The final paragraphs of the book constitute an elegant defense of his creed from the reproach that it is based on thought as well as on intuition, and point, in support of his thesis, to clear examples from among the great figures of the past. It is indeed lamentable that such a defense should need to be made at all. A profoundly conscious attitude toward art has repeatedly been one of the attributes of greatness, though by no means necessarily a sign of it. This writer possesses photographic facsimiles of certain of Beethoven's sketches for the finale of Opus 106 that show beyond all doubt the conscious and even methodical testing of the various possibilities of his fugue subject, which can scarcely be other than a relatively cold process of technical modification. In such a case it is discrimination, not "creation," in the usual grotesquely misunderstood sense, which is inspired; the titanic power of this whole movement is quite evidently in no wise softened by the composer's complete awareness of his procedure, which appears in black and white on his manuscript pages.

One takes exception therefore not to the fact that the twelve-tone composers are conscious and reflective in their methods, but to the intensely abstract nature of their thought. In a remarkable passage Krenek demands not a "natural" (*Naturgegebenen*) but an intellectually determined basis (*Geistesbestimmten Voraussetzungen*) for music. This writer's antipathy for the twelve-tone system is expressed precisely in these terms, provided that by "nature" is understood not physics but the response of the human ear and spirit to the simplest acoustic facts. He is profoundly out of sympathy, therefore, with the conception which Krenek boldly avows, of music as an abstract system like geometry. On the contrary it seems to him that its human meaning—and this has nothing to do with "success," "conformity," or any of their current and more pretentious synonyms—lies ultimately in the fact that such elementary musical phenomena as the fifth, and the measurably qualitative distinction between consonance and dissonance, are psychological as well as physical facts, out of which a whole language has grown, and which even in music based on the twelve-tone system seem often more powerful binding forces (*Relations-momente*) than those inherent in the system itself. As a result of an intensive and painstaking study, undertaken over a period of years in good faith and with the best means at his disposal, this writer has come to the conclusion that this is so; that what one hears in twelve-tone music is often plainly at variance with the conceptions that go into its construction.

The Limits of Theory

The criticism which he would make is thus one not so much of the music as of the abstractions which lie behind it. What seems to him an esoteric conception of form, based not on the psychological process of association but on what may be called abstract literalistic procedures (e.g. the *cancrizans* and its inversion) seems to belong quite in the same category. Space does not permit the detailed discussion of these points, and the reviewer is all too conscious of the fact that by their very nature they cannot in any sense be proved. He adduces them only in order to explain and perhaps in some sense justify the recalcitrance of his instincts in regard to a musical tendency for many of whose representatives and creative products he has a genuine and deep admiration and respect.

His final question relates to the basic assumption of Herr Krenek regarding the historical inevitability of the system, as the latest embodiment of a constant tendency toward intensification of "expression"—what Herr Krenek terms the *Espressivo-Haltung*. The reviewer's question is whether this intensification has not been carried to the breaking point, where real expression is vitiated by an over-abundance and excessive elaboration of detail. The history of art shows clear instances of such exaggeration in the past, as well as of the inevitable and fundamentally healthy reaction against it, somewhat as natural history shows instances of over-development of this or that biological trait, ending, however, in this sphere tragically, in the annihilation of a species. Here again the reviewer must abandon proof and fall back on a tenacious and undeniable instinct.

Herr Krenek in some measure seems to answer and justify this charge at the end of his fifth chapter where he admits the fragmentary impression created by his "new music" which he considers part of its character as the "innermost expression of reality" (*das innerste Ausdruck des Wesens*). But is it not precisely the nature of art to transcend this fragmentary reality and to give it significance through synthesis—through the creation of a spiritual world in which "the unattainable" in Goethe's words "becomes event" and the fragments achieve a unity impossible in the real world? The significance thus attained is no doubt never a truly definitive one, but it is perhaps in a still deeper sense the *innerste Ausdruck des Wesens* since it represents the creative embodiment of the most constant even if ultimately the vainest aspiration of mankind—that of transcending itself and approaching something like divinity. Is not art therefore, significant precisely insofar as it is not fragmentary, and are not the greatest works of art those in which completeness, not so much of form as of range and depth and intensity, is most fully attained?

Escape by Theory
[1938]

HEINRICH SCHENKER's *Der freie Satz*, subtitled *Das erste Lehrbuch der Musik*,[1] is difficult and unfortunately, in large part, repulsive and sterile reading. It is, in the first place, pathological in the most obvious sense; unfortunately its author lays great store by the general, pseudo-philosophical assumptions which form the background of his thought, and these are in the most self-revealing manner the outcome of personal frustrations and fantasies. His megalomania alienates even the patient and open-minded reader by its constant effort, a tendency all too frequent in contemporary German writing, not to convince or illuminate, but to intimidate him. Herr Schenker's obvious self-adulation, the endless polemic against the ignorance, venality, and bad faith of, it seems, all of his colleagues in musical theory, and his contemporaries in music, grow quickly to seem petty and dull. The recurrent note of cultural nationalism—an aggressive Germanism, somewhat stretched in order to include Scarlatti, Chopin, and obviously and above all Herr Schenker himself—strikes a thoroughly repellent note today, in its insistence not so much on the primacy as on the eternal exclusiveness of German musical culture—of Germanism as such, in Schenker's own definition. This is all, of course, implicit in the subtitle of the book; the reader is never allowed to forget that Schenker, for the first time and quite alone, has made clear the true nature of music, that he alone understands the genius of the masters, in whose closed and

[1] *Neue Musikalische Theorien und Phantasien, III: Der freie Satz*, Vienna, 1935 (rev. 1956).

From *Modern Music*, vol. 15, no. 3, pp. 192-197. Reprinted by permission of the League of Composers—International Society for Contemporary Music, U.S. Section, Inc.

inaccessible company he belongs as a kind of supreme arbiter of musical values.

In other words, Herr Schenker demands of his reader a great deal of patience, and a certain amount of tolerance and urbanity. It is true that a serious reader may to a large extent be expected to give this; but it is scarcely avoidable that, after twenty-nine pages devoted largely to this sort of thing, he begin to demand something a little more serious of Herr Schenker himself. Unfortunately the chapters that follow—comprising, with the above mentioned, nearly half of the book—are precisely the most abstract, profoundly questionable, and obscure part of it, and for this reason serve simply to create new problems and difficulties for the reader. It is this portion in which Schenker establishes his theory of the *Ursatz*, or basic formula, which constitutes the "background" of music, and in which he formulates principles relating to what he calls the "middle ground," in its various and, according to Schenker, clearly definable planes (*Schichten*). It is not, certainly, the existence of a "background," or even of a "middle ground" that one would deny; musicians do not need Herr Schenker to tell them that a fully realized work of art is organic and the product of a "conception" in the truest sense of the word—an indivisible impulse, in which all parts contribute to the whole. One can appreciate, too, the immense amount of ingenuity and scholarship which has gone into Schenker's effort to lay down the formula of the *Ursatz*. This very ingenuity however confirms one's doubts in regard to what he has achieved. The formula is so attenuated, so inflexible, and so devoid of any dynamic quality that it is quite impossible to regard it as the kind of musical spermatozoon which Schenker conceives it to be; and however ingenious his adductions to it, they produce too often precisely the effect of being in given cases not only far fetched but quite extraneous to the object. It must not be forgotten that a living seed contains not only the possibility, but the determining elements of organic development along a certain predestined line;

it is these determining elements, and not the inert ingredients of which they are composed, which indeed make a living organism possible, and which must form the basis for its study as an organism. It is therefore of no fundamental interest, even from the analytical point of view, to find a formula which lies at the basis of, say, the first movement of the *Eroica* Symphony, Bach's Passacaglia, and Chopin's E-major Etude; the interest of these or any other works begins precisely at the point where their individual qualities begin to appear and to grow in an inevitable manner. It is only at this point that organic life may be said to begin; and in a more specific sense it is at this point—the composer's *conception*—where music begins to exist as such. For this reason, even if one considered Schenker's conclusions as proven beyond all manner of doubt, one could regard them as possessing possibly a certain academic interest, but as fundamentally irrelevant to living music; one would still be obliged to deny categorically their applicability as anything like invariable laws of art. At best they would be merely observable facts, subject to modification at any time.

In the second half of the book, where Schenker discusses the "foreground" of music, the reader fares considerably better, and if he can ignore the author's thoroughly offensive style and manner, may find much even to delight him. It is true that these chapters to a large extent presuppose the earlier ones as their foundation, and this "background" is never wholly lost from view; but here Schenker is in the immediate presence of concrete objects, rather than theories, and his first-rate powers of observation and keen analysis often appear here freed from the megalomania which drives him, in the earlier chapters, towards the establishment of "eternal laws." It would be futile to attempt much particularization in this regard; many of Schenker's observations, especially in the chapters relating to what he calls "Diminution"—the individual features of a musical work, in their relation to the whole design—to "Articulation," and to "Metre and Rhythm," struck the writer as genuinely profound, illuminating, and hence, in the only true meaning of the term, important.

The reviewer does not wish to lose sight of this fact in making general observations which express his quite radical dissent from the values on which Herr Schenker bases his system. He has repeatedly paid tribute to Schenker's analytical penetration and insight, and does so again, acknowledging gratefully that his own conceptions of certain technical and pedagogical problems owe a great deal, by way of clarification and precision, to certain of Schenker's earlier writings. But it is partly for this very reason that he feels the more strongly a fundamental divergence of viewpoint in regard to a system which aims to establish values and criteria which he cannot regard as other than categorically false.

He regards them as false first of all because they are based exclusively on "form"—form taken, in spite of Schenker's protestations to the contrary, not in the all-embracing individual sense, in which form is the complete, fully integrated, and all-inclusive embodiment of the composer's ideas, inseparable from and fully identical with them, but in the purely material sense of acoustical logic. Schenker frankly wishes to establish his principles as criteria, not only of the degree of *realization* of a musical work, but of its intrinsic value. The *Urlinie* becomes more than the final essence of musical logic—it becomes a touchstone of genius. It is unnecessary to repeat the reasons, given above, why the reviewer and, he is confident, most of his colleagues, find it quite inacceptable as either the one or the other. "Form" on this plane, or constructed on this basis, seems to him non-existent because the living germ—the musical impulse—is absent; just as form in the abstract, as a point of departure, is in any artistic sense non-existent.

It is inevitable that on this basis Schenker should give

an inordinate importance to musical theory. If, as this writer is convinced, musical logic is by its very nature dynamic and concrete, existent as a reality only in the successive embodiments created by the genius and imagination of composers, theory is properly not a code of external laws but a compendium of known and discoverable materials and usage, of practical value to the teacher and student, and in a far more questionable and restricted sense to the mature artist. It is thus strictly descriptive in character, and is useful precisely insofar as it is accurate and complete. It has no reality or significance whatever beyond this; and a theory which pretends to establish "eternal laws" is always suspect —not because there are no eternal laws, but because these are the affair of God, not of man, who can approach them only through the embodiment of a creative instinct in *works*, manifold in aspect and subject only to the limitations of human powers and imagination.

For these reasons such a system as Herr Schenker's is only possible *after* the fact—never before it. It becomes essentially the grammar of a dead language, being based inevitably on the music of a given, strictly circumscribed time and place. In Schenker's case this is, roughly speaking, the period which nearly everyone would concede to have been the greatest, even though Schenker's company of geniuses, which includes, apparently, Clementi and certainly Mendelssohn, nevertheless excludes Wagner and Berlioz and Verdi. Schenker not only practically ignores whatever is in any sense evolutionary in this period, and treats it as something purely static, but seems to imply that its greatness was based primarily on its embodiment of certain principles of craftsmanship, and that the art of music can be revived by a reapplication of principles which he believes himself to have derived from it. The reviewer is heartily in agreement with Schenker's distaste for a false and destructive historicism which finds in history justification, through false parallelism, for any and every possible idiocy, and for the lack of standards which a too great "catholicity of taste"—meaning in reality a lack of essential conviction—has engendered in our time. But his static theory has little or no relevance to the actual situation of music today, and even takes no regard of the causes—inherent already partly in the music of the "great period"—which have brought it to this situation. This constitutes both its fatal weakness and its appeal for a certain type of mentality. It is all too easy for those incapable of meeting the creative problems of a period like our own, to take refuge in a contempt for the present and its struggle, and a highly specious identification with the great masters of the past, through the false profundities of an analysis which is always excessive and often sophistical.

For it should properly be a truism that analysis, however brilliant and even imaginative, can never penetrate below the surface of a work of art. It is possible approximately—though only approximately—and valid pragmatically, to demonstrate some of the connections and syntheses that go into a work of genius. The work itself, however—and this is true of the humblest as well as of the greatest—remains still inaccessible and mysterious, and above all unique—a *deed* of which the attempted reconstruction is, and must perforce always be, a mere reflection, without content or value of any genuine kind. To a large extent Schenker would admit this. What he seems not to admit is that an art, a culture, is organically attached to the time and place that produces it, and that even the greatest culture of the past can serve at best as an example and an ideal, not as a model. His motto, *Semper idem sed non eodem modo*, is of course in the deepest sense true; it says little however that is definite, since there is no way of establishing theoretically the exact point of divergence between the two categories which it sets up. One can admit gladly that artistic values—since they are human values—are inherent and in the last analysis unchangeable; their living embodiment however must come from within—through the gradual growth and development of a tradition from the means at its disposal; it can never be imposed from without by the adoption of "standards" conceived in a purely static sense, and taken over from a period which, as Schenker himself would have us believe, is closed. The composer of today must, and at his best does, strive, as composers have always striven, to embody in his art the qualities of synthesis, of range, of intensity for which he must perforce strive as a human being; he would only face hopeless and inevitable defeat were he to ignore the continuity which binds him to the great period of the past, even if that continuity has been primarily destructive of the older synthesis. It is his task, in fact, to build, as far as he is able, in the spirit of his titanic predecessors, but with the materials, vastly different from theirs, which his time and destiny have put at his disposal.

The Function of Theory
[1938]

I**N** the preceding articles of this series the writer has attempted to form a judgment of what seem to him three highly significant contributions to present day thought regarding music. Two of these were the work of eminent composers (Hindemith and Krenek); the third (by Schenker), was the product of a mind of unquestionable brilliance and insight, and profound scholarship—one of the outstanding figures in contemporary musical theory and one, in spite of exclusive preoccupation with the past, quite capable of holding its own among the various involutions and complexities of contemporary speculation. Not only did it seem to the writer almost inevitable that he should compare them; also they led him, or at least accompanied him, very logically along certain trains of thought which seemed to him significant, regarding the condition in which music finds itself today.

What is musical theory and what is its function? For the musician, at all events, it has absolutely no other than a practical purpose—that of helping him more easily to grasp and hence to master his materials. It must therefore in overwhelming measure consist of a compendium of known materials and known procedures—that is, materials and procedures which have been given genuine artistic effect—the result of actual creative experience. Its validity lies precisely in the extent to which it faithfully reproduces the results of this experience and lays the foundation for further discovery on the basis of what is already known. It is, in other words, nothing more, in essence, nor less than a demon-

From *Modern Music*, vol. 15, no. 4, pp. 257-262. Reprinted by permission of the League of Composers—International Society for Contemporary Music, U.S. Section, Inc.

stration of actual results obtained and effects achieved. It is difficult to see how any more than this can be of value to the serious musician, whose self-educative task is, solely and unceasingly, that of gaining fuller control of his materials, both technically, in being able to use them as he will, and imaginatively, in apprehending their unexplored possibilities and above all in embodying in them his individual creative vision. But creation—the end—is a subconscious process, while technique—the means—is the conscious or superconscious one; musical theory therefore that is before the fact can have no conceivable value to the musician, and can only be poisonous to him if he allows himself to be really exposed to it.

In other words, musical theory is valid for the musician only insofar as it is practical and not speculative, in regard either to the nature of musical material or the establishment of abstract values. It must base itself on music in the concrete, and not on physics or history or aesthetics. If the latter are adduced it must be by way of confirmation or analogy, in support of observed facts, not by way of exposition or deduction as to the inherent nature of music itself. Since physics and history belong in categories completely different from that of art, anything whatever—and, of course, nothing—can be proven from them.

If this is the case, and musical theory is a compendium of results obtained, it is clear that a successful theory must consist of clearly demonstrable data, accessible and readily recognizable to all competent observers. It will in other words exist in a reasonably impersonal sphere in which not one style or tendency but all conceivable styles of a given time and culture are included. Otherwise no longer materials alone, but highly imponderable and inevitably shifting criteria are certain to become operative. Theory so based is, by just so much, rigidly circumscribed in value and applicability. At worst it favors a highly self-conscious and ultimately sterile attitude toward music, which is forced into channels of an academic and artificial nature.

The Limits of Theory

The three books in question are interesting, then, because each in its own way tries to meet this test of universal applicability. Hindemith's book, *Unterweisung im Tonsatz*, comes, at least in tone and intention, the nearest to meeting it. It is less a "system" than the other two, and is by comparison remarkably free from aggressive polemics. But neither does he succeed in convincing the reader by his demonstrations, nor does he establish his thesis on a clear and indisputable definition of fundamentals. The result is a sense that, yes, music can no doubt be conceived in this manner, and move in this direction, but why must it do so? The end sought and obtained seems to be that of facility in Hindemith's own manner, the exploitation of musical materials rather than their real mastery. Should it be applied, the result would be a virtual adaptation of Hindemith's style—no doubt not a fatal, but certainly—because it is strictly personal—a far from inevitable or profoundly motivated direction for music to take. It is, fundamentally, the direction of "Gebrauchsmusik," produced according to formula and lacking the profundity and differentiation which only creative necessity can give. Certainly, far from Hindemith's intention, which was obviously a quite objective one. The book, however, is the most personal of the three—as completely personal, in its own way, as *Das Marienleben* or *Mathis der Maler*.

Krenek's *Über neue Musik* is the exposé of a system—a system not constructed, to be sure, quite out of whole cloth, but one inextricably bound to a definite interpretation of musical history and a marked aesthetic bias. On this level, already, the system is suspect. This particular type of preoccupation with history, on the part of creative artists, is a quite recent development, and is all too often a symptom of profound inner insecurity. It is far different from Wagner's serene, magnificently and naively impudent assumption that all of his predecessors were in the last analysis but forerunners—an assumption that sprang not from any need for "rules" to support or to clarify his procedure but from an exclusive absorption and intense belief in his own partially fulfilled creative tasks. The twelve-tone system is bound to the past not by ties of continuity—which might conceivably lead in a thousand directions—but by the far more restricting one of opposition. History itself, after all, is based necessarily on abstraction, and the interpretation of history as the development of any single tendency is preeminently abstract. In the case of the *Espressivo-Haltung* the abstraction becomes even more arid since "expression" or "expressiveness" is hardly conceivable without an object, and the ultimate question involved regards not the manner and intensity, but the quality and the content of expression.

This to be sure goes beyond the specific realm of the musical theory embodied in the system itself. As propounded in Krenek's book this is far more consistent and more refined than Hindemith's theory; it is however at the same time more stuffy and more remote. Again, though by the mere fact of being a self-contained system, it is more impersonal, this same quality renders it, like the other, fatally insufficient as a solution of contemporary musical problems. Once more, it is at best possible, not inevitable. It stands fatally before the fact; its principles are, quite frankly and from the beginning, based on abstract reasoning rather than on concrete and demonstrable experience of effect. The music toward which it ineluctably tends is one in which "expression" and form (since the latter is bound by strict, pre-determined and invariable rules) belong in quite different categories and in which the former resides in dynamics, register, accent and color rather than in the specific musical content as embodied in an organically developing tonal pattern.

Of the three books, Schenker's *Der freie Satz* is the most pretentious and, in spite of its exclusive preoccupation with the past, the most provocative. It deals with more fundamental questions than Hindemith's, and its approach to musical problems is far more concrete than that of the "twelve-tone system." This latter quality is obviously due in part to the fact that it deals exclusively with problems of analysis, and takes as its basis the postulate of a past, complete in itself and sealed, so to speak, at both ends. But as opposed to Hindemith, it faces fully the problem of musical continuity—the continuity of organic growth and not merely that of succession, while as opposed to the twelve-tone system it takes as its point of departure the ear in its manifold discriminative and synthesizing functions, and not a set of arbitrary relations between tones. The writer has expressed himself fully in judgment of Schenker and does not feel inclined to modify his considered opinions. Theories such as those of Hindemith and Krenek are pertinent and vital, whatever their limitations, because they represent serious attempts to deal with actual problems; Schenker's goal, on the other hand, evades these problems and successfully vitiates the fundamental soundness of his approach.

The books raise, however, other questions than those inherent in their contents. Why, above all, do composers occupy themselves with musical theory? It is true that present day conditions force many of them to become teachers and hence into the necessity of organizing their material into a consistent and presentable form. Such treatises as those of Schenker and Krenek and even Hindemith, however, go far beyond this necessity and manifest both a preoccupation with theory as such, and a dogmatic, even a polemic, spirit in regard to it, which is one of the curiosities of the present day—one of the distinguishing symptoms of the somewhat anomalous situation in which art, like everything else, tends to find itself today. Like so many other forms of intellectualism it is to some extent a sign of profound inner insecurity—on the part of society perhaps, rather than the individual; a search for forms, external imperatives, to reinforce and direct confused or wavering inner necessities. After all, the composer's real task is to discover and utilize, not to classify and rationalize, his materials. He achieves form through the necessities of a clear and directed intensity of vision, not through molds into which his ideas can be poured, or recipes according to which they can be fabricated to pattern. If such rationalizations are to have validity even for the student—and they can certainly have no other—they must be deduced from the plenitude of actual creative achievement, not evolved in the factory of facile classification or the laboratory of a priori abstraction. It was not really Fux, after all, but his far greater contemporaries who, through masterpieces—deeds, not theories— brought order into the "chaos" of his time.

There remains, to be sure, a very real task for the theorist —that of deducing and finding principles from contemporary musical procedure and putting them into a form that will be clear and intelligible to the musicians of the present and future. It is, no doubt, not a task for the composer, whose approach and point of view, in our day above all, is an eminently personal one. In any case such a theory would seem to require, as its basis, a genuinely penetrating, all inclusive, and unbiased study of the musical ear in its varied responses and coordinating activities. As far as this writer knows, this has never been done with anything approaching adequacy, though all reputable musical theory deals with its problems. It is in truth a task of heroic magnitude, and one requiring a variety of attitudes very rarely met with in combination—psychological insight and tact, ability for exact analysis, as well as profound and genuinely imaginative musicianship. It should, it would seem, irresistibly tempt musicians or musicologists whose interest in their art is more than a purely historical one. It should not however be attempted by anyone not fully aware of its pitfalls, or unwilling to reconsider in full the cherished concepts of existing musical theory. Above all it must aim, in the spirit of the practical artist, and not that of the speculative student, at demonstrating facts, not establishing laws, and at the enhancement of a musical language capable of meeting all of the varied demands which the composers of today place upon it.

V

Music and the World Conflict

Music and Nationalism
[1933]

SOME NOTES ON DR. GOEBBELS' LETTER
TO FURTWAENGLER

Soon after the Nazis came to power in Germany, Wilhelm Furtwaengler, conductor of the Berlin Philharmonic Orchestra, wrote to Dr. Paul Joseph Goebbels, Minister of Propaganda, in protest against the policy of discrimination against Jewish musicians. Dr. Goebbels replied at length, defending the Nazi position. (The correspondence in its entirety was published in the New York Times, *April 16, 1933, IV, 1-2.)*

IT is hardly any longer necessary to discuss the practical workings of the policy of the present German government in regard to music and musicians; the outside world has been kept closely in touch by its informants with developments in Germany, and whatever inaccuracies may have been reported involve only the details and not in any sense the essentials of those developments. The policies of the government have been proclaimed in quite unambiguous terms, as has the mélange of "ideas" which underlies them; in Berlin last spring one could often hear the opinion expressed by well-informed foreigners that a page from either one of the official Nazi organs, translated each day in the foreign newspapers, would prove a far more effective argument against the Nazis than any number of chronicles of terrorism.

From *Modern Music*, vol. 11, no. 1, pp. 3-12. Reprinted by permission of the League of Composers—International Society for Contemporary Music, U.S. Section, Inc.

The effect of the government's policy on cultural activities, too, is well-known. It has not been limited to the exclusion from musical activities of real or suspected Jews, pacifists, or so-called Marxists and *Kulturbolschevists*—a term which has been applied to practically all, if not all, those whose practice or even whose opinions are contrary to the wishes of the party in power at the moment. The storm of execration which burst from the already *gleichgeschaltete* musicians last spring against Thomas Mann for having used the expression "dilettante," in an extremely qualified sense, in connection with Wagner—their manifesto was signed even by Richard Strauss—may be taken as a slight indication of the lengths to which the conception of *Kulturbolschevismus* may be carried.

In practice, Germany has been deprived of such personalities as Walter, Klemperer, Schnabel, Busch, Schoenberg and dozens of others, whose offenses range from *Kulturbolschevismus* and "non-Aryan" descent to unorthodox opinions in regard to Wagner or Beethoven or merely to personal affiliations of an unorthodox nature. In one case a singer was consistently baited by the Nazi press because, herself a Czechoslovakian, she dared to sing, in her native country, in a performance of Beethoven's Ninth Symphony in the Czech language. Such a classic as Mendelssohn's Violin Concerto has been banned from certain concert programs, not to mention modern works which, in the opinion of the present arbiters of such matters, depart from the true German tradition, while it is rumored that even Brahms' music has become suspect on account of a Jewish strain in his ancestry. In a survey of the theatrical situation made in private conversation with a well-known German conductor last April, the writer of this article was able to verify the fact that even at that time there was not a single opera house of importance in Germany which had not suffered severely through the loss of intendant, régisseur, or one or more of the leading conductors or singers. Other musicians, who had taken little or no interest in politics, found themselves in a position of the utmost and most painful moral uncertainty through being forced to come to terms with a set of conditions and standards entirely extraneous to those which had previously concerned them, as performers, composers, teachers, or critics, in the practice of their art. Musical education has been weakened, and the situation of the musicians affected made incomparably more difficult, by the denial to Jewish musicians even of licenses to engage in private teaching in their own homes; while discrimination on racial or political grounds in the matter of the payment of royalties and the fulfillment of contracts of all kinds has become increasingly general with the virtual cessation of legal protection for persons belonging to the affected classes.

These conditions which now prevail and which seem for some time likely to prevail in the country which has (together with its neighbor Austria) for the past two hundred years led the world in musical culture and activity, raise in a most intensely actual form the question of the relationship of music and of culture to nationality, race, and political and economic ideas in general. The following notes make no claim to originality nor exhaustiveness; they are simply the expression of an attitude which the writer believes to be true, and as true in this age as in any other. Their point of departure is an exchange of letters which took place on April 6th of this year between Wilhelm Furtwaengler and Reichsminister Dr. Goebbels, in which the latter, replying to Furtwaengler's protest against the exclusion of such personalities as Walter, Klemperer, and Reinhardt from the artistic life of Germany, defines the Nazi point of view in regard to German music and to art in general.

Furtwaengler's thesis may be summed up in the following quotation: "In so far as the struggle against Jewry is directed against those artists who, uprooted and destructive, seek to assert themselves through 'Kitsch' (i.e., bad taste, banality, sentimentalism), dry virtuosity, and the like, no one could take exception to it. The struggle against such elements and the spirit which they embody—a spirit which also has its representatives of Germanic blood—cannot be waged energetically or consistently enough. When the attack, however, comes to be directed against the true artist, it does not operate in the interest of the artistic life." To which Goebbels replies: "The task of art and the artist is not only to bring diverse elements together (*verbinden*); it is, far more, to give form and shape, to remove what is diseased, and to create a free channel for what is healthy. For this reason I, as a German political man, cannot recognize only the one line of demarcation which you would establish: that between good and bad art. Art must not only be good; it must be conditioned by the needs of the people—or, to put it better, only an art which springs from the integral soul of the people can in the end be good and have meaning for the people for whom it was created. Art in an absolute sense, as liberal Democracy knows it, has no right to exist. Any attempt to further such an art would in the end cause the people to lose its inner relationship to art, and the artist to isolate himself from the moving forces of his time, shut away in the airless chambers of 'art for art's sake.' Art must be good; but beyond that must be conscious of its responsibility, competent, close to the people, and combative in spirit.

"I admit gladly that art is not in any condition to be made the object of further experimentation.

"It would, however, have been fitting to protest against artistic experiments at a time when the artistic life of Germany was governed almost exclusively by the experimentalism of elements foreign to our people and our race, and when therefore the prestige of German art was discredited and compromised before the whole world. . . .

". . . it is my opinion that the way to unhampered activity should be freely opened to every true artist.

"But—as you yourself say—he must in that case be a constructive, creative personality, and may not range himself on the other side—that of the elements which you

274

yourself decry as rootless and destructive, levelling and dis-
integrating in tendency, and for the most part grounded in
a merely technical proficiency. . . .

". . . Artists of real ability, whose extra-artistic influence
does not conflict with the fundamental standards of state,
politics, and society, will, in the future as always in the
past, receive from us the warmest encouragement and support. . . ."

It is difficult not to agree to a large extent with the letter,
at least, of much that Dr. Goebbels says in his definition of
"good art." Such considerations as he implies in his elaboration of the words *volksmässig* and *volksnahe* would seem
to be fundamental to any such definition. Who would deny
that art must have vitality, as well as perfection, originality,
or any other of the current criteria? Indeed the whole
essence of artistic form is the intensity of the artist's creative
vision, and such a vision cannot grow and develop in isolation, in the dusty atmosphere of esoterism and of theory,
either conventional or "radical." Art must certainly be "near
to the people," but in the sense that it must be rooted in
the soil, and in the deepest human impulses that spring from
man's contact with the soil and with other human beings;
in the sense that the complete development of a personality,
and therefore of the art into which it pours itself, cannot
take place in a void, and that the richness of a personality
is to be measured not so much by the variety as by the
depth and warmth of the contacts which nourish it. Like
every other living thing, it may and indeed must grow far
out of the specific range of its roots, but as soon as it ceases
to be nourished by them it will inevitably begin to wither
and to die.

To say this, however, is very different from saying that
art must subject itself to the momentary passions or whims
of whatever modern demagogues may choose to call the
"people." The artist, like any other complete human being,

must remain autonomous, at least in relation to his art, and in his highest development is at least as much a leader, in the deepest sense of the word, as is the political man. This is of course the reason why modern political men of the type of the Nazi leaders, whose power must ultimately rest on their ability artificially to stimulate and direct or even to manufacture popular passions, concern themselves inevitably with art and with culture in general. In its essence art reveals the inner nature of life and of men, and must thence be eternally opposed to those who are trying to force human impulses into purely interested channels. That art may sometimes be inspired by enthusiasm for a cause may be readily admitted, just as it may be inspired by any really profound feeling whatever. But when it remains on the level of an organ or reflection of popular prejudice, the artist has "made the great refusal" and abrogated his responsibility as a man and therefore as an artist as well.

Dr. Goebbels also insists that art be "combative in tendency" (*kämpferisch*), thus espousing the much mooted conception of art as propaganda. He also implies that what is "close to the people" (*volksnahe*) will also of necessity be *kämpferisch*, as if the ultimate interests of any people lay in the theories and slogans which their leaders impose upon them.

It is true that art is the product of intense feeling; it is also true that art—bad as well as good art—reflects in large measure the personality, and therefore the multifold background of the personality that produces it. But the impulse to create has nothing whatever to do with the impulse to proselytize: it is far more elementary and far more direct. The conception of art as propaganda appeals either to the type of artist who is so childlike as to be incapable of self-analysis, or to minds so academic, sterile, and tortuous as to be incapable of any but purely interested reactions. Propaganda is inevitably self-conscious, secondary—while art, if it is genuine, is from its very nature primary and spontaneous, and this will be found to be true even in the case of living works of art which have an apparently "propagandistic" coloring. It is the vivacity and completeness of the artist's vision, and not his subject-matter, that give a work of art both its character and its significance.

It is true, of course, that the vision of the artist develops only through contact with the world and experience of its offerings. If *l'art pour l'art* means the isolation of the artist it is quite as sterile as Dr. Goebbels maintains. But propaganda does not offer the only, nor the principal, point of contact with his environment possible to the individual, nor the only—or the most essential or infectious—means of communication.

The strictures of both Herr Furtwaengler and Dr. Goebbels on "experimentalism" should need no qualification, did not the actual performances of the present German régime give one cause to doubt either their sincerity or the clarity of the definitions behind them.

Without doubt, art is not produced in laboratories, and is not genuine except when it proceeds from a living impulse. The conscious effort to produce novelty as such, at all cost, is, as the years immediately preceding and following the war should have proven, a sterile one and one which has nothing to do with the demands of a living personality. It springs rather from impotence, disorientation, and fundamental embarrassment, as does indeed every purely self-conscious approach to art. The truly creative artist is guided only by the necessities of his inner vision and is really creating only when he feels himself possessed by it. When the artist ceases to feel these necessities and be guided by them, then art will have ceased to exist. It is hardly necessary to add that he is thus often inevitably led to means of expression which are unfamiliar and which to the superficial observer may look like experimentalism; but it cannot be too often emphasized that here the impulse, the psychological process, is entirely different from a self-conscious effort to produce novelty for its own sake.

But just as experimentalism is never the ally of art, neither is it hostile to art. It belongs, purely and simply, in a different category, and is useless rather than harmful. It may for the time being confuse standards of judgment, as indeed it has done, but this danger can be met only by the production of living and healthy works of art, by opposing something positive and living to all that is dry and negative, and hence born dead.

If one cares for historical generalizations, one may perhaps legitimately feel that the wide prevalence of experimentalism is a sign of decadence. So is perhaps the prevalence of criticism, of *Kunstforschung*, and kindred approaches to art. Gibbon reflected this feeling when he wrote, in connection with third century Rome, "a crowd of critics, commentators, and compilers darkened the face of learning." But true productiveness is not to be legislated into—nor sterility out of—existence; and furthermore one cannot always be sure that those who emphasize a campaign against "experimentalism" will distinguish over-nicely between what proceeds from a drily experimental attitude and that which springs from a truly creative one—especially since the latter is far more powerful and far more "dangerous." It is obvious that those now in power in Germany have not made the beginnings of such a distinction. And truly creative power, when it exists, never needs to be on the defensive, or to achieve success by means outside itself.

It may be added that the "experimental period" which Dr. Goebbels pictures as having injured the credit of German art abroad has been, on the contrary, precisely one in which the outside world has turned with deep interest to German achievements in many fields of art. Whatever one's opinions of many of these achievements may be, or whatever their ultimate value, it should be obvious to anyone that Germany's cultural prestige has been raised and not lowered by them. The same can hardly be said of the contemporary productions which have thus far been given the stamp of official approval by the National Socialist government.

Dr. Goebbels' strictures against *volks- und rassenfremde Elementen* are of course directed primarily against the Jews; taken in this sense it could be met with a list of names whose service to German culture is unquestionable, and was indeed unquestioned till a short time ago. It is hardly necessary to repeat them here. There is also, however, the oft-mooted question of foreign influence in art. A truly creative period worries little about such influences; for a relatively sterile one their danger lies not in the fact that they are foreign, but is rather that they are likely to remain superficial and half-digested.

Handel and Chopin were both profoundly influenced by Italian music, but no one would attempt to deny the German nature of Handel's art, while the Slavic nature of Chopin's is almost proverbial. These composers in other words succeeded in making the "foreign" traits present in their works entirely their own—so much so, in these cases, that they tower far above their models in a way to recall Emerson's saying, apropos of Shakespeare, "The greatest genius is the most indebted man."

An artificial shutting off of "foreign contacts" will not therefore necessarily deepen the indigenous ones, nor will it give roots to those who have not got them. If a healthy art cannot absorb "foreign elements" it will throw them off spontaneously, and without external and self-conscious pressure.

It is hardly necessary to point out that Dr. Goebbels' letter contains other elements and raises other considerations than those of a purely musical nationalism. It is interesting,

for instance, to note the cleverly graded crescendo of qualification applied to the term "true artist" in the last three
paragraphs quoted. To the qualifications, taken literally as
principles, it is difficult to take exception. That only good
artists deserve encouragement most people would agree. It
is also fairly generally admitted that a state has the right to
protect itself. Nevertheless it is a rather striking fact that
the highest cultures of the past have been those in which
the artist has enjoyed a very large measure of freedom of
imagination and expression and the possibility of a rich and
varied life, unhampered by the constant pressure of political
or other dogma and theory. One thinks readily of the
Athenian and Florentine republics, and if the musical florescence of eighteenth-century Vienna may seem to be an
exception, it is as well to remember that music was not in
those days regarded as potentially dangerous to any national or political idea.

In critically examining any program which has to do
with "cultural defense" it is necessary to raise first of all
the question as to what culture it is that is being defended,
secondly as to the forces against which it is defending itself.
In the case of present-day Germany these questions hardly
bear examination. The German musical tradition that is being so assiduously "defended" is apparently that of the middle and late nineteenth century; indeed, it seems at times as
if it were, more specifically, precisely those elements of German music which seem most circumscribed by the limits of
time and place that the directors of German cultural policy
now desire to nurture and perpetuate. As a writer in a
Königsberg paper explained a few months ago in discussing
the importance of Hans Pfitzner for the "new" Germany,
"The best part of German music is its Romantic period."
It is Wagner, not Bach or Mozart, who is the spiritual father
of the National Socialist musical ideal; only one of several
Wagners, moreover, and that the most purely subjective,
visionary, and barbaric one. Beethoven is conceived according to the Wagnerian tradition as the foreshadower of

Wagner rather than as the heir of Mozart and Haydn. The Nazi movement, then, is, from a musical standpoint, the victory of a distorted Wagnerism; its spiritual "enemies" include whatever fresh impulses have been alive in the world since Wagner's time.

The above considerations do not, of course, apply to Germany alone; nor are the policies which are now being carried out there the exclusive property of the National Socialist party. They constitute, in fact, the basis of polemics, slogans, and theories which are being everywhere increasingly resorted to by advocates of one or another extremist solution of our contemporary distresses. It would be well for those who have adopted the view of art as a function of the political state, whatever form that state may assume, to reexamine their theoretical position in the light of the abuses attendant on its practical realization in Germany— abuses which are inherent in such a program and are not merely of a temporary and tangible nature, but in the deepest sense destructive of the integrity of the artist and of the art which he serves.

Vienna—Vale, Ave
[1938]

In March 1938 German troops occupied Austria and Hitler proclaimed the Anschluss, uniting that country with the Third Reich. These events and their tragic consequences occasioned the following letter to the Editor of Modern Music. *It is dated May 1, 1938.*

O NE evening last month I heard, for the first time in nearly ten years, *Die Zauberflöte*. My feelings, as I listened, were inevitably colored by the world events of the preceding week, and took on an almost intolerable poignancy from my awareness of all that these events mean, both as concrete facts and as symptoms for the present and the future of music. Not unnaturally, my first thoughts were connected with the incomparable music to which I was listening. The performance was an amateur one, for which its participants would be the last to claim more than a relative adequacy. I had heard, to be sure, performances before which, though far more pretentious, were perhaps less satisfactory. This one, at all events, brought back to my mind so many unforgettable experiences in the city where *Die Zauberflöte* was born, where the music of Mozart, like that of few others, even among the "Viennese" composers, seemed so much a part of the air one breathed, so completely an embodiment of all that Vienna gave, or aspired to give to the world. I asked myself if this work should ever again be truly understood; I found myself dwelling with perhaps pardonable exaggeration on the, so to speak, accidental and circumscribed by-products of an

From *Modern Music*, vol. 15, no. 4, pp. 203-208. Reprinted by permission of the League of Composers—International Society for Contemporary Music, U.S. Section, Inc.

art which in its deepest essentials is limited only by the limitations of humanity itself, and growing perhaps unduly wistful over certain aspects of the tragedy, which is at the same time both far more intimate and more appalling in its immediate aspects, and far less irrevocable in its more distant and profound ones, than that which my fantasies of that evening chose to envisage and to contemplate.

Yet the latter, too, is not without its reality and its pertinence. Awareness of the intimate tragedy of Vienna is accessible to us all through the reports of the newspapers, through eye-witnesses, and through the many individual cases of which we happen to have direct knowledge. Though it has been more terrifying, in its suddenness, in its violence, and in the value of all that has been destroyed, it is only in detail and degree different from that of many another city in Europe, in Asia, and even, here and there, nearer home. It has, however, an obvious and inescapable significance for the musician; in spite of the fact that the masterpieces of music, unlike those of painting and sculpture and architecture, are not localized in space, it is still true that for at least one hundred and fifty years Vienna was, for us musicians, a symbolic counterpart of all that Florence or Athens represented in other fields of culture.

First of all, it was here that during those years the greatest masters lived and worked, and that their memories, intimately associated with a thousand backgrounds, remained vivid and intense. From Mozart and Haydn through Beethoven, Schubert, and Brahms, to (let us for once ignore petty qualifications and admit a juxtaposition, the limitations of which we perfectly well know) Schoenberg, Webern and Berg; when one thinks of these and the many other names which I have omitted, one wonders not only at how few of the truly great names are absent, but perhaps above all at the variety, the vastness, and the depth of invention and expression which it includes. Here the greatest composers grew and were nourished by the richest blend of European spiritual streams; not only north and south, but many elements also from the east, met in Vienna and combined to form a musical tradition which was genuinely European and therefore genuinely human.

It is of course the earlier composers that I have in mind as I write this. The art of Mozart, Beethoven, Schubert and their contemporaries, speaks, with an unfaltering voice, for the whole Western world, and covers this world completely. It is true also that later in the century, music, like European culture in general, tended gradually to disperse itself. Music became, as we all know, more and more local and in the deepest sense provincial—no longer European, but German and French and Italian, and even Bohemian and Hungarian and Russian—even Finnish and Rumanian and Yugoslavian. Nietzsche pointed out some fifty odd years ago that Schumann, already, and first among the great German composers, was no longer a European but purely a German event.

In contemplating the tragedy of Vienna, therefore, we are forced to ask ourselves, what, in such a world, Vienna had become. You asked me for an article on the *Götterdämmerung*; and perhaps it might even seem a little inopportune to question what, with the "gods" or their successors scattered here and there over the European landscape, actually remains in Valhalla. Was the music of latter day Vienna not, after all, simply one among many provincialisms, and even the least fresh and attractive among these? Is it not true that twentieth-century Viennese music—and I mean not only musical production but the whole of Viennese musical activity—was more than that of any other place haunted and overawed, to the point of paralysis, by the stubbornly exacting ghosts of its own great past, of which the consciousness seems never absent, least of all even in the work of those who sought to rebel against it?

It seems to me however that this is a very shallow, or at least an impossibly incomplete view of what Vienna was, and of what we now feel may have been irrevocably lost. For whatever the eventual judgment may be of the last phase of pre-Hitlerian Vienna, it is certain that its influence was an inestimable and quite irreplaceable one. For long after Vienna ceased to be the external center of musical activity, she kept her character in a very true sense as the most intense spiritual center of the musical world. Her musicians through their spiritual aristocracy, their seriousness, their integrity and their disdain for any but the highest conceptions of art, set a standard which was true to the example and tradition of their great predecessors, and one which must easily put to shame any similar group in any other land. They supported the rôle of a kind of conscience of the contemporary composer, even a kind of touchstone by which he might judge himself, not so much as a creative force but as a fully mature, completely integrated personality. For these musicians probed more deeply —even though one utterly disagreed with the method and the result of their probing—into the problems and dilemmas of the contemporary musical soul than any other group. Even their tragedy, if one choose to regard it as such, is not that of having probed unsuccessfully so much as of having been so placed, in time and space, that such probing was inevitable and therefore necessary for them. For my part I cannot consider it as a tragedy, even though I have often expressed myself as being of a quite different mind from theirs. At the very least it is a vital and inescapable part of the leavening process out of which music must and will continue to be born. Possibly it is more than that.

So it is Vienna as the center of all this that belongs now so definitively to the past—not because of the personalities that have been thrust out, since after all the exodus began long before this last March, so much as because the whole aim of the totalitarian state is to destroy the integrity of the individual and the spirit of truth and of disinterested effort on which integrity depends. This, infinitely more than anti-Semitism, imperialism, or reaction, is the real menace of Fascism—its implacable hostility to everything toward which Western civilized man, pagan or Christian, has striven in the last three thousand years. It is this spirit to which the living artist, even more than other men, must remain mortally hostile, since, whether he be aware of it or not, it strikes at the foundations on which all spiritual activity rests, and which have never before been seriously threatened. Unfortunately the menace is by no means confined to Germany or even to adherents, national or otherwise, of the totalitarian creed. It is rather a malignant and ubiquitous infection to which the whole contemporary world is dangerously exposed.

You will see that what I have tried to outline has none of the tempting Wagnerian contours of a *Götterdämmerung*. I have not a moment's doubt that the destruction of musical life and tradition in Vienna is final and complete; my experiences and observations in Germany during the first half of 1933 showed me how speedily and how effectively the wreckers do their job. And let us never forget that in Vienna it did not begin only this year. But what is lost to Vienna is not necessarily lost to the world. As far as I know, the outstanding figures in Viennese music are all of them still living and presumably will still be able to function. But unless their tradition—so important to music's future—is to die a completely barren death with them, it must find organic and revitalizing growth elsewhere.

That this will take place is perhaps far from certain; but I believe it is quite clear that if music is to have a future, it lies in the United States. Most European musicians, I believe, are coming to realize this, and many of them are coming to join us in a spirit of genuine collaboration and constructive action in building gradually a real and profound musical tradition on our side. Europe's loss is therefore America's gain, and, I may add, America's responsibility. Let us not forget the numberless instances in the past where such an infusion has taken place, and a tradition been, as it were, transferred from one locality to another.

As far as I am concerned I welcome it from the bottom of my heart. The American musician will rapidly cease to be an isolated figure, both forced, as it were, and enabled, to retire behind a wall of protective isolation; he will meet his European colleagues on equal ground, standing or falling by virtue of his achievements alone. I am sure you hope, as I do, that we will prove equal to our opportunities, though I have my moments of feeling that it is almost too much to hope. At all events profound changes will have to take place. The American composer above all, must learn to take a more mature and serious attitude towards his art and abandon the postures which, as we all secretly know, have offered such convenient havens of refuge up to this time. You realize, of course, that I am not speaking of a few outstanding and ripened personalities, but of a bewildered and groping "rank and file." The postures of which I speak are familiar enough—they take the form of feebly conceived artificial and quasi-academic standards, before the fact and beside the point, of the pseudo-provincial dilettantism of the "typically American style," of self-conscious conceptions both of form and content, quite unnecessary to enumerate. Above all American composers will have to abandon resolutely chimerical hopes of success in a world dominated overwhelmingly by "stars," by mechanized popular music, and by the box-office standard, and set themselves to discovering what they truly have to say, and to saying it in the manner of the adult artist delivering his message to those who have ears to hear it. All else is childishness and futility —and unquestionably the moment has arrived when a real choice cannot be postponed much longer. It is our opportunity, and our responsibility, to carry on.

On the American Future
[1940]

Like the preceding essay, this one appeared as
a letter to the Editor of Modern Music. It is
not dated, but it was written during the first
months of the war in Europe.

THE piece for which you have asked this time takes me
back to the letter which I addressed to you a year ago
last spring, when Hitler marched into Vienna. It takes shape
as a sort of companion piece, since its subject is so nearly
related. Since that time the totalitarian flood has gathered
momentum and is now far more widespread, more powerful, and infinitely more threatening. In spite of the wars
which are being waged against Germany, Russia, and Japan,
it seems likely if not certain to spread still further before
it is finally crushed. For all of us, and for our children, life
has suddenly become problematical—even in the United
States. The luxury which we could at that time allow ourselves, of genuine optimism regarding the survival, at least
in this country, of the values which totalitarianism aims to
destroy, has dwindled to a somewhat grim hope—not a for-
lorn hope, certainly, but one which can be maintained and
realized only at the price of intense and ceaseless struggle.
It has become fairly evident, too, that if these values are to
prevail—and prevalence means always constant, creative renewal, not merely conservation which is bound to fail—
then initiative and leadership must come largely from this
part of the world. Europe's agony is but one phase of a
much vaster situation in which we, too, are involved, and
in which ours may very easily be the last word. In any

From *Modern Music*, vol. 17, no. 2, pp. 71-75. Reprinted by permission of the League of Composers—International Society for Contemporary Music, U.S. Section, Inc.

event the final responsibility will in all probability be presented to America, to accept or reject: whether or not the basic human liberties, envisaged by the men who created America, shall become securely established in the world. This is the real issue at stake today; around it all the economic and political problems, however urgent, group themselves with reasonably clear logic.

Unhappily, this issue has not yet been thoroughly faced. Totalitarianism has won its victories, and still continues to win them, as a result of the cowardice, the short-sighted greed, and above all the mental and moral confusion of its enemies. Under the stress of war and possible danger, this confusion seems greater, at times, than ever. We see and feel every day the temptation to grasp at dubious straws, to contract strange and dangerous alliances, and above all to risk refuge from sheer fatigue and lack of staying-power in the delusions of isolationism, together with the many convenient fictions which enable us to forget, for a little while longer, the real but not yet inexorable demands of the situation. Very often this takes the form of a reconditioning of older escapist attitudes; it brings with it the real danger of fixing more firmly attitudes and complexes which should normally be outgrown.

It is for this reason that I feel genuinely concerned over the present trend towards nationalism and cultural isolationism among American musicians. This tendency is nothing new; I used to be aware of it twenty-five years ago when, as the extremely youthful editor of a short-lived Harvard undergraduate publication, I occasionally tilted with it. Today, however, it is becoming a very real problem. A certain number of our musicians, together with a not negligible part of our musical press, is demanding with a voice quite reminiscent of various totalitarian phrases which we have heard, that music which shall "express the national feeling," "reflect the American scene," "establish an American style"—as if these were in any sense measurable or specific quantities, or as if they were in any sense criteria or even basic ingredients of musical quality. We hear frequent statements to the effect that "European music is played out," that "American composers are doing in every way better work than their European contemporaries." I was asked recently at a Forum-Laboratory "question period" if I did not think that American music is in an improved "strategic position" as a result of the war—as if American music were in some sense embattled against "European music" and as if the present situation in Europe represented in some way a victory for the American cause. Why, one might well ask, drag in Europe at all? What has the state of music in Europe to do with the achievements of American composers? One sees, finally, a none too clearly expressed, but none the less unmistakable hostility to the "foreign" musicians who have settled here during the last few years—as if (and here I hope I may be forgiven for speaking with the authority of one whose American ancestry has been "uncorrupted" by "immigrant" blood since the early seventeenth century) the very essence of Americanism were not the coming together, on our soil, of a thousand different elements, united by the single bond of a common love of liberty, so often the result of exile from lands where life had for some reason become intolerable. One of our recently acquired compatriots has defined an American as a man who was himself unhappy in his native land, or who possessed forebears who were unhappy in theirs.

The tendencies which I have enumerated are of course quasi-fascist attitudes—*Blut und Boden!*—but they are dangerous for other reasons as well. First of all because they reveal and tend to perpetuate through cultivation, a lack of inner security on the part of American musicians which is the greatest possible obstacle to healthy creation. The demand for "national" art is fundamentally a defensive attitude, the reflex action of a pervasive inferiority complex. If American composers tend to think of musical life in terms of competition, it is not merely a quite false analogy taken over from the business world, but a sign of their own self-con-

sciousness which may make them think of musical development in egocentric terms rather than in terms of music itself.
If they are self-conscious and hypersensitive with respect to
"European" music it is only to a very small extent because of
real or fancied slights which have been dealt them in the
name of European tradition; for these would prove largely
quite illusory and in any case quite negligible if they had
really found themselves and were primarily absorbed in
their own creative impulses. But just as the valetudinarian
frequently becomes, through excessive preoccupation with
his health, the victim of his own hypochondria, the artist
who is excessively afraid of "influences" or insistent on the
purity of his origins tends to wither from lack of nourishment. A consciously "national" style, in any field, inevitably
becomes a picturesque mannerism, a kind of trade-mark,
devoid of significant human content irremediably outmoded
the moment its novelty has gone. Of the Russian "Five"
how much music remains in the vital repertory? And in the
music of Moussorgsky himself is it not precisely what is
most specifically "Russian" which has aged most quickly?
How much remains of the French "school" which throve
with such apparent luxuriance as a spiritual result of the
disaster of 1870, in seeming unawareness that Chopin and
Berlioz and Bizet were also Frenchmen though quite un-
preoccupied with the idea of a "national" style?

For vital music is characterized far less by the somewhat
academic purity than by the range and depth of its expression; great composers have been so by virtue of influences
absorbed and transcended, not through scrupulous avoidance
of contagion or through self-conscious direction of their
impulses into channels "national" or otherwise. They have
expressed themselves, in other words, as men, and have not
scrupled to draw their nourishment from all promising
sources, since it would never have occurred to them to
question their own digestive capacities.

My second cause for concern is that the nationalistic attitude tends to remove composers, through the artificial

isolation which they thereby assume, from the realities of their art, since it is indeed to a considerable extent a pretext for escape from those realities. Especially in a country like ours, in which development has been inevitably so rapid, there is always the danger of superficiality; and the establishment of specialized critera leads all too easily to a neglect of the fundamental requirements of the art. Hence in asking that music be American we almost inevitably neglect to demand that it be music—that it spring from a genuine and mature impulse on the part of the composer and be more than simply a more or less promising attempt. I am not speaking here of technical inadequacy but of the half-baked quality, the undefinitiveness, which we so often tend to mistake for vitality. No amount of "technical" proficiency can compensate for a lack of the basic spiritual discipline which alone can produce a mature artist. Composers, to be sure, are born, not made. But once born, they must grow; and far more composers are born than ever come to real fruition. "Talent" and "promise" are exceedingly common, and one need not be unduly impressed by them when they so often remain at that primitive stage. They can never get past that stage unless artists demand of themselves something more than provincialism.

For nationalistic criteria are in the last analysis quite unreal. I do not really believe that our advocates of "American" music would be seriously content with a picturesque folklore or with the musical reproduction, either specific or general, of American scenes or landscapes—we are quite adequately supplied with these in our popular music and various other manifestations. A nation is something far greater than that—it is rather the sum of a great many efforts towards goals which are essentially human and not parochial. It gains much of its character, no doubt, from the conditions of time and space under which those efforts are made. But it is the efforts and the goals which are really essential. So how on earth can we demand in advance qualities which can reveal themselves only gradually, in works, the products of clear artistic vision? It is such works which, if and when they come into existence, will reveal America to us, not as the mirror of things already discovered, but as a constantly renewed and fresh experience of the realities which music alone can reveal. It seems to me so clear that this was the real achievement of the great music of the past. Bach and Mozart and Beethoven did not *reflect* Germany, they helped to create it; they brought in each instance new and unexpected, but essential, materials to its construction. And only after the picture had really begun to take clear shape, through the influence of their finished work, was it possible to point with some certainty to specifically German characteristics in their art. It is not, moreover, as "German" composers that we value them, but rather we value Germany because of them, as creators of immortal music. What is "German" in their works and that of their lesser colleagues is purely incidental, an inevitable but unimportant by-product of music that is real and complete. So what we must ask of our composers is not "American music," but something much more exacting and at the same time essentially simpler—*music* in the only real sense of the word—music, that is, which is deeply and completely conceived, the product of a mature vision of life.

I have said nothing about my recently acquired colleagues or of the "problems" which some American musicians feel they have brought to our shores. You will understand, I am sure, why I have not done so; it would be inconsistent with my whole mode of thought were I to regard them as anything but welcome collaborators. It would seem to me, in fact, inconsistent with everything which I have been taught to regard as American, besides involving subtle distinctions of priority for which I have certainly no taste. I believe we need them and the contributions which they have for us in the crisis which we are now, I hope, gradually learning to face. Any other attitude would be not only repulsive but unthinkable; and I believe that the truly representative musicians of America will eventually feel as I do, if indeed they do not do so already.

Certainly we, too, will create a "tradition" if civilization is saved, and if we really wholeheartedly desire it. It will come, not through cultural isolationism or consciously nurtured "Americanism" but through men who, having listened to the music which sings within them, are willing to let themselves be guided by it, wherever it may lead them. Such music, and only such music, will be truly and profoundly American.

American Music and the Crisis
[1941]

A third letter to the Editor of Modern Music.
*It is not dated, but it was written during the
early part of 1941, before the United States
entered the war.*

THE request that I write "an appeal to reason" invokes
in me the feeling that I should, perhaps, offer something
other than has been asked for. The question of musical nationalism is of course paramount; it constantly comes forward in a time of crisis and in many forms even as applied
to music. But after all is it "reason" which is fundamentally
involved? Reason is impossible without premises, and in
most of the discussions which take place today it is our
premises that are insufficiently considered. I am perhaps
being very blunt, or very arrogant, in calling for an appeal
not so much to reason as to reality, if you like, to facts.
Nothing less, however, seems likely to lead to anything but
wishful thinking and confusion.

Then again, I have a little the feeling that I am writing
primarily not about music at all, but about National Defense. For inevitably any thoughts which one may have
about American music, about the conditions which prevail
in American musical life, and above all, of course, about the
relation of both to American national feeling, must lead to
the general question of the crisis in which we find ourselves,
our inner preparation to meet this crisis, and the possible
future of our country, once the crisis is past. To pretend,
as some still do, that no serious crisis exists, is of course
fantastic. But it seems to me equally fantastic to persuade

From *Modern Music*, vol. 18, no. 4, pp. 211-217. Reprinted by
permission of the League of Composers—International Society for
Contemporary Music, U.S. Section, Inc.

ourselves that we are at the present time meeting it adequately, either in its external or its inner aspects. It is of course not for me to write here on Defense Production, Aid to England and China, or the grand strategy of American Defense. Music has nothing to do with these things, nor can a musician as such contribute much to them except his voice as a citizen of a still democratic country.

But if anything should be obvious, it is the fact that the crisis is above all an inner one. It is a commonplace, of course, though as generally stated an inaccurate one, that the present struggle is a "world revolution." The inaccuracy derives from the fact that neither are the revolutionary issues often stated very clearly, nor is the challenge of "Fascism" (I insist that H. G. Wells is right in refusing to admit any such thing as a Fascist "ideology") even recognized, let alone squarely faced. In many quarters, to regard Fascism as a challenge is to find oneself immediately dubbed a Fascist.

Yet is it not plain that Fascism, far from being a doctrine or even a "movement" in the usual sense, is simply the uprush of the more ruthless and resentful elements into a void which has been created in modern society by the prevalence of nihilistic cynicism, by economic, intellectual, and moral disorder, and by a crassly competitive spirit in human relationships? To insist that Democracy and Freedom can prevail only if we rediscover and make effective our democratic convictions, our sense of social responsibility, and a greater spirit of cooperation, is neither Fascist nor defeatist —nor is it compatible with an unwillingness to resist Fascism also from without, in spite of Messrs. Thomas and Hutchins[1] and others who like them seem to be doing their best, in their several roles, to repeat here the exact German pattern. Unfortunately we are obliged to fight on at least two fronts, and failure on either the one or the other means inevitable disaster.

What has all this, one may ask, to do with music?—espe-

[1] Norman Thomas and Robert Maynard Hutchins, who were articulate "isolationists" before the United States entered the war.

cially with contemporary American "serious music"? For, while we admit that great art in the past has often helped to build a national spirit, American music has certainly not yet begun to play any such role.

Yet if my diagnosis of the Fascist challenge is correct, our musical problems are wholly relevant to all that I have said. For while I do not believe that building a national spirit is the main function of great art, it has certainly always been one of its by-products; and the failure of existing art to achieve that effect is almost certainly a symptom of the inner problems which the country faces.

In our case many of these problems are certainly due to the organization of our musical life. For the latter has become a vast and complex profit-making structure, which has literally no relationship to the creative composer. That this has happened is, of course, nobody's fault—not that of managers, critics, or musicians, or of that perennial scapegoat, the public. It is rather the result of forces in our society that lie entirely outside the artistic sphere, and can only be understood or dealt with in terms of those forces.

But the situation bears, certainly, all the earmarks of an *impasse*. Consider only one of its implications, in the light of the present crisis. Our musical life is built largely around "stars"—that is, around personalities whose musical achievements may be very great but whose position rests certainly upon other factors as well. The glamor of the stars is enhanced by a tendency to what may be called an "economy of scarcity" in this connection. Manifestly, the fewer the stars, the brighter they shine; and, partly because of the need to attract as great a multitude as possible—partly also because the supply of potential stars is far greater than the number of available places in the galaxy—the distance between the stars and their nearest competitors tends to become ever greater. Hence an enormous waste of talent, and, above all, since stardom is based, except in the rarest cases, on established reputation, an ever-increasing diminution of opportunities for younger artists to penetrate the charmed circle, or even to survive. I often wonder where the conductor will be found who will be capable of leading the Philharmonic Orchestra in, say, 1960, and how, if the present trend should continue, artistic standards can possibly be maintained. The remedy, of course, can only come through far-reaching reorientations, in the direction, I should say, of decentralization and, if I may coin the word, deglamorization. But that, of course, is not my story here.

The composer, however, is placed by this state of affairs in a serious dilemma. Either he will come to terms with it, or he will be obliged to find some kind of *modus vivendi* outside the system, and without regard to it. He will either accept its standards—those of "success" measured in terms of practical and immediate sales value—and try to conform to them; or else he will pursue a more independent course, one which does not bind him to the system in any way. Naturally I am over-simplifying. Each course of action which I have suggested contains many gradations of possibility, as may be readily seen in the careers of our various composers.

Both courses, however, have their dangers; and it is these that I think we should face clearly, in order really to appreciate the problems facing the composer today. I believe that any attempt on the part of the composer to come to terms with present conditions is bound to prove, in the end, a losing fight, and for very simple reasons. First of all he is subjecting himself to standards which are by their very nature alien to him. It is all very well to preach the duty of the composer to write for a public; but this is successful only when one can assume a community of tastes between composer and public. It presupposes a state of culture and society, in other words, rather than a type of art—a culture that is both sure and conscious of its aspirations, which are shared generally among its members. In such a culture the creative artist is, so to speak, at one with his public, and expresses its aspirations because it expresses his own. But in such a society creative activity flourishes to such an extent that the commercial exploitation of art becomes irrelevant, and the conditions of which I have spoken become inconceivable.

Under present conditions, however, the relation of the public to music becomes inevitably a trivial one, since what exists is something very much like a planned rationing of musical sensations, in the interests of maximum profits. In times of economic plenty, the public is given a considerable proportion of novel sensation, in the effort to attract it, while in lean years the effort is inevitably to prevent it from shrinking beyond the danger point, with the result that caution and eclecticism become the rule. Our own twenties and thirties form unsurpassable examples of both states of affairs. The result however is that the *grand monde* of music satisfies the real aesthetic needs of no one, since its moving forces have little, fundamentally, to do with aesthetic necessities, but are primarily concerned with selling goods, with all the devices that salesmanship uses for that purpose. Since the nature of the goods in question makes public consumption far more profitable than private consumption, it is inevitable that a high degree of standardization must be the result; and standardization thus becomes the contemporary substitute for the real community of spirit that existed between the eighteenth-century Viennese composer, or, later, the nineteenth-century Italian opera composer, and their respective publics—both smaller, by the way, than is often supposed.

The composer is thus faced by the impossibility of finding his public within himself, and any attempt to conform to the standard will therefore mean that he no longer demands the most of himself—already a literally insuperable obstacle in the way of worth-while achievement. To render his position the more hopeless, however, his work is inevitably compared with the greatest works of the past— works which had their origin not in an effort at conformity, but in a vital creative impulse which still glows in them. The result is obvious. It is true that some of our conformists have achieved a certain abstract reputation; but the public remains politely unresponsive to the actual music. In this respect they fare certainly no better, and in others certainly less well, than their bolder colleagues.

Yet the alternative course is also dangerous. Its dangers are not, I believe, inevitable; otherwise the situation would be indeed hopeless and the outlook desperate—not only, indeed, for music, since the conditions which I have described are general and in no way limited to the musical world alone. The dangers are fairly obvious. They are those of what I may call individual isolationism on the one hand, and, on the other, of a quasi-political, back-door conformism which accepts all of the premises which motivate the *grand monde*, rejecting only its commercialism and its genuine, if falsely applied, standards.

Of "individual isolationism" enough has been said, and the attitude is so comparatively rare by this time that it is hardly a danger now. The other attitude, however, is less rare and in fact quite popular in certain quarters; it is therefore worth analyzing a little, simply because it too is a blind alley. For it is based on the fallacy that "style," conceived in a purely materialistic sense, and external association form the real content of music, and that musical expression apart from them hardly exists. At least, though this is seldom expressed so crudely, it is clearly implied in the basic assumptions of such music—assumptions which find still clearer expression in the writings of some of our exponents of a music—not yet existent—that shall "reflect the American scene," or embody an "American idiom"—not yet discovered, at least by "serious" composers.

This of course raises the basic question as to what *is* genuinely American music—or, how can music be achieved which really represents us, as Americans? I am not satisfied with this manner of stating the question; and yet I think the true answer will nevertheless express the essential nature of my reservations. The question is not a peculiarly American one, and yet the answer is clearer, stated in terms of America, than it would be in the case of any other people.

For, after all, we are Americans not through a purely geographical accident, but through a profound faith in certain human principles which were affirmed as the basis on which our nation was founded; a faith which we have sometimes allowed to slacken grievously, but to which we always refer in times of stress. It is this faith above all which constitutes Americanism, and which has thus far made us stronger, not weaker, than other peoples. If we have at times tended to confuse equality with lack of discrmination, justice with unwillingness to face the facts of real evil, and freedom of conscience with competitive disorder, we have, to be sure, imperilled our democracy, but we have done so within a characteristically American pattern. We can avert that peril only if we are willing to rediscover once more the true meaning of those principles, and to build a social order that shall more adequately embody them. I believe we will do this, and do it successfully, if we will only become aware of the real threats which face us.

For, once more, these principles are the core of our national being. The Polish farmers who have revitalized the soil of my Connecticut Valley have learned to love that soil, just as I and my ancestors have done. But like my ancestors, and those of all of us, they were Americans already before this conversion had taken place, through their basic American faith.

This is one specific reason why I refuse to conceive of Americanism, in music or otherwise, in purely materialistic terms. It is not an American "idiom" that composers should seek, nor even a definitely American "content." For neither idiom nor content, in any genuine and significant sense, is achieved by any external means. They are not measurable quantities nor are they embodied in formulae of expression or in "subject matter." They become so only in the spurious sense, in what is essentially "applied art"—art which is no longer genuine expression but rather the imitation of expression, for purposes which have nothing to do with expression as such. Basically this implies a denial of expression —a denial that it is relevant to the purpose in hand. And if all art be relegated to this status, it is a denial of the human spirit itself which is involved.

Here is where the question of National Defense crops up again. For the kind of implicit pessimism which I have described is obviously inconsistent with the vision of an American future. It is true that the prevalence here of such conceptions of art is due not entirely to pessimism regarding the future creative potentialities of America, but in large part to a lack of education, especially among "educated" people, which leads them to think of all music as a kind of applied art which possesses what significance it has through sheer association. That is, of course, as fallacious as anything could be. It is not the forests of Finland which give the music of Sibelius any significance it may have, but rather the accents and gestures of Sibelius, the man, speaking on whatever subject happens to stir his imagination.

These are the reasons why I believe so profoundly that the problems of American music can and will be solved only by the simplest of attitudes on the part of American composers. First of all, they must abjure "success" as a goal and strive rather to be significant individuals instead. Do you remember the story of Alexander the Great who, after conquering Darius of Persia, ordered his followers to elect him a god? All, I believe, complied with his wishes except the Spartans, who stated the crux of the matter in saying, "When Alexander wishes to be a god, let him be a god!"

Secondly, they must become significant musicians instead of mere "talents." Of course you know I do not mean to imply that there are as yet no significant musicians among us already. It is only that we still tend, a little, to be over-impressed with "talent" in the raw, and to confuse mastery with academicism. As a matter of fact, what I mean by mastery is the very reverse of academicism, which is not mastery but slavishness, and essentially one of the commoner forms which incomplete development—or amateurishness—may take. But the composer needs, and if he is a mature composer will achieve, the resourceful command of musical materials which will enable his imagination to identify itself with these materials and to express itself fully through them.

Finally, they must learn to write music which is a genuine expression—music in which they are fully themselves, music which has been a real, important, and primary experience to them. Music so produced will vary in quality, as individuals vary; it will vary in style and form, with the immense variety of America itself. But it will embody the authentic accents and gestures of American individuals. And what other Americanism do we want, or can we demand, in our music?

No More Business-as-Usual
[1942]

Written shortly after the United States
entered the war.

B Y the time that these lines are written, most of us will
have become fully aware of the fact that the United
States is engaged in a desperate and prolonged struggle
which involves the ultimate conditions of our existence. It
is not true, certainly—or at least it is no longer true—that
the American people is "complacent," or unaware either, of
the magnitude of the task ahead of the nation, or of the
fundamental issues involved. Rather we are adjusting ourselves, not without many difficulties and even some inner
resistance, to the necessities, psychological and otherwise,
of total war. This adjustment is being made with extraordinary speed; and those of us who, like this writer, have been
apprehensive lest the war should not be fully enough understood, or who have been profoundly alarmed by the be-
havior of some of our public men, must nevertheless take
much heart at many signs, which they may see on every
hand, that the national will is firm, and that the American
people is not going to be misled for long by either the
traitors, the profiteers, or the cowards among us.

The above refers, of course, to the conditions of the
present moment; and the above-mentioned process of adjustment is that which the present very grave military situation demands. It is, in other words, in a certain sense a preliminary adjustment—an adjustment of mind and will. It is
basically a recognition of concrete and urgent perils and

From *Modern Music*, vol. 19, no. 3, pp. 156-162. Reprinted by
permission of the League of Composers—International Society for
Contemporary Music, U.S. Section, Inc.

tasks, and a gradually focusing determination to clear the way for the larger task of complete and effective victory.

One may well ask at this point what such considerations have to do specifically with music. Why in fact, does one discuss music at all, at such a moment?

Like every one of his colleagues the present writer has asked himself these and similar questions, and he must confess candidly that he has found the usual answers quite unsatisfactory. He does not, for instance, regard the activities of serious musicians today as having any very important connection with "morale," and he in fact has a strong objection to the word "morale" as belonging to a purely defensive and hence dangerous war psychology, and as being at the same time a profoundly undemocratic conception. Wars are won, not by "morale," but by people, possessed of guts and imagination.

It is also in his opinion childish, if not worse, to speak of "keeping alive the flame of culture" or any similarly disguised plea for artistic "business-as-usual." Culture, in so far as such an abstraction exists at all, is not "kept alive"; it either lives or dies. And if it survives this upheaval, in any form whatever, it will do so as a direct consequence of the spirit in which the war is waged and, above all, of the transformations which the effective conduct of the war demands and achieves.

Only on this level, it seems to me, should the question of musical activity in wartime be discussed, if it is to be discussed at all. For more than any other war of at least the last three hundred years—perhaps more than any in all history—the present conflict, total in extent as well as in depth, is basically a conflict in the human spirit. Its inception and its course have been determined not nearly so much by international or even ideological tensions as by basic weaknesses (or, if you like, conditions) in modern society and eventually in the structure of the modern individual spirit. Its winning, as the experience of the Russians, the Chinese, the Dutch, and the British has clearly shown, depends primarily on the total mobilization of the spiritual resources of the people—of their insight into the nature of the conflict, of their will to resist and to destroy and to produce, of their powers of endurance. In the absence of this, as recent events in particular have shown, even the "unlimited material resources" of which we and our allies boast are in serious danger of crumbling gradually but surely away under the blows of an intensively prepared enemy. For nothing is so obvious—it is, or should be, practically a truism by this time—as the fact that the most vulnerable points for the United Nations have been precisely those at which they have felt themselves most complacently secure.

If the serious artist, then, is to have a valid place in the urgent necessities of the present, he must find that place not as an entertainer, a professional propagandist, or a mere curator; but rather as one who, along with the millions of his fellow-countrymen, helps to achieve the transformation which these necessities demand, and, in his more specialized function as an artist, to make this transformation articulate and manifest.

For there is no doubt that transformations are required. A healthy will to victory demands, in every sphere of our life—spiritual as well as material—a resolute abandonment of "business-as-usual" and the cheerful adoption, whenever necessity demands it, of a pitiless "scorched earth" policy. Even many of those among us who have been most ardent in their hatred of tyranny and their support of anti-Fascist causes, have not completely understood this; and it is possible that each one of us has to struggle to some extent—consciously or otherwise—against the desire to preserve at all cost his own pet corner of a status quo—which, however, the very existence of the present crisis has proved to be not only rotten and corrupt but, still more accurately stated, *false* in so many of its basic premises.

For Fascism itself is only the logical conclusion, as it is certainly the result, of what one might all too easily regard as the dominating tendencies of our time. Its ultimate horror is not the fact that it is cruel beyond all conception but the fact that from beginning to end it is *phoney*. It is an almost inevitable product of a culture which contains so much that is phoney as does that of pre-war Europe and America. This fact—the core of the present situation—is the primary key to the understanding of the war; it is the key also to the contradictions and the embarrassments of American and of so much of Allied policy, which have led us directly to our present painful situation. In the United States, for example, one of our most serious inner problems is that created by those divided minds who wish certainly to defeat Hitler and the Japanese but who would like to include if possible in the defeat some of our Allies as well—the Russians, the British, "Labor," or Roosevelt, or any others whom they are determined to dislike.

But such confusion is an inevitable result of many phases of the contemporary spirit: for example, a spirit in public life which has identified values with the "business boom" and thus encouraged the belief that nothing is fundamentally serious except the type of material comfort furnished by the latest automobile model or the latest headache remedy; of a spirit in education that under the pretext of objectivity has aimed at strictly neutral *classification* and often quite irrelevant factual knowledge, while regarding with suspicion or even scorn the far more exacting problems of insight and discrimination; of a spirit in human relationships that regards "success" as the one worthwhile goal and which has even developed a prevalent and ubiquitous technique of success, based on a scientifically calculated art of misrepresentation and systematic obfuscation.

It is not simply that Fascism has, as has so often been pointed out, "used" these and other phases of modern life; rather a large part of its essence lies in the complete acceptance of all their implications and the logical and ruthless exclusion of all premises which still challenge them. In this sense, Fascism is something quite other, and even more sinister than the vehicle of sheer reaction which some people on both sides imagine it to be; and it is certainly quite other than the new economic and social principle which its adherents and even the more naïve of its opponents imagine. Rather it is the final enthronement, by terror and blood, of all that is spurious in contemporary life, and the attempt to make of spuriousness itself the basic principle of the future. Its essence is the principle of the *hoax*. It is in every respect a move away from Nature, not towards it.

For these reasons it is urgently necessary that everyone— the artist no more and no less than everyone else—examine candidly the shortcomings of the present state of society, as a preliminary step toward the achievement of a more honest and more human future. Let us leave aside for the moment the question of whether the United States is to "lead the world"—in culture or in anything else. At this moment the Russians, the Dutch, the Chinese, and the Filipinos are fighting superbly—as the British on occasion have also certainly done—and are carrying the main brunt of Allied war effort. The British and ourselves have made costly mistakes and even been guilty of spectacular cases of almost criminal neglect. No doubt we, too, will, long before the war ends, be "all out" in our efforts and our sacrifices; but until that time it is not only futile but ungallant to talk of world leadership—on the other hand we will not yet be even winning.

Nevertheless, we have our responsibilities, which we must fulfill, or perish; responsibilities which go with our immense power, but which ever since the end of the last war we have tried to dodge and to postpone. It is quite impossible however for us to live as a nation any longer, in the vague world of future potentialities. Our hour is at hand, and either we must begin to live seriously as heirs of a great civilization, or we must, in refusing this role, face destruction.

I have said that we must face our shortcomings. What does this mean in terms applicable to musical life?

Music and the World Conflict

American musical life is convention-ridden as has been that of no other modern nation. Having received our musical education largely during the seventies and the eighties of the last century, it is natural that the prevalent values should be still, even among many "advanced" musicians, to a very large extent those of the Wagnerian and post-Wagnerian heyday. This does not of course imply that our composers all write in the "style" of Wagner's followers —that question is not even particularly important. The prevalent attitude towards music, however, is that of the late nineteenth century. Our standards are very largely external ones. We demand music that, whether "programmatic" or not, is evocative rather than inwardly expressive; or profess a "nationalism" which we conceive in terms of association or recurrent mannerisms rather than of the traditions created by mature and significant works. We still worship "instrumentation," "thematic material," "technique," and all the other conceptions proper to a time when music was conceived chiefly in terms of material splendor or subtlety or strangeness, and comparatively little account was taken of the spirit that animated the composer's materials and gave them whatever significance they possessed.

Musical life today is theory-ridden and musicology-ridden. The radio and the publishing houses swarm with well-intentioned *words* about music, and the attitude of the *music-lover* is more and more replaced in our musical life by that of the musical *student*. Everything possible is done to deter the layman from listening to Bach's work spontaneously as the glorious and timeless music that it is; instead, he is never allowed to forget Bach's exact historical position, the number of his wives and children, the structure of "the Fugue" (as formulated a good half-century after Bach's death), his place in the society of his time, or a thousand interesting but—as far as the essential impact of his music is concerned—irrelevant and even disturbing particulars. Worse than this, even our contemporaries are carefully docketed, assigned "tendencies," and provided with dossiers; they even sometimes provide dossiers and classifications of their own. Very rarely indeed are they regarded as human beings writing music for the joy of it, to be heard for whatever direct and clear message their music may be able to convey in its own right. In very many cases they perhaps do not even expect to be so regarded; and in such cases the result can be only confusion both of musical feeling and of musical utterance.

Our musical life is propaganda-ridden. This is of course partly an inevitable result of the situation which has made "American music," as such, a *cause* to be promoted. The result has been to a very large extent to place emphasis on "personalities," "tendencies," a "movement," rather than on music itself, which seems at times almost to be relegated to the status of a by-product. More than one esteemed colleague has on occasion confessed to this writer that, in spite of his professed admiration for this or that younger colleague, he had not received genuine musical pleasure from a single bar of the latter's work. Whence, then, the "talent"? Yet such cases are far from uncommon; and one frequent result is an intense though futile factionalism. And while the spectacle of jealousy and partisanship among musicians is always disagreeable, it becomes ridiculous among "serious" composers in the United States, none of whom has achieved so large a following as to interfere seriously with the prestige or success of any other.

We are in fact prone, in our musical life, to a kind of fetish-worship which is at best a provincial mannerism and at worst a provider of alibis. We are a "young country," so we say, without any place in European tradition—therefore our most "vital" composers are expected to write music which, artistically or otherwise, is something less than mature. (They do not, of course, always oblige.) Or we dig into the unpretentious music of the American past, recent or otherwise, hailing all crudities and gaucheries as signs of originality and of the emergence of an "authentic" American style. Of our living composers, however, we consistently demand something less than their best, both damning and excusing them on the ground that no "tradition" has yet developed on American soil—as if "tradition" were something abstract and mysterious and localized, instead of, purely and simply, successive generations of musicians engaged always in doing their best.

I have said little, obviously, of the all-important question of the economics of our musical life. It might easily be shown that it is this, above all, which has been responsible for most of the evils which I have mentioned, and given our musical culture such a large admixture of "phoney" elements. It bears moreover, many of the symptoms of an "impasse"; it is characterized by a lack of foresight, an expenditure of existing resources, and a failure to build up reserves, which remind one of other phases of our economic life, at its worst. How the "star system" with all of its by-products can long survive the collapse of Europe, even under the most favorable future conditions, is difficult to see. But its disintegration will solve no problems unless new and sounder values are found, to replace those which it embodied; and the establishment, through vital musical production, of these sounder values is precisely the task—both at short and at long range—of the American musician as such.

This task is, to be sure, scarcely definable in more concrete terms. Valid works of art are produced, not because the composer should or may produce them, but because he *must*. If he produces because he *should*, the result is almost sure to be weak and lacking in conviction; if because he *may*, it belongs certainly in the category of unnecessary luxuries. Were American music to be based on no deeper necessities than those, there could be but one answer to the basic question posed at the beginning of this article. Music would have ceased to be relevant either during the war as in the following peace. At the very least it would have degenerated spontaneously to the status which the Nazi plan has prescribed for it; it would have become mere propaganda, mere innocuous and uncharacteristic entertainment, or an academic reminder of a once living culture.

Our composers will, of course, be serving the country in ways immediately relevant to the conduct of the war. The situation is too immediate and too urgent for any thought of "business-as-usual" even for the most gifted, for the American composer any more than, for instance, Shostakovitch in the siege of Leningrad. But in doing their share for the common cause they will not cease to produce. According to talent and inclination they will be moved, as many have been already, by the tragic events which we are living through; many of them, certainly, will re-examine, even more or less consciously, the premises on which they have based their works; and some at least will learn to eliminate whatever is inessential or irrelevant. They may learn, too, to be even more completely aware of what is essential—of what their real inner necessities are. It is this result, I believe, for which composers should strive.

If they can succeed they will have performed the greatest possible service. For, once more, our survival itself depends on a total mobilization of human resources, both during the war and after. And the artist does not so much reflect the spiritual climate of his age as help to create it, in proportion to the vitality and real inwardness of his product. Even the size of his public is irrelevant; the greatest art has, in fact, always been, and perhaps always will be, accessible to the comparative few.

The task of the American musician is, then, now as always, to *create*; to help build a really new and better inner world.

Artists and This War
[1942]

A LETTER TO AN IMAGINARY COLLEAGUE

Dear————:

Yes, it is true that I am forty-five years old, that I have two small children, and that I am, as far as we can now see, unlikely to be fighting in the front lines. It is also true that at the beginning of the last war I was a pacifist, and remained so until Mr. Wilson "talked me around." Let me say that I have since remained firmly convinced that Mr. Wilson was right. Having decided that I really cared about the outcome of the war, and after having been rejected for all forms of service by my local draft board, I took real, though vain, steps toward obtaining a passport to the one allied country whose army would have admitted eyes as defective as mine.

I mention this simply to remind you that although, as you have hinted, we two are not in identical situations today, your problem is not entirely unfamiliar to me. Exactly as is the case today, we in 1918 had been shown during three and one-half years what war was like; and though the experiences which we faced were different from those of this war, they were certainly intrinsically no more inviting. No man of imagination was precisely amused by the prospect of standing in muddy trenches, devoured by lice, waiting for weeks and months at a time, or even occasionally going over the top to face what the newspapers described as "a solid wall of steel" from machine gun bullets.

When I made up my mind, therefore, that I must get into the fighting, if possible, I did so with the most unheroic

From *Modern Music*, vol. 20, no. 1, pp. 3-7. Reprinted by permission of the League of Composers—International Society for Contemporary Music, U.S. Section, Inc.

feelings imaginable. What impelled me to do so was simply the sense that I would have been unable to live at peace with the self that had willingly allowed others to leave me behind in offering their lives in a cause in which I was vitally interested.

Well, the story of my relation to the last war is a trivial one with a decidedly weak ending, and has no interest whatever except to show that I have some basis for understanding your present situation. Let me go farther and point out the obvious fact that you are now far more than the aspiring but thoroughly untried sub-beginner that I was in 1918. You have already large works to your credit, and have earned a following, both professional and lay. Above all, you have learned to know, basically at least, what you want, both as musician and as a human being.

So I am sincerely honored and touched that you should care for my opinion of artists in war time, especially since, the policy of our Government being decided beyond your power or mine to change it, any such discussion is bound to be purely academic.

But let me point out another difference, more apparent than real, but still desperately apparent, between my position of 1918 and yours of 1942. We agree fully that this war is only the most urgent and, let us hope, the most tragic, phase of a much larger crisis of civilization. While this also was true in 1918, only the wisest and most far-sighted of men realized it. Otherwise we would be in a far different position today. This time it is evident to all of us.

That, in fact, is the basis of your questioning. Since it is civilization itself, you seem to ask, that is in danger, is it not the duty of artists and all who possess creative potentialities to give their energies exclusively to their art, forswearing other service in order that life and culture may survive?

In giving you my own answer to this question I do not mean to imply that mine is the only one. I must confess, too, that my thoughts about our situation have undergone a considerable evolution since, in Berlin in 1933, I first began to realize that a world showdown might be in the making.

And first of all, I am afraid that I do not feel that any of us are very good guardians of culture. For after all culture is not an objet d'art, or a set of books, or a manufactured product made to order by specialists; rather it is the total spiritual product of any given time and place. The terrible but inescapable fact remains that the culture of which you and I are a part, which we have helped to maintain, and for the preservation of which a few of our colleagues would like to be excused from military service, is the fertile soil from which Fascism and all that it implies has sprung. For you, if you have followed attentively the development, or observed attentively the nature, of Fascism, must have seen written on every page of every comprehensive view of recent history, that this "Fascism" is not at all a localized symptom, but only the localized accumulation of all the symptoms of the diseases from which a sick civilization was already grievously suffering: diseases against which all the most far-sighted men of the past century and a half have constantly warned us, but against which we—not only Neville Chamberlain and his like, but you and I and all the rest of us—failed to react strongly or promptly enough. Not even those of us who knew of the menace of imperialist Japan, of Nazi and Fascist Germany and Italy, or who saw and understood similar threats within each nation including our own, summoned ourselves quickly or energetically enough to realize the total revolution in our own lives that the decisive victory must ultimately involve. Most of us are far from realizing it yet. Instead, we have each in his own way complacently accepted the lazy self-deception, the frigid professionalism, the cynical misrepresentation, the competitive savagery, and the carefully nurtured and pervasive triviality which have characterized not German or English or French or American life, but modern life as such —which "Fascism" has simply carried to logical and conscious conclusions, and with the aid of which so many of our compatriots seem still to think that victory may be won.

Please don't misunderstand me. I am, first of all, not pleading for a return to any state of society, of mind, or of culture, that has ever existed in the past, or anything remotely resembling this. You know I have been sometimes taxed with this and other such attitudes, but I believe you know how and why I have, in respect to certain published estimates of my work and my attitude, preferred always "to let nature take its course" rather than to complicate matters still further by trying to correct obvious misapprehensions. But in the present connection it seems to me so clear that, as modern men, we have passed the buck pretty generally and consistently in regard to the real problems of our society. We have never had the courage to face basic human questions in terms of the actual conditions of existence, but instead have lived on unearned wealth, both inner and outer, provided by the past, by technique, by stereotyped and often outworn ideology and by the subtle uses of publicity, which suffuses our commonest activities and to such a large extent even our most intimate thoughts. If other times and other places have a preponderant advantage over our own, it is entirely because they have been, in matters of the spirit, self-supporting where we have so often been asked to be paid in advance without the obligation of delivering the goods.

Secondly, I am not referring, by any means, to only the slowest witted among us when I say that nearly all of us are still hugging some cherished status quo. That this is true in a very obvious sense of certain large political, social and economic groups hardly needs mentioning. But in a subtler sense many of us, too, are cherishing our own ideological or spiritual status quo and trying desperately to squeeze some kind of aggressive juice out of it. We are afraid, above all, of abandoning doctrines which once may have seemed richly promising, but which may very well stand in the way of the real necessities of the present and future. So musi-

cians, too, behave as if the aesthetic attitudes of the last
twenty years were still valid, as if an agonized world could
possibly remain patient with what have been on the one
hand essentially private attempts to find some kind of private solution to problems which can only be solved in terms
of general validity, or on the other hand, the specious universality of generalized matter and form devoid of any real
content whatever.

I hope this will leave in your mind no doubt of my conviction as to the supreme task which artists of today must
face, or of the supreme importance of that task. It is, in
fact, a vital part of that conviction that artists are not merely,
as a decadent aesthetic would have it, reflectors of a time
and place; instead it seems so clear that they help very powerfully to create eras and localities by giving concrete form
to their visions. Certainly this has always been true in the
past. As for the present, never have we artists had so clear
a vocation. For if our successors are to find the world a
tolerable world to live in, it is a new world which we have
to create—there is unlimited space to be filled. It can be
filled only by the most complete implementation of human
constructive imagination; a task so difficult that, were it less
than utterly necessary for human survival, one might well
dismiss it as beyond conceivable possibility. It may require
the full energies of several generations, and the achievements
of creative artists will certainly be largely interdependent
with what other human beings achieve. What you and I
and our contemporaries can contribute may well be, when
viewed in later perspective, of value chiefly as a preparation, even a mere slight change of direction. Who can tell?
But it has to be done and requires, in categorical terms, the
best energies of which we are capable.

Meanwhile, however, we have an immediate and im-
mensely threatening crisis to meet. In view of this, can any
of us, without becoming ridiculous and pitiable in our egocentric irrelevance, do less than try to fulfill with credit
and without complaint whatever task is assigned us? Are

you and I really, as individuals, so indispensable that we can with any possible justification ask for exceptional treatment? With all possible sincerity, I think not. I feel passionately that, should any of us do so, we would be advertising ourselves and our art as a mere commodity capable of possible minor utilization in the war effort, or as a curiosity to be kept going as part of a kind of fluid "time capsule"—one of the articles of no intrinsic value to be preserved for posterity as a curious survival of a superseded civilization.

On the contrary, let us be, frankly, men, and accept our destiny as other men are doing, and fight without respite the enemies who have to be fought. The survival of culture seems to me to depend to a far greater extent upon the ability of artists to do this than on their physical survival as individuals.

This is, for better or worse, the best wisdom I have to offer. Were the world other than it is, my solution might be a more ideal one. You know that as well as I. Meanwhile, all my affectionate thoughts and my brotherly wishes go out to you.

Roger Sessions

Europe Comes to America
[1945]

An address delivered at the Music Institute of Kenyon College, Gambier, Ohio, in August 1945, just after the close of the war.

WHEN I began reflecting on the subject on which I was asked to talk this evening, it quite naturally occurred to me how vast were its implications. I might conceivably take as my point of departure the year 1492, when Columbus discovered the new world; or 1519, when Cortez scaled the sheer wall of the Mexican tableland with his horses and his cannon, and, after overthrowing the native American civilization, established in its place his most curious mixture of oppressive greed and Christian idealism. Or, I might jump forward another century to the founding of Virginia and New Amsterdam and the Plymouth colony by the ancestors of those who later founded the United States.

Other dates also come to one's mind—the Irish potato famine, or the revolutions of 1848, in which our country became a refuge for thousands who were fleeing from hunger or political oppression. Or the period in our history —so dreary in some aspects—during which millions of Europeans were brought here to man America's rapidly expanding industrial machine, lured by the promise of a richer and freer life than they could find at home.

Of course the title "Europe Comes to America" does not in this present case refer to any of the above events, but rather to events of the last twenty years, which, though similar in certain respects, differ in two essential respects from the ones which I have mentioned.

In 1492, and 1519, though European culture was at one

319

of its great turning points, it was not, in any conceivable sense, in mortal danger; and in the early seventeenth century, in some degree as a result of the expansion of Europe's boundaries, the crisis had been to some degree overcome, at least in appearances. In 1848 Europe was already dangerously ill, but the chances of recovery looked by no means hopeless.

This time, of course, it is quite different. It would be bold indeed should I try to estimate the full extent of Europe's catastrophe. But it is hardly necessary to stress the fact that one must speak of the years since October 1922, when Mussolini "marched" on Rome in the night express train from Milan, in terms of catastrophe and not of crisis; or to recall the fact that the catastrophe—so nicely symbolized by the fact that it was the King of Italy who met the train—that the catastrophe was an inner catastrophe, brought about by the treason of Europe's rulers. That is to say, it was in a certain very real sense an act of suicide, from which the patient could and can recover, if at all, only with considerable help or at least support from outside its own borders.

The future of Europe is in other words dependent on the will and wisdom of three great powers, none of which are more than partly European, and those who have come to us are as surely deprived of the possibility of turning wholly backward. Those Americans who have for so long accustomed themselves to look to Europe for final authority in cultural matters, or even for what is vaguely known as "tradition" or "atmosphere," will find themselves to a large extent deprived of these commodities in a Europe which at best will be wholly occupied for many years to come with absolutely vital tasks of sheer resuscitation.

Secondly, it is to a large extent precisely the best of Europe which has come to us—that part of Europe which Fascist Satanism could not tolerate, and which, as the first condition of its own existence, it was obliged to exterminate. It is quite unnecessary to me to give here a detailed list of names of those leaders of European culture who have come to us, as a result of this situation, thus demonstrating so clearly what a tremendous portion of the very best and most vital blood of Europe is now with us and, with very few exceptions, of us. But the list would extend into nearly every intellectual field or spiritual realm of activity—scientific, literary or artistic. These men and women have come to share our lives and fortunes, and to place their wealth of creative resources at our disposal. The victories which we have recently won, to which Americans of foreign birth have made spectacular contributions, are themselves testimony to the vast contributions which these new Americans have brought us.

It is of course unnecessary here to draw attention to the term "new Americans"; but it is not perhaps irrelevant once more to recall that America is a land based not on race—for we are many races, or even all races—or on land—for the land is ours by right of conquest and settlement—but on an idea. This is not the place to define that idea, and perhaps it cannot fundamentally be better or even by implication more profoundly expressed than in the words of a very brilliant friend of mine who once defined an American as one whose ancestors were unhappy, or who himself was unhappy, in his native land. The "American Dream" of which we so often have heard, especially in recent years, is of course—America itself.

There are those, to be sure—and all too many—who believe that the presence of so many new Americans, of so great distinction, will in some way impair the integrity of our "native culture"—that some especially American quality is threatened by the influx of so-called "foreign ideas." We are told, for instance, that a budding musical culture stands in the gravest danger from the encroachment of so-called "European tradition." Such people, it seems to me, forget, or perhaps misunderstand, two things. First of all they misconceive the nature of tradition itself. During a recent lecture Erich Leinsdorf asked for a definition of tradition, and none of the answers, mostly flippant, satisfied him. One reason perhaps was that most of us were defining a certain traditional*ism* which is the opposite of productivity, but which we too often confuse with the genuine tradition which has made European music great. This latter is something quite different, of which I should like to offer a quite other definition, and a very simple one: tradition seems, to me, to be nothing more nor less than the accumulation of many generations doing their best.

Furthermore, if we examine a little the history of music or art, we see that no great culture has ever developed on a basis of isolationism or exclusiveness. The great musical tradition of the Renaissance, as Alfred Einstein and others have abundantly proven, was founded very largely by Netherlanders—Josquin des Prés, Verdelot, Arcadelt, Willaert, Cyprien de Rore, Orlando di Lasso—of whom no one thought of asking whether they were native Italians. The great Germans of the eighteenth century—Bach, Handel, Mozart—were never tired of studying Italian models, and they and their successors were in fact the inheritors of the Italian musical tradition, which was, in fact, European music. Vienna itself was the crossroads of European culture where currents from South and East and West met and mingled in the greatest musical culture the world has known. And French musical culture was largely, through two centuries, the creation of foreigners—Lully and Cherubini the two Florentines, Gluck the South German, and Chopin the Pole, in whose style are mingled influences from his native Poland, from Italy, and even from the Irish composer John Field.

If we are some day to have, as all of us hope, a great and luxuriant musical culture in America, it will be not because at one period in our cultural existence we became nervous and timid and exclusive and therefore impoverished, but because we always had the courage and the affirmative imagination to take and absorb whatever can be genuinely nourishing from any source whatever, to accept it and let it exert its leavening influence to the enrichment of our national inner life. For of great cultures the same must be true as of great individuals, as Emerson described so beautifully when he wrote "the greatest man is the most indebted man."

Thus, when a singer recently spoke to me about a recital of "American" music, I encouraged her to do exactly what she wished to do—to arrange her program entirely according to artistic principles and to make no artificial separation into "native" and "foreign-born" groups of songs. For I felt that any such separation of the native and the voluntary children of America is in the truest sense of the word un-American. Let us once more face this great fact— which is the ultimate source of all that has made our country great, either in material or moral power: America is, and always has been, not primarily a land but an *idea*. Its very name is the name of one of a series of European dreamers who dreamed of a greater Europe extending beyond the seas. Cortez himself destroyed an American empire based on mystical conceptions of "blood and soil"—especially, and in the most drastic sense, blood. He brought to take its place a spiritual framework which aspired, as it still aspires, to include all mankind.

I am quite aware that Cortez and his warriors were human beings, and that their motives were as mixed as was their Christianity. Something quite similar is true of the founders of our nation. What I want to point out is that when Europe first came to America, she was in fact even consciously serving the ends of a vast historic process— that of creating something which is greater than either Europe or America; and it could, I think, be shown that each successive decisive movement in our history has continued to serve that end, often in spite of ourselves.

If this is true, there can be only one conclusion—America's finding itself means nothing more nor less than the discovery that mankind must be one, and that Americanism is by its very definition inclusive, all-inclusive, not in the smallest degree exclusive, and that loyalty to America means nothing less than a consistent devotion to the human principle in that inclusive sense.

Let us, then, put away childish things; or rather, more seriously and more accurately, let us put away childish attitudes toward things that are of a truly deadly seriousness. Nationalism or nativism in music may seem a far cry from political nationalism, and there are even real anti-nationalists (or, as they are quaintly called, internationalists), who believe that a kind of cultural nationalism and exclusiveness must be maintained. Believe me, this is the most dangerous of yearnings. It is on the basis of precisely such yearnings that dangerous illusions such as that of the master race are born, even though they develop by slow and almost imperceptible degrees, from apparently harmless and even well-intentioned beginnings.

So when one hears, as every one constantly does today, of positions for which only native Americans need apply, or when one hears even the slogan "play American music," the only adequate reaction is a shudder of apprehension, and the only adequate response is a redoubled effort to fight this poison. Aside from the overwhelming human menace which such slogans or programs carry with them, they carry a deadly danger to American music, and by implication, a fundamental offense to American musicians. For the implication is clearly that American musicians can not endure honest competition even when the scales are heavily weighted, as they inevitably are, in their favor. It implies that music by American composers is tainted by reason of its origin, and that as inferior music it needs to be "protected."

Let us freely admit that in the past artificial attitudes and illusions have been fostered, that Americans have been over-impressed, and not always by what is best in Europe. It is true also that musical culture in the United States is still in a very early stage of development, and not to be compared with the European past, even that of the immediate pre-war days. But is that not all the greater reason why we should welcome the presence among us of so many of the greatest musicians of Europe, and be thankful that they are with us?

And, to my friends of European birth and origin, I make, above all, one plea, from the bottom of my heart, even though I know that those of you who are present do not need it. This plea is that you should be as true in America as in Europe to what you have always considered the indispensable demands and criteria of real artistic achievement. I say—give us, or continue to give us, the best you have, and only the best you have according to your own standards; and demand in your turn the best from us. For too many of your fellow Europeans, in the past, have come to us for the money and success America has to offer, and offered us something very shoddy in return, on the pretext that this is what America wants, instead of offering us what they know is the best, and what they should consider it their obligation as artists to give.

And so—the idea "Europe comes to America" contains by implication the essence of America itself. Not only is the situation of which I have been speaking in line with American tradition and history—we are in fact capable of making of it a great phase of the realization of America's destiny. For is it not true that that destiny, as dreamed by great Americans of all times, is to assume its real responsibility in bringing about a world in which men of all nations and races shall work together in a common human effort toward a common human fulfillment? Perhaps it is part of our destiny, too, to help to bring once more to existence something like that "good European" of whom Goethe and others dreamed, and whom our common late enemy has sought, above all else, to destroy.

325

VI

Five Composers

Ernest Bloch
[1927]

Sessions had been a pupil of Bloch, and later
his assistant at the Cleveland Institute.

AMONG the European musicians who have made the
United States their home, Ernest Bloch is a unique
figure. Not only is he, aesthetic controversies aside, in-
dubitably of the first rank; he has gone farther than any
other in a conscientious effort to identify himself with our
musical life and future. His part has been a more active one
than that of an independent purveyor of musical wares. As
musical director of the Cleveland Institute of Music, and
later of the San Francisco Conservatory, he has established
himself in the country at large as an important influence
in our artistic development, and has at the same time acquired an intimate knowledge of "American musical life":
that odd conglomerate of women's clubs, music "weeks,"
music memory contests, and other earnest efforts of which
the average composer remains in happy ignorance. It was
in the United States, moreover, that his most mature work
first gained performance and recognition. Thus it is not
merely through his assumption of United States citizenship
that we are privileged to consider him as an American musician, and to regard his personality and achievement as in
a most real sense identified with the development of music
in his adopted country.

The principal facts of Bloch's career are fairly well
known. The earliest which need concern us here is the
completion in 1903 of his first important work. The Sym-

From *Modern Music*, vol. 5, no. 1, pp. 3-11. Reprinted by permission of the League of Composers—International Society for Contemporary Music, U.S. Section, Inc.

phony in C♯ minor while by no means free from "influences," is prophetic in that it not only reveals a consummate mastery of technique, but sketches in its main aspects
all that future works will confirm as the temperament, the
"artistic personality" of the composer. The opera *Macbeth*
followed; four years were required for its completion, and
four more elapsed before it was finally performed at the
Opéra-Comique. In the meantime Bloch had composed
Hiver-Printemps, two short movements for orchestra, and
a cycle of songs, *Poèmes d'Automne*. These four works
must be considered together as what Wilhelm von Lenz
would have called Bloch's "first manner." *Macbeth* in particular is interesting, not only because of its own great
qualities, but because of the light which it throws on certain
aspects of his later development.

Indeed, it is difficult at some moments to resist the temptation to regard *Macbeth* as Bloch's masterpiece. Since writing the Symphony, he has obviously become acquainted
with *Boris* and *Pelléas*; but while he has been deeply impressed by both styles, he has molded them to his own uses,
with a result that is neither Moussorgsky nor Debussy. One
is aware of a new personality, full-blooded, uninhibited, and
conscious of its own strength. The irony, the violent and uncompromising sincerity, the profound pessimism of Bloch's
later works, are already here, transmitted through the impersonal medium of the Shakespearian tragedy. This is not
the place for an analysis of this very remarkable work, nor
could the criticisms of Lalo, Gatti, and Pizzetti[1] be easily
improved upon. But to those who know *Macbeth* it must
remain a mystery why it has not been revived, or performed
elsewhere than in Paris.

It seems to us that while Bloch's more mature works
show an enormous advance in originality, force, and sharpness of contour, there is in *Macbeth* a freshness of mood,

---

[1] Pierre Lalo, French critic; Guido M. Gatti, Italian critic; Ilde-
brando Pizzetti, Italian composer.

an exuberance and fecundity alike of spirit and of musical invention, which do not again fully appear. Is it possible that this later music does not completely contain the whole man? It is as though in becoming more conscious of his personality, his "message," he had almost deliberately thrown aside the serenity—one is even tempted to say the universality—of his native musical impulse.

The projected opera, *Jézabel*, still today only a mass of remarkable sketches, served as point of departure for the Jewish Cycle: the *Trois Poèmes Juifs*, the *Psalms* for soprano and orchestra, *Schelomo*, the *Psalm 22* for baritone, and finally the unfinished symphony, *Israel*, which filled the years from 1912 to 1916. In these works, Bloch's style defines itself with splendid assurance.

Wherein, exactly, lies the specifically "Jewish" character of this music? Bloch has stated his aims clearly enough: "It is not my desire to attempt a 'reconstitution' of Jewish music. . . . It is the Jewish soul that interests me, the complex, glowing, agitated soul that I feel vibrating throughout the Bible. . . . All this is in us, all this is in me, and it is the better part of me. It is all this that I endeavor to hear in myself and to transcribe in my music: the venerable emotion of the race that slumbers way down in our soul."[2] It would be difficult indeed to find a better statement of the aesthetic which underlies these works. His music is self-revelatory, and quite consciously reveals an ideal self rather than an actual one. His role is prophet or orator, rather than lyric poet; least of all is it creator of objective aesthetic worlds.

Materially, this music is above all sumptuous and grandiose; rich and exuberant in color, luxuriant and full-blown in form. Its austerity, if such it can be called, is a pagan austerity of mood; intensity and concentration rather than

[2] From a communication by the composer to Guido M. Gatti. Quoted in the latter's article "Ernest Bloch," *La Critica Musicale*, Apr.-May 1920 (translated in *Musical Quarterly*, vol. 7, no. 1, Jan. 1921).

essential restraint, a quality of his soul rather than of his art. Indeed, the overwhelming power not only of the Jewish works, but of Bloch's music as a whole, is perhaps attributable before all else to this extraordinary directness and intensity of feeling, together with the splendor of its material embodiment. And if we speak of body and soul as more or less separate existences in art, we do so in deference to Bloch's own thought, the consistent basis of his whole creative activity.

More specifically, the orientalism of the Jewish works shows itself in certain melodic and harmonic traits. The trumpet calls, for instance, with which they abound, give them a character at once barbaric and ritualistic. Actual Jewish melodies, on the other hand, occur but rarely and incidentally, and not as the result of a desire on Bloch's part to reproduce folklore. What he has done is to allow his imagination to play on the embodiment of a truly Jewish spirit in music, and in so doing he has created a style which is entirely personal. His orientalism is a part of the fully assimilated substance of his music, and in no sense a pseudo-oriental décor. To his work as a whole it lends a singular freedom which, as Guido Gatti has well said, is "before the schools and not after them."[3] Thus the use of a single quarter-tone in *Schelomo* is in no way disturbing to our sense of a style in which, through the completeness of its imaginative mastery, the utmost freedom of melodic line becomes natural and in the aesthetic sense inevitable.

More profoundly individual, perhaps, than Bloch's orientalism is the quality which arises from its amalgamation with an element of quite different origin. He is not only a Jew, but a European. The solid fruits of his musical culture are everywhere present in his work. Years ago he startled a critic by acknowledging the influence of Beethoven in *Macbeth*; yet this influence, with that of the other classics, has persisted in his later music, and is a no less living force in *Schelomo* than in the C♯ minor Symphony. Above all, in

[3] *Ibid.*

his approach to the problems of form, he is a traditionalist in the best sense of the word. As truly as his orientalism, his classical culture is something inherent in the nature of his art. Even when, in his less felicitous moments, two different aesthetic impulses seem to conflict in his music, one cannot question the reality of either.

An increasing affirmation of this cultural heritage is evident in the four large works which follow the Jewish Cycle. The Quartet, the Suite for Viola and Piano, the Sonata for Violin and Piano, and the Quintet were composed at intervals of approximately two years, the three last-named in moments literally snatched between hours of teaching or administrative work. All four reveal a progressive tendency toward more closely-knit formal construction.

In these works he gradually divests his style of its Jewish garments. In the first movement of the Quartet they are still very much in evidence; indeed nowhere are they more perfectly fused, more profoundly felt in the aesthetic sense, than here. In the finale of the same work they appear episodically; and there are still traces of them in the Suite, however, they are merged in a style of altogether different character. In the Sonata and the Quintet they have virtually ceased to exist; Bloch's style, even his attitude toward his art, has undergone a radical change. If, in the Jewish Cycle, he gave voice to a positive belief in the value, the grandeur, of human suffering, in the greatness of his racial tradition and hence, by implication, the essential greatness of the human spirit, in these later works his dominant moods are those of pessimism, irony, and nostalgia, felt with the utmost intensity and embodied in works whose emotional or even philosophical tendencies are defined with unmistakable clearness.

It is significant that he writes no longer primarily for the orchestra. The Suite, to be sure, is orchestral in its final form; but here his conception of the orchestra differs in essentials from that which had produced *Schelomo*. Although the Suite has the same richness and depth of coloring, it is astonishingly different in texture. *Schelomo* is conceived on the broadest and grandest scale; for all its wealth of color, its power lies above all in its largeness of utterance. The Suite, on the other hand, retains its character as chamber music even in the orchestral version. Individual timbres, finely wrought details, a texture reduced to barest essentials, make it the most delicate of Bloch's works. On the piano this consummate transparency is lost. The proportions are completely altered through the undisputed supremacy of the solo instrument.

The smaller medium in which these works are cast is the logical vehicle of a more personal mode of speech. Bloch no longer writes as a Jew, but rather as a solitary individual. His language becomes, in fact, at once more individual and more detached. In abandoning the expression of a collective faith, he grows increasingly aware of the menace of superhuman forces over which he has only a limited control. The violence of his later music is ruthless and mechanical; it is no longer the voice of human suffering and revolt. It externalizes itself more often in brusque and vehement rhythms, insistent sometimes almost beyond endurance, than in the sharp and broken pathetic accents of his earlier style. Irony, of which there is hardly a trace in the Jewish works, becomes one of his characteristic moods, manifesting itself above all in a fondness for the grotesque, for caricature; the *allegro ironico* of the Suite, like its Lisztian prototype, is the embodiment of the "Spirit that denies." In the moments of rarest beauty, disillusion becomes resigned. A serenity akin to that of the end of *Israel* returns, deeper and richer in true eloquence, in the wonderful last pages of the Violin Sonata; but whereas in the earlier work this serenity arises from faith and ultimate confidence, it is in the later one imbued with profound sadness.

The nostalgia at which we have already hinted grows out of this disillusion. A longing for distant lands, softer

climates, simpler conditions of life, shows itself in the guise
of an increasing fondness for the exotic, quite different in
essence from the orientalism of the Jewish Cycle. For many
years Bloch has been an ardent collector of exotic music
from all parts of the world, and his later style is interspersed
with conscious borrowings from this source: it abounds in
sonorities, modes, rhythms, actual musical fragments, of Far
Eastern origin or suggestion. The parallel with Gauguin
immediately suggests itself; there is no doubt that the same
moment in the history of the human spirit produced both
artists, nor that the bitterness and despair which led Gauguin to the islands of the Pacific have taken Bloch there
many times in thought.

From the purely musical standpoint, the exotic elements
in Bloch's later works tend sometimes to assume the character of external bodies, absorbed into his style by sheer
force of will and technical mastery. We have spoken already of the rare moments in the Jewish works when the
European and the oriental elements in the music seem to
clash with one another. At its best, when the elements are
most perfectly fused, this duality of culture and sensibility
gives Bloch's work its most profound character. But the
exoticism of the Quintet and the Sonata is more essentially
picturesque, felt less through its sounds and rhythms than
through its powers of evocation; and at certain moments,
enchanted by the rare and beautiful sonorities, one suffers
a passing resentment when an architecture belonging in essence to our own time and place—an architecture of which
Bloch is preeminently a master—begins to assert its sov-
ereign rights.

Since 1916 Bloch had lived in the United States. The experience of American life, with its ruthless impersonality,
its restlessness and confusion, intensified the pessimism, the
sense of a decaying culture, which had been part of his
European experience. In the Suite, the Sonata, and the Quin-

tet, however, he was still the spectator. His real contact with American life began in 1920 with his appointment as director of a Middle Western conservatory. This chapter is most illuminating; from a distance it assumes the form of a sort of panorama of American provincial life in its most characteristic phases, thrown into clear if lurid relief by the apparition of a personality such as Bloch's. Starting with the highest artistic ideals, Bloch soon became aware of the tendency to institutionalize which in the newer parts of the United States applies itself no less ruthlessly to education and culture than to industry. His very name was from the start capitalized for advertising purposes; he was, moreover, expected to devote to the gaining of enrollments or subscriptions his force of conviction, and his immense persuasive powers—powers already strained in the defense of fundamentals of his educational policy. Even his proposal to establish a Theory Department met with some opposition at first; it was considered a quite unwarranted addition to a "practical" curriculum. What, then, of solfeggio? What of the "fixed *do*," long established in Europe as the basis of musical instruction, but regarded in America as difficult and unproductive of quick results? The convincing demonstration, by means of musical tests, of Bloch's accuracy of judgment in these matters, was of no real avail in lessening the obstinacy with which certain of his pedagogical principles were opposed. A system of instruction which, eliminating "marks" and textbooks, took as its point of departure the direct musical experience of the pupil, and sought constantly to enlarge, to co-ordinate this experience through observation rather than rules: such was Bloch's aim. But to the majority of those with whom he had to deal, such a conception was quite incomprehensible, and its methods of procedure unheard-of innovations.

In the end, one is forced to conclude, Cleveland's rejection of Bloch was a rejection precisely of the best that he had to give—that, as all who were with him can testify, he wanted so passionately to give. His very geniality, his force of conviction, his ironic laughter—his richness of temperament and culture, in other words—stood in his way. The city which had summoned him, at first disarmed by his magnetism into partial capitulation, took alarm before the full impact of his personality. It was not, in the last analysis, an individual, a style, or an aesthetic that went down to defeat in Cleveland; it was rather just those disinterested and humane conceptions which form the indispensable background for artistic creation of any kind. The story of this episode deserves to be written more fully, and with more detachment, than is possible here; its value as documentation to some future historian of American culture would be inestimable.

Could it be wondered at had the chief protagonist emerged from such a struggle for the moment a little wearied, a little less prodigal of himself, a little on his guard? When we consider the music which Bloch has written since the Quintet it is impossible to escape some such conclusion. Certainly it contains fine pages, but little that is intrinsically new. Four years, however, may count for little in the sum of an atrist's work. One has only to look back over Bloch's most memorable works: the *Cortège Funèbre* of the *Trois Poèmes Juifs*; *Schelomo*; the Quartet, on the whole his most deeply beautiful work; the slow movement of the Sonata; the massive opening movement of the Quintet—but why enumerate them?—to realize all that it is one's right to expect, and one's duty to hope for in the future, from an artist of such stature. Let us then content ourselves for the present with the fact that he now lives in the mellower and more congenial atmosphere of San Francisco, where he is allowed comparative freedom from administrative details, remembering that the career of a man like Bloch is inevitably full of surprises.

Since the critical moment of Bloch's artistic life, the moment at which his mature style formed itself, changes

have taken place—changes which penetrate to the very
depths of the soul of Europe and America. Art, too, has
felt the fatal impact of these changes, and it has become
increasingly evident that the future must see either the
death of Western culture or a supreme effort toward reconstruction. Younger men are dreaming of an entirely
different type of music—a music which derives its power
from forms beautiful and significant by virtue of inherent
musical weight rather than intensity of utterance; a music
whose impersonality and self-sufficiency preclude the exotic; which takes its impulse from the realities of a passion-
ate logic; which, in the authentic freshness and simplicity
of its moods, is the reverse of ironic and in its very aloof-
ness from the concrete preoccupations of life, strives rather
to contribute form, design, a vision of order and harmony.
Such a music, like all that is vital in art, seeks affinities in
the past. Bloch, in his splendid enthusiasm for the masters
of the sixteenth century, for Bach, for Haydn, has helped
more than one of his pupils to comprehend the true nature
of such an art, and to appreciate the forces in the culture
of today which make our impulse toward it inevitable. Of
a passage in the *De Profundis* of Orlando di Lasso he once
said, "I can conceive of a day when Beethoven will seem
old-fashioned; even Bach may one day seem old-fashioned,
while Wagner has begun to seem so already. But this can
never grow old." The newer music, so radically different
from his own, owes then something very concrete to the
culture which has gone into the making of Bloch. And if
the effort of a different conception to assert itself has temporarily seemed to isolate him, to deprive him of adequate
recognition, there can be no doubt that the adjustments of
history will restore to him his true place among the artists
who have spoken most commandingly the language of conscious emotion.

On *Oedipus Rex*
[1928]

Stravinsky's opera-oratorio Oedipus Rex *received its premier in Paris, in May 1927. It was performed in the United States (Boston and New York) during the following season.*

ERNEST ANSERMET remarked some years ago on the good fortune of Stravinsky in having had his works become known before they were commented on. *Oedipus Rex*, together with the rest of Stravinsky's later music, has not shared this good fortune. The comparatively small number of his works, the rapid evolution of his style, and his own increasingly enhanced reputation have all contributed to a widespread curiosity in which comment has often preceded thorough acquaintance or even in some cases the actual performance of his works. It is not surprising therefore that each new work is hailed as an entirely new departure, the starting point for new catchwords and generalizations by admirers and detractors alike. Such generalizations no doubt often contain some truth, but they must be understood with caution and accuracy if they are not to mislead. Above all they must be considered as no more than indications of a rather general character.

This was the case with the well-known "Return to Bach" which was seen in the *Octuor* and the Piano Concerto is equally true of the "Return to Handel" which *Oedipus Rex* is said to exemplify. *Oedipus* preserves in a general way the formal lines of the oratorio, of which it also reembodies some of the solemnity and stateliness of spirit. But it is the oratorio of Handel, impersonal and almost ritualistic in char-

From *Modern Music*, vol. 5, no. 3, pp. 9-15. Reprinted by permission of the League of Composers—International Society for Contemporary Music, U.S. Section, Inc.

acter, rather than the more dramatic Passion music of Bach, that has served as a general model for Stravinsky—a model to be studied and understood, but to be readapted rather than imitated in any but the broadest fashion.

The result is the "opera-oratorio," a form which while preserving the general lines of the dramatic action, makes possible the most complete freedom of musical development. The whole work is divided into two acts, each of which contains three main sections separated by the successive appearances of a "speaker" whose ostensible function is to elucidate the drama in order that the hearer may concentrate attention upon the essential drama rather than upon the text. This drama unfolds itself in a series of musical movements, each fully developed, but bearing its definite musical relation to the formal plan of the whole. Keys, metres, tempi are balanced and contrasted with the utmost nicety; in the first act the alternation of chorus and solo passages produces an effect similar in kind to that of the older concerto form, where orchestral masses were brought into contrast with the solo instruments. The whole is in other words as closely knit, as organic a unit, as a large instrumental work. The somewhat loose oratorio form is thus merely a point of departure; the division into arias, choruses and concerted numbers is preserved in some general fashion, but the total result is something essentially different in character and effect.

The "speaker" as we have already hinted not only elucidates the action of the drama; he performs the important function of helping to clarify the general musical lines by his regular appearance between the main sections. This was not clear at the premiere in Paris, owing to the very unsatisfactory nature of the performance as a whole. In Boston and New York, however, the effectiveness of the contrast between speaking voice and music became evident, and added to the solemn and dignified impression of the whole work.

The music of *Oedipus* is built on a strictly harmonic

basis; in this respect it stands in striking contrast to the other recent works of Stravinsky, which are primarily contrapuntal in character. This is moreover its second and final point of contact with Handel—here, too, with the spirit and method but in no sense the actual musical personality of Handel. Polyphony exists, and to be sure, is almost constant; but it is always subordinate, rather serving to accentuate the harmonic or rhythmic context than existing in its own right.

Arthur Lourié has acutely pointed out that the harmonic structure of *Oedipus* is *tonic* rather than tonal in the ordinary sense of the word. As in nearly all of Stravinsky's works, the shifting harmonies move around a clearly established harmonic axis. In *Oedipus* the harmonic axis is nearly always a tonic triad. Whole sections may be found which are thus constructed on a single fundamental tonic harmony. To give but one instance: the musical pages which embody the crucial moment of the drama are based on a persistently reiterated D minor harmony. The effect of such a style is one of great deliberation and stateliness of movement. Tonality, as expressed in the harmonies of the perfect cadence, is to be found only occasionally in isolated phrases. It is in no sense a part of the structure of the whole.

Modulations, generally effected through the shifting of the harmonic poles, are fairly frequent and often most striking in their boldness and freedom. The quoted example is one of the finest from the choruses of the opening scene.

This tonal freedom is characteristic of all of Stravinsky's more recent music, only in *Oedipus* one is conscious of greater simplicity as well as greater flexibility in the whole tonal scheme.

The orchestral style is characterized technically by the nearly complete equality of the three main instrumental groups. One is tempted to add to these a fourth consisting of piano, tympani and harp, which have important roles to fill, generally in combination. The scoring is at the same time simple and daring. It is as bare, as free from prettiness

or mere brilliance as the music itself. Often two or three instrumental voices will carry the entire weight, as with the pages accompanying Oedipus' first appearance, where clarinets two octaves apart play a rhythmic and harmonic figure above a single bassoon; or the opening of Tiresias' long air, accompanied by first and second violins in unison from two to three octaves above a flowing figure in the bassoon, or like the accompaniment for two bassoons of the Shepherd's song. All of these passages are of the utmost simplicity, yet their effect is extraordinarily rich and full. In many of the tutti passages the instruments are strongly individualized. The music which accompanies the duet of Oedipus and Jocasta, for instance, achieves its extraordinary crystalline effect largely through the individual exploitation of single timbres—the trumpet, the clarinet, the piccolo. The score is full of masterly and subtle detail: the horn, an octave higher than the tenors of the chorus, adding a brilliance which almost suggests the presence of sopranos; a single pizzicato chord accenting a phrase of the trumpets; a horn sustaining the upper notes of a strumming accompaniment. Every instrument is exploited to the full extent of its characteristic possibilities; even the contrabassoon, two octaves below the voice, accompanies the first words of the messenger with an effect which is both completely novel and apposite.

The rhythmic element is, superficially at least, far less striking in *Oedipus* than in either *Le Sacre du printemps* or *Les Noces*. It is, however, not less important in the construction of the whole. A constant metrical unit is preserved with only the slightest variations from strict regularity in accordance with the necessities of expressive contrast. The transitions from one tempo to another are always carefully and delicately wrought. The above quotation furnishes an excellent example, though Stravinsky's mode of procedure is quite familiar by this time. Rhythmic freedom in the sense of constantly shifting accent is rare and confined wholly to the scenes of the Messenger and Shepherd, which form an interesting though perhaps quite unconscious parallel with the general form of Greek drama in the introduction of complex and agitated rhythms at the moment when the tragic suspense is at its height. Otherwise the rhythmic effect is concentrated in certain persistent orchestral figures, such as the constant and regular pulsating of tympani, harp, piano and pizzicati beneath the choruses of the first act; in certain rhythmic effects arising directly out of the Latin text; and in a very different sense in certain pages of a quasi-declamatory nature, such as the long passage beginning with the words *Sphynga solvi* in the Latin text. Here one may speak of a kind of rhythmic modeling which is of extraordinary and subtle beauty.

The use of Latin as the language of the text has aroused an astonishment for which it is difficult to account. The text of a vocal work is of the utmost importance to the total effect, as any one can testify who has attentively listened to the performance of vocal music in other than its original language. In planning a vocal work in which the music should retain its complete supremacy it was natural that Stravinsky should choose a language which combines extreme vocal effectiveness with freedom from associations which would offer any distraction from the music. Latin as a "dead language" is in a sense a passive medium which can be used with respect to its timbre alone to a far greater extent than would be possible with French, Italian, Russian, or German, each of which has certain definite local connotations that could not be ignored.

The musical language of *Oedipus* is at first baffling through its apparent mixture of styles. The musician, according to the degree of his culture, may pick out "reminiscences" on every page, and is disconcerted not so much by the fact that they exist as by their apparent inconsistency. A dozen centuries, a dozen localities will seem to him to be clamoring for recognition. Then gradually on closer acquaintance this impression disappears almost completely. The truth is that the elements involved are of the most general nature, belonging to no time or place in particular, but rather to the common fund of European musical culture. Stravinsky has reabsorbed them into a style which is his own, working in some such manner as the composers of the eighteenth century, who likewise wrote, not each in a separate, individual language, but in an idiom which he inherited and developed, according to his own talent and the unconscious dictates of his sensibility.

It is thus a mistake to think of Stravinsky's later music as in any sense "archaistic." If *Oedipus* tempts one on first acquaintance to various analogies with the music of the past, it is because of a lingering tendency, contrary to the whole spirit of Stravinsky's art, to seek impressions in music which are evocative rather than direct. The power of *Oedipus* never depends on effects of association. In each case the analogy holds good only up to a certain point, beyond which we find ourselves in the presence of a style whose individuality is so pervasive and compelling as to thoroughly escape analysis.

Like the other recent works of Stravinsky, indeed to a certain extent like all his works, *Oedipus* is the direct result of a certain aesthetic faith, a faith which regards works of art as objects existing in and for themselves apart from the limitations of purely personal emotions. An art which is impersonal, objective, is certainly not to be judged by the standards generally current today.

One even suspects that many of the older composers are accepted now only because current standards of aesthetic value are not applied to them. The reader of Mozart's letters, for instance, can hardly fail to be struck by this difference in attitude. His art, one is tempted to think, was for him in part at least, a commodity which was very much in demand, and which he could supply in large quantities with a maximum of assured quality. There is no trace of exhibitionism, of preoccupation with self-expression, individual exaltation, or any of the other attitudes which characterized the literature and the music of the nineteenth and early twentieth centuries. The emphasis was entirely on the work, not on the composer. His personality, in so far as it appears at all in his music, shows as a vitalizing but unconscious and inevitable factor. What he sought unceasingly was perfection of form and style—clarity and solidity and equilibrium.

It is a similar aesthetic that underlies Stravinsky's later music. If personality consists in the exaltation of everything that is particular, eccentric, "personal" in the narrowest sense, or in the discovery and exploitation for their own sake of novel effects, *Oedipus* is certainly the least personal of works. But a quite different conception is possible. In seeking objective musical realities, concerning himself solely with concrete problems of form and style, his sensibility, his musical instinct is still the court of last appeal. Instead of affirming his own peculiarities he brings a complete personality—its general as well as its particular elements—into his work. It is this completeness which *Oedipus* achieves, and this quality above all which makes it similar in kind to the art which is generally called "classic."

Hindemith's *Mathis der Maler*
[1934]

Hindemith's symphony Mathis der Maler, *derived from his opera of the same name, received its first complete performance in Berlin, in March 1934. (There had been a partial broadcast performance over the B.B.C. in December, 1933.) The work was performed in New York the following Fall.*

HINDEMITH's symphony, *Mathis der Maler*, which Otto Klemperer introduced to the American public at the first Philharmonic concert this season, has already made history in one respect. It was performed in Berlin last season by Furtwaengler in the face of Nazi opposition, and in fact is said to have been the only work by a composer of not strictly conservative tendency to be performed at one of the more important concerts in Germany since the present government assumed full control of German musical life. The unprecedented enthusiasm with which it was greeted forced the authorities to give it and its composer a certain measure of recognition, a recognition that represents in some measure a victory for the cause of contemporary music and contemporary culture on the very soil where these are being most vigorously suppressed.

The New York performance, while not a sensational event in any respect, achieved a victory which was similar in kind if not in extent. More than one hearer who had begun to be discouraged by the paucity of real achievement in the music of the last few years must have felt considerably heartened to hear, in a new work, music of real power, of clear con-

From *Modern Music*, vol. 12, no. 1, pp. 13-17. Reprinted by permission of the League of Composers—International Society for Contemporary Music, U.S. Section, Inc.

347

ception, and of legitimate and full-blooded relationship with the central current of Western music. One was reminded once more that however barren an artistic epoch may seem, through the quality of its inferior productions, it is, nevertheless, by its best and not by its worst that it must, and ultimately will, be judged.

This symphony is based on excerpts from an opera dealing with the life of Matthias Gruenewald and consists of three movements each of which bears the title of one of the paintings in the famous altarpiece by that master. The first, entitled *Concert of the Angels*, is an allegro movement preceded by a slower introduction; the second, *The Entombment*, lento molto, is a short and deeply expressive slow movement, elegiac in character. The third and last movement bears the title *The Temptation of St. Anthony*; it is the longest and most complex of the three, and contains striking formal features. There are five sections, clearly differentiated in tempo and character but closely related thematically in such a manner as to form an organic whole which, however, represents a real innovation in respect to recognized formal patterns. A slow recitative for the strings in unison is followed by a fast and impetuous movement in nine-eight time which presents three new themes; this in turn is followed by a slow section in which additional material is introduced on the strings alone. The third section, in fast two-four time, recapitulates in radically modified form material from the preceding two sections, while the last section, a still faster movement, brings back as a kind of ostinato the theme of the opening recitative, which here serves as a background for the hymn *Laude Sion Salvatorem*. The movement closes with a triumphant *Alleluia*.

Mathis der Maler has on several grounds been hailed as a new departure in Hindemith's work. Two points in particular have been stressed in this regard.

First of all, critics and musicians have professed to find

in it a "return" to a simpler harmonic style, to "tonality" and "consonance." Secondly, much stress has been laid on the fact that it is in a sense "program music." It has thus been acclaimed as heralding another type of "return" for which certain sections of the public have long been clamoring. It would be idle to deny that there are grounds for each of these views; but like all snap judgments—and what such neatly expressed critical opinion is not, perforce, a snap judgment?—both need considerable qualification before they can be taken quite seriously.

The case is a reasonably simple one, complicated largely by the fact that Hindemith's output is so large, so varied in character and even in its aims, and (let it be frankly stated) so uneven in quality. In America this state of affairs is considerably complicated by the fact that performances are comparatively rare, and the difficulty of forming a true conception, not only of the music itself but even of the real development of the composer, becomes very great indeed.

In regard to the style of *Mathis der Maler* it must be said that the features noted above have been increasingly evident in Hindemith's music in the last years. It was evident, for example, to a very large extent in the oratorio *Das Unaufhörliche* or, farther back, in such works as the two concerti for viola, the concerto for piano, brass, and harps, or the concert piece written for the fiftieth anniversary of the Boston Symphony. In all of these works the composer has shown himself preoccupied with the necessity of establishing his music on the basis of a solid and unmistakable tonal center. While the music is not perhaps tonal in the strictest classic sense—what contemporary music is, after all?—and while the tonal procedure is often complex, constantly shifting, and sometimes even angular and apparently arbitrary, the ear always keeps its orientation, with the tonic triad in the background as a point of departure.

In *Mathis der Maler* the use of the hymns *Es sungen drei Engel* and *Laude Sion Salvatorem* in the first and last movements respectively, tend to make the tonal design even

349

simpler than in the former works, since their extremely simple lines make such treatment inevitable. For the rest, Hindemith's melody shows the same characteristics as may be observed in his other works. The main theme, alla breve, of the first movement is an obvious example of this, in its general line as well as its details.

As far as "program music" is concerned it may be pointed out that this symphony is in reality an excerpt from an opera and not in the strictest sense of the word an independent instrumental work. This however does not dispose of the question. The quarrel of contemporary composers has not been with program music as such, but simply with music whose impelling force, instead of lying in the melodies, rhythms and harmonies themselves, is borrowed from images or ideas which are outside the music, which are not organic parts of it but which nevertheless, to an overwhelming degree condition its form. This produces a type of music whose interest depends in overwhelming measure on such features as tone color, texture, and dynamic accent taken in and for themselves and not as an element of a complete musical impulse. Such distorted emphasis is to be found not only in "program music" but in many works which profess to be free of all extra-musical associations. In a work like *Mathis der Maler*, on the other hand, the titles of the various movements have no function except that of giving a definite direction, so to speak, in time and space, to the emotions aroused by the music; the music, however, in no sense depends on the title either for its impulse or its development.

To say this is not to deny *Mathis der Maler* a special place in Hindemith's work, even though it makes it a little more difficult to define precisely what that place is. Here again we are confronted by the mixed and uneven quality of his work as a whole. Those who find this music more human, more tender, more profound than his earlier music must be reminded perforce of many pages in the *Marien-*

leben, of the Third Quartet, of the concerti for viola, and
of many truly moving pages scattered throughout his other
work. *Mathis der Maler*, also, contains some pages which
are less satisfying than others. The main body of the first
movement, in spite of some beautiful moments, is in what
has come to seem a rather conventional Hindemithian manner, and though it is probably, through its freshness and
simplicity, one of the best of such movements, it has less
interest than the other two. Again, the last movement, in
spite of the great beauty of the opening measures, the im-
petuousness of its rhythms, the real power of its climaxes,
is too long and becomes less convincing because of the
comparative flatness of its texture, which until near the close
remains prevailingly homophonic. Its general formal design,
though interesting to the highest degree, therefore seems
looser and less convincing than would otherwise be the case.
The slow movement, on the other hand, with its simple and
deeply moving accents, is not only one of the most beautiful
things which Hindemith has written but one of the finest
pages in contemporary music.

Local comment on the work stressed as usual the "dry-
ness" of Hindemith's music which it contrasted unfavorably
with the Second Symphony of Sibelius on the same program. It is highly unfortunate that such comparisons be
made, largely because they lead to such false conceptions
not only of the personalities involved but of music itself
and its true relation to life. It is fortunately not necessary
to make a choice. They also force a perhaps undue emphasis of the fact that for all the fine pages and eloquent accents in his work, Sibelius remains, in the deepest sense of
the word, a provincial composer. It is not merely that his
music is essentially music of a special landscape and climate,
and that landscape and climate, which are subsidiary factors
in the work of any artist, play a preponderant role in his
music. It is above all that his music faces none of the issues and poses none of the problems, the experience of
which has formed the sensibilities of contemporary men

and women. He has remained aloof in his Finnish forests, and what he offers his hearers is, precisely, a refuge from these problems and issues.

The music of Hindemith, too, has its limitations; and since they are limitations of a totally different order it is quite idle to argue a comparison on the basis of abstract "greatness," "genius," or merit. Hindemith's limitations are to a certain extent those of his goal, that of the artist who aims first of all at perfect and expert workmanship, accepting his ideas as they come to him, and leaving the rest to Providence, Destiny, or God. At the best such an attitude produces supreme works of art; at the worst it is certain to produce good ones. And if Hindemith's work never achieves the force of ultimate revelation, it always rests firmly on the ground of musical reality, never giving less than it aims and pretends to give. And occasionally what it gives is of a very high order indeed.

Schoenberg in the United States
[1944, revised 1972]

AUTHOR'S NOTE. *This article was written in 1944 (the year of Schoenberg's seventieth birthday) and must of course be understood in the context of its time. Since then my perspective has naturally changed: first, simply because twenty-eight years have passed; secondly because Schoenberg's death in 1951 imposed on all of us the obligation (which the passage of time has given us ample opportunity to fulfill) of considering his achievement as a whole rather than merely as a succession of "phases"; thirdly, because, partly as a result of this article (which, somewhat to my surprise, pleased him) I acquired a very satisfying and quite unforgettable personal relationship with Schoenberg, never as a "disciple" but rather as a loyal friend. Finally, I have since become acquainted with several of his most important earlier works, notably* Der Jakobsleiter *and* Moses und Aron, *which were not then available to me, and also the* Orchestral Variations op. 31, *which I knew only from a first perusal of the score. I have therefore made a few minor revisions in the original article and have appended to it a series of critical comments from my standpoint of today (1972).*

IN any survey of Schoenberg's work one fact must be emphasized above all: that no younger composer writes quite the same music as he would have written had Schoenberg's music not existed. The influence of an artist is not,

From *Tempo*, no. 103 (1972), pp. 8-17.

even during his lifetime, confined to his disciples or even to those who have felt the direct impact of his work. It is filtered through to the humblest participant, first in the work of other original artists who have absorbed and reinterpreted it for their own purposes; then through the work of hundreds of lesser individuals, who unconsciously reflect the new tendencies even when they are opposed to them. For genuinely new ideas determine the battlegrounds on which their opponents are forced to attack. In the very process of combat the latter undergo decisive experiences which help to carry the new ideas forward.

In Schoenberg's case this process is clear. The appearance, around 1911, of his first completely characteristic works, and of his *Harmonielehre*, marks the approximate beginning of the years that were decisive in the formation of contemporary music. True, these works—both music and book—only carried to more radical conclusions tendencies already present in the music of the time; these manifestations, then hailed as revolutionary, seem to us now more like footnotes and queries to established modes of thought than integral and challenging steps toward new ones. What was new in Debussy and Ravel and Scriabin seemed more fundamental and far-reaching than it does today.

But in the Three Piano Pieces, op. 11, and the Five Orchestral Pieces, op. 16, a much more thorough-going challenge became evident. What led in Wagner to an enlargement of musical resources, in Debussy and Scriabin[1] to the cultivation of special and restricted corners, here openly insists that new resources, having multiplied to an over-

---

[1] This rather casual statement was not, of course, intended as a reflection on the artistic stature of either composer—particularly that of Debussy, whose rich and unique achievement, throughout the whole length of his career, is incontestable. I add this note of caution simply because of an all too prevalent tendency (to which further reference will be made in the course of these notes) to confuse questions belonging to the realm of historical development and categorization—essentially arbitrary, though convenient and presumably unavoidable—with those of inherent artistic value. (R. S.)

whelming extent, demand a logic of their own, depriving the earlier principles of their validity even in music of a relatively conventional[2] type. The *Harmonielehre*, which exerted its influence on some of the least likely persons, raised the same questions in the realm of theory, deducing them from the very logic of previous practice. The musical status quo has never completely recovered from the blow.

In 1933 Schoenberg came to the United States and ten years later became an American citizen. In the country to which he came, musical activity is intense on many levels, and despite many necessary reservations the development within the last generation has been phenomenal. Musical education has penetrated everywhere; both the general level and the quality of instruction available on the highest level of all have risen to a degree amazing to all who confronted the musical conditions of thirty-five years ago. American composers of serious intent have begun to appear in considerable numbers, and to achieve an influence and recognition undreamed by their predecessors; moreover, they have become aware of themselves, of their inner and outer problems, and better equipped to face these. Above all it has become evident that musical talent, the raw material from which musical culture grows, is strikingly abundant.

It is, however, clear that the institutional structure of music in the United States has not yet been established in definitive outlines.[3] The relationship between the art and the business of music, and of both of these with the "public"; the role and direction of musical education; the influence of radio, gramophone, and amateur musical activities—these are questions which in the United States are still fundamentally unsettled. There is similar confusion as to what we

[2] Not "conventional"—which implies motivation through sheer convention—but rather simply "unadventurous." (R. S.)

[3] The situation has developed very considerably in the United States since 1944, of course. Were I discussing it today I would write somewhat differently. As of 1944 I find my remarks fairly accurate. (R. S.)

may call the structure of musical effort: the respective roles in musical culture and production of the composer, performer, critic, and scholar.

These latter observations are true of course not only of the United States but of modern civilization in general. But conditions here differ from those elsewhere in the fact that whereas elsewhere the forces of opposition are those of an established cultural tradition, here there is a perceptible undertow in the growing musical consciousness of a culture still in the making. It is this which keeps the musical life of the country in a state of constant change and flux, and which makes the situation chaotic but far from hopeless.

It is not surprising therefore that Schoenberg should have found himself in a quite new relationship to his environment and that his impact should have taken on a new significance. I do not mean to minimize the importance of either the revolutionary or the specifically Viennese Schoenberg. The former has already affected the course of music in a profound sense, and though possibly the first full impact of a composer's work is the most immediately powerful one—think of the *Eroica*, of *Tristan*, in contrast to the last quartets or *Parsifal*—nevertheless with the constant ripening of his art, the latter imposes itself in another, more gradual and more definitely constructive, sense. But that is a task for the composer's successors, and is even independent of his purely historical importance.

As for Vienna, Schoenberg has outlived it as he has outlived Alban Berg. Had he not done so his position might be today less evident than it is. There are other musicians from Central, also from Western and Eastern, Europe, whose impact has been purely provincial; they have conceived their mission as that of winning spheres of influence for their own native background; and have found—by an inexorable law of human polarization—the most sympathetic acclaim often in circles most tenacious in the pursuit of an American "national" style. Undeniably Schoenberg is a product of Vienna, and of a Viennese tradition with which he is as

deeply imbued as anyone living. But it is characteristic of
the man, the situation, and possibly of the Viennese tradition itself that his impact on the United States has been that
of a third Schoenberg—one by no means unknown in Europe
nor difficult to find for those who sought him, but one
often obscured in the heat of controversy and the battle
positions which his followers were led to assume in his behalf. For in coming to the United States, he left the scene
of his most bitter struggles; he came with the prestige of a
fighter of distant and only dimly understood battles, with
the respect and admiration of a few to whom the battles
were neither so distant nor so dimly understood. Others
recognized the achievement of the composer of *Verklärte
Nacht* and other early works, and were ready to acclaim
him as at least an asset to American musical life.

He taught and lectured in Boston and New York and
finally was appointed Professor of Music, first at the University of Southern California, later at the University of
California in Los Angeles. His music received sporadic performances; he found himself frequently quoted, frequently
in demand as a writer and lecturer. His main influence, however, has been exerted through his teaching, the musicians
with whom he has come in contact, and finally the series
of works composed in the years since he has lived in the
United States—works which in my opinion represent a separate phase and a new level in his music as a whole.[4]

[4] This final clause, and the following paragraph, need some clarification. First of all I have never regarded the Suite for Strings, the
Variations op. 43, or the *Kol Nidrei* as being in the mainstream of
Schoenberg's development. The Second Chamber Symphony I find,
on the other hand, a rather important piece, precisely because of
what has sometimes been considered a flaw: the fact that it harks
back—as it necessarily must—to an earlier Schoenbergian manner.
It seems to me that it does so successfully, even though it does not
fit into the "period" of his work—as we have chosen to conceive it—
during which it was completed. It is still unmistakably Schoenberg;
and perhaps we should learn, now that he has passed the "controversial" stage, to regard his work as a whole, laying less stress on its

These works include a Suite for strings, written in 1934; the Fourth String Quartet written in 1936 and performed by the Kolisch Quartet in 1937; the Violin Concerto, performed in 1940 by Louis Krasner with the Philadelphia Orchestra; a second Chamber Symphony; a setting of the *Kol Nidrei* for chorus and orchestra; Variations on a Recitative for organ, first performed by Carl Weinrich for the United States section of the I.S.C.M. in March, 1944; the Concerto for Piano first performed by Edward Steuermann and the Philadelphia Orchestra in the spring of this year; finally two works shortly to be performed, the *Ode to Napoleon*, after Byron, for *Sprechstimme*, piano and strings, and a Theme and Variations, written originally for band and later arranged for orchestra.

Of these works, the Suite is consciously in an "old style," and the Second Chamber Symphony is the completion of a work left unfinished some forty years earlier. With the latter, the organ Variations have given rise to rumors of a "conservative" trend in Schoenberg's music—a "return" at least to "tonality" and to a more "consonant" style. No doubt, the new Variations and possibly the *Ode*, both shortly to receive their world premières, will add to these rumors which purport to herald a "capitulation" on Schoenberg's part. The organ Variations are extremely freely but none the less unmistakably in the key of D minor, though also

---

individual phases, and on what once seemed, fundamentally on purely technical grounds, sharp differences between them.

The organ Variations and the Ode I knew only slightly at the time of writing this article. They both still seem to me somewhat problematical, perhaps because I have not heard them or studied them in recent years. My remarks in the article apply principally to the Fourth Quartet, the Violin Concerto, and the Piano Concerto; but they apply also to *Moses und Aron* and to the Orchestral Variations op. 31, which were both composed several years before Schoenberg came to the United States; and they apply most emphatically to the String Trio, composed three years after this article was written. The Trio seems to me in some respects the most perfect embodiment of Schoenberg's essential musical character. (R. S.)

influenced by serial thinking; the orchestral Variations are in G minor, signature and all, and definitely in a simpler style. The *Ode to Napoleon*, though still in the twelve-tone system, is superficially more "consonant" than many of Schoenberg's earlier works in that, to a very large extent, its style[5] is characterized by the superimposition of triads and their derivatives. It is, however, doubtful if either the *Ode* or the organ Variations will prove comforting to those who pretend to see any reversal on Schoenberg's part. They are presumably quite as "forbidding" as any of his reputedly "atonal" works.

"Atonality," in fact, is a conception which Schoenberg has never accepted and which has certainly no relationship to the experience of a practiced listener to his music. If "tonality" means anything in other than academic terms it must certainly denote the *sensation* of relationships between tones, and of functional differences arising from these relationships. The tonic, the leading tone, and so on are sensations habitual in all listeners. In no sense are they mere theoretical abstractions; they are not inextricably bound up with any systematic formula yet established nor are they in the last analysis definable in terms of any such formula alone. The prevailing harmonic concepts or definitions of "tonality" are inadequate not only to the music of contemporary composers, but to many elusive problems in classic music. It should, however, be clear that these inadequacies are in no manner to be conjured away through the adoption of the essentially meaningless term "atonal," any more than the presence or absence of an occasional triad or sixth-chord is of more than incidental significance in determining the characteristics of a style such as Schoenberg's.

I believe that in these works written since 1936 Schoenberg has achieved a freedom and resourcefulness which car-

---

[5] Not "style," of course, but "vocabulary"; however, this question should be discussed only with reference to the tone-row on which the work is based (see Joseph Rufer, *The Works of Arnold Schoenberg*, New York, 1963, especially the facsimile facing p. 64). (R. S.)

ries them in this respect far beyond his earlier works, especially those in the twelve-tone technique. Regarding that technique itself much misleading nonsense has been written. I am in no sense a spokesman for it; I have never been attracted to it as a principle of composition.[6] But one must

---

[6] I used the twelve-tone principle for the first time in 1953, in my Sonata for Violin Solo, and have used it to various degrees and in various ways ever since—always, of course, in my own terms. My first use of it was, at the beginning, quite involuntary. I had at various times, for my own self-enlightenment, carried out quite small-scale exercises with the technique, but I still envisaged it as not applicable to my own musical ideas. It was therefore a surprise to me when I found the composition of the Sonata flowing easily and without constraint in its terms. I used it consistently in several well-defined sections of the piece; but on several grounds I decided not to mention this to anyone. However, a colleague to whom I showed the piece immediately recognized the twelve-tone procedures, and afterwards observed, with some surprise, "But it's still *your* music." This of course is the crux of the matter; I would not have adopted the principle had it been otherwise. It is a mistake to regard the adoption by an artist of a new technical procedure, or even a new "manner," as in any way changing his essential artistic nature.

Once—in 1948, I believe—in the course of a long conversation with Schoenberg, I told him of my opinion that the "twelve-tone method" had been over-publicized and, in the process itself as well as in the controversy which resulted, had become grossly distorted in the minds of many people; and that this had led to strained and artificial attitudes towards the music itself. He replied, somewhat glumly, "Yes, you are right, and I have to admit that it's partly my fault." After a pause he recovered his animation and added, "But it's still more the fault of some of my disciples."

I cite these incidents not in order to play down the importance of the twelve-tone principle—or "method" as Schoenberg insisted on calling it—but rather to place it in its proper perspective as a means and not an end or—above all, at this late date—a "cause." Obviously it is a fact relevant to the music of composers who adopt it—one fact among others, after all. But in no sense does it determine musical value, still less can it be regarded as a quasi-historical end to be pursued for its own sake. In my view it is an all too common error of our times to invoke a facile historicism as a valid basis for both musical effort and musical judgment. One should never forget that it is music, and music alone, that determines musical history; in Schoen-

distinguish carefully between technical principles in the abstract, and the works in which they become embodied; even a great work does not validate a dubious principle, nor does a valid principle produce in itself good or even technically convincing work. It would for example be easy, though basically irrelevant, to show that Beethoven's *Heiliger Dankgesang* in the Lydian mode, like most other modern "modal" works, is based on a technically specious conception of the nature and function of the modes. Similarly, assuming the fugue or sonata to have been valid as principles of musical structure, how many grievous sins have been committed in their names!

One can not too often insist that in music it is the composer's inner world of tone and rhythm which matters, and that whatever technical means he chooses in order to give it structure and coherence are subject to no a priori judgment whatever. The essential is that structure and coherence be present; and the demand which art makes on its creator is simply that his technique be sufficiently mastered to become an obedient and flexible instrument in his hands. True, the twelve-tone technique became at one time a fighting slogan; this happened under the stress of combat, the inevitable result of bitter opposition met by Schoenberg and his disciples. Today, however, it is no longer invoked as a universal principle; it is recognized for what it is as a mode of technical procedure, a principle which evolves and becomes modified by practice. Once more—the significance of music springs solely from the composer's imagination and not from ideas about technique. The latter are merely tools which he forges for himself, for his own purposes. They gain what validity they possess from the results, in music, to which they make their imponderable contribution.

---

berg's case, *Moses und Aron* and the String Trio and many other works are more important facts, historically as well as musically, than the discovery of the twelve-tone method. The same is of course true of the music of Berg and Webern, not to mention Stravinsky and many others. (R. S.)

Five Composers

In regard to Schoenberg's work it may also be stressed that the twelve-tone technique is a part of the *process* rather than an essential element of the form.[7] It is not essential or even possible for the listener to apprehend it in all its various transformations. He must listen to Schoenberg's music in exactly the same spirit as he listens to any music whatever, and bring to it the same kind of response. If he is fortunate he will from the first discover moments of profound and intense beauty which will tempt him further. He will always find that the music makes the utmost demands on his ear and his musical understanding, and he will probably find that with a little familiarity it begins to impose itself. In any case, esoteric notions or strained efforts will, as in the case of all music, serve as a barrier rather than as an aid to his understanding.

So if in some works of the 1920s one feels a certain tenseness and dogmatic insistence, one must regard that as a necessary phase in Schoenberg's development. At the time he was exploring and mastering the resources of the new technique. In the works of the last ten years one feels no such limitation. The technique is used with the ease of virtuosity, with complete resourcefulness, and with such freedom that it is sometimes difficult to discover. The Fourth Quartet, the Violin and the Piano Concertos are, as far as I can see, his finest achievements of these years, perhaps of his whole work. They are larger in scope, if not in gesture, than the *Ode to Napoleon* or the organ Variations; like these they are in no conceivable wise more "conservative" than the

[7] This statement, as it stands, seems to me clumsy and self-contradictory. To be sure, the sentences which follow help to make my meaning somewhat clearer. The idea that twelve-tone manipulation as such can—and should—account for every factor that is embodied in a piece of music belongs possibly to the time, now fairly well past, when the "system," or derivatives from it, aroused the kind of heated controversy that leads to overstatement and misunderstanding on both sides. However, the idea that "process" and "form" are separate and isolable elements strikes me as palpable nonsense, which I'm guilty of having perpetrated here! (R. S.)

earlier works even though they differ from these in several essential respects.

They differ first of all in their longer and broader lines. This is not simply a question of "continuity"; Schoenberg has always been in this respect a master of form, and in no work known to me can he be accused of a lack of logic. But—with those qualifications and exceptions—the individual details are underlined to a degree that they, rather than the larger lines, seem to bear the main expressive burden.[8]

[8] Here too I would change the emphasis to some extent. The better I have learned to know Schoenberg's work as a whole the more I have become aware of the breadth and the power—and the uniqueness in character—of the larger lines, more pronounced in the later works but by no means limited to them. I have also realized that it is precisely this aspect of Schoenberg's work that has contributed strongly to the curious phenomenon of a very great composer, each of whose most distinguished—and devoted—disciples achieved general recognition before him, and each of whom (literally as well as figuratively over their dead bodies) has been used as a weapon against him. This has certainly been as basically unjust to Webern and Berg as to Schoenberg himself, and is mentioned here in full appreciation of the achievements, the individuality, and the stature of both composers. The point is that Schoenberg was a genuine and original master of large musical design, and that this becomes clearer as his work, in its totality, becomes better and more generally known.

One may note too that regardless of the musical vocabulary involved, the emphasis on large design as above detail is in some quarters held to be in itself a symptom of a "conservative" trend. This reaction to the fact that the lines are necessarily broader and the relationships farther-flung than in works of smaller format and shorter duration, is just as superficial as the associated use of terms like "conservative" and "radical," which have little relevance to the development of a mature artist intent on the problem which the evolution of his own work sets for him. If one follows Schoenberg's development as an organic unit, it should be easy to see that, having established the twelve-tone method to his own satisfaction, he inevitably applied it to problems of genuinely large musical design, while avoiding the easy pitfall involved in regarding the tone-row, in and by itself, as (automatically, as it were) furnishing the whole and exclusive answer to these problems. Composers, after all, are primarily concerned with writing music, not in solving technical theorems. (R. S.)

It is a question of emphasis; the "fragmentary" impression that disturbs many listeners results from the fact that every sensation is intensified to the utmost degree. All contrasts are of the sharpest kind, and it is not surprising that they strike the hearer most forcibly, even after familiarity with the work has brought their essential continuity more to the fore. In the later works, above all in the Piano Concerto, the expressive emphasis shifts strikingly to the line as a whole. A sustained melodic line becomes the rule rather than the exception. The melodic style itself has become more concentrated, less extravagant and diffuse in detail. I am tempted to cite examples: the graceful melody which opens the Piano Concerto; the declamatory opening phrase of the slow movement of the Quartet; or the haunting and tender Andante of the Violin Concerto.

The very adoption of the concerto form, with the predominance of one instrument, underlines this tendency. Though Schoenberg's uncompromising polyphony results in a large measure of obbligato treatment of the solo parts, especially in the Piano Concerto, this treatment is nevertheless on the broadest lines, the constant tone quality contributing unmistakably to the architectonics of the works. Equally consistent is the orchestral dress. Though certainly as vivid as in the earlier works, it contrasts strikingly with these in that it, too, is laid out on broader lines. The constant and kaleidoscopic change so characteristic of the Five Orchestral Pieces or the Bach transcriptions, has been superseded by a style in which tone colors, in all their characteristic boldness, remain constant over longer stretches, and are opposed to each other in sharply defined and large-scale contrasts. Needless to say, the instruments are employed with complete freedom from preconceived ideas and with full awareness of the relationship between ends and means. While it makes extreme demands, technical and otherwise, on the performers—the solo parts of both concertos are truly formidable—it does so always with full awareness; the demands lie in the musical ideas themselves and are in no way superimposed on them. They pose new problems for the performers—but they have this in common with much of the best music of every generation.

These works possess other and more elusive characteristics, at some of which I have already hinted in connection with the *Ode to Napoleon*. It is not easy concretely to demonstrate, in the two concertos and the Quartet, a still wider range of harmonic effect—one which includes all the simplest as well as the most complex relationships—or a much vaster harmonic line, at the least suggesting a new tonal principle, powerfully binding like the old but embracing all possible relationships within the chromatic scale. As far as I know, no adequate study has yet been made of Schoenberg's work in its harmonic and tonal aspects—aspects which lie deeper than the twelve-tone system or the individual sonority, and guide the ear of the listener in his real apprehension of the music. The above-mentioned qualities seem to me, however, strikingly present in all of this later music and a most important element in the effect of unity, sweeping movement, and concentration which the works produce. If I express myself cautiously in this regard it is because they raise questions of capital importance, for which nothing less than a painstaking effort of research, and a totally new theoretical formulation, would be necessary. Meanwhile the works are there, with a new challenge, different in kind but perhaps not in importance from that embodied in the Three Piano Pieces and the Five Orchestral Pieces thirty-odd years ago.

The above remarks are at best cursory and convey all too little idea of the works themselves. It goes without saying that performances have been very few, and their real impact limited. The scores are available, however, through the foresight of G. Schirmer, Inc. The enthusiasm of many of the most gifted among young musicians as well as the gradually deepening interest of their elders is one of the striking phenomena of a period in which the prevailing trend seems superficially to be all in the direction of a not entirely genuine "mass appeal," facile and standardized effect, and a kind of hasty shabbiness of conception and workmanship.

As a teacher Schoenberg has fought against these latter tendencies with undiminished energy. Here, too, his influence has been both direct and indirect. In New York and especially in California considerable numbers of Americans have passed under his instruction. At one time he even was in demand among the composers of film music in Hollywood; his demands, however, proved too high, and composers in search of easy formulas of effect withdrew in disappointment. The same thing has happened to those who have gone to Schoenberg in the hopes of learning to compose in the twelve-tone system or in the "modern idiom." Nothing is farther from Schoenberg's ideas than that sort of instruction. He does not, in fact, preoccupy himself with "style" at all, in the usual sense of the word. What concerns him is the musical development, in the most integral sense, of the pupil. He insists on the most rigorous training in harmony and counterpoint; those familiar with his *Harmonielehre* must needs appreciate the extent to which this is true. For one who has never been his pupil, the striking feature of his teaching is precisely that it is systematic without ever becoming a "system" in any closed sense; that it is almost fanatically rigorous in its ceaseless striving after mastery of resource; logical and clear in its presentation of materials, but as free as teaching can be from any essential dogmatic bias. It is based on constant experiment and observation; theoretical comment is offered always in the most pragmatic spirit—as an aid to the clarification of technical problems and not as abstract principle. They are literally, as with many such features in the *Harmonielehre*, the observations of a keen and experienced mind with reference to a specific matter in hand, to which they are completely subordinate.

Musical experience, and development through experience, is Schoenberg's watchword as a teacher. His pupils speak of his boundless love for music—the energy of his enthusi-

asm for a classic work as he analyzes it in his classes, or of
the demands on which he insists in its performance by them.
They speak of his tireless energy in asking of them—above
all the gifted ones—that they bring into their work the
last degree of resourcefulness of which they are capable.
It is not surprising that under such instruction they learn
to make the greatest demands on themselves, or that their
love of music and sense of music is developed both in depth
and intensity as a result. It is this which distinguishes Schoenberg's pupils above all—their training is not merely in
"craftsmanship" but an integral training of their *musicality*,
of ear and of response. The conceptions which they have
gained are rounded and definite; they have not only gained
tools of composition, but have developed also their own
individual sense of the purposes for which these tools are
to be used.

In complete agreement they testify to the fact that nothing has been taught them of the twelve-tone system or of
"modern" composition as such. Schoenberg's attitude is that
musicians must come to these things, too, through development and necessity or not come to them at all. Having given
them a basis on which they can develop further, and a sense
of the demands of art, he insists that they must find for
themselves their path in the contemporary world. He is
fond of telling them that there is still much good music
to be written in C major, and offering them no encouragement to follow the paths he himself has chosen.

Perhaps it will be seen from this what I meant in speaking
at the beginning of this paper of a "third Schoenberg." In
his educational tenets he has not, of course, changed through
living in the United States. But he has brought these tenets
from the principal stronghold of a great and old tradition
to a fresh land which is beginning slowly and even cautiously to feel its musical strength. He has given to many
young musicians by direct influence, and to others through
his disciples, a renewed sense of all that music is and has
been, and it is hardly over-bold to foresee that this is going

to play its role, perhaps a mighty one, in the musical development of the United States. A small testimony to what this new contact may produce may be seen in a very valuable little book—*Models for Beginners in Composition*[9]—which Schoenberg prepared for students in a six-weeks' summer course in California. Certainly the eagerly awaited treatise on counterpoint, and the one also planned on the principles of composition, based on Beethoven's practice, will furnish deeper insights; they cannot fail to prove to be works of capital value.[10] But the little book has for me a special significance as a moving testimony to Schoenberg's relationship to the American musical scene, and his brilliantly successful efforts to come to grips with certain of its problems.

In this essay I have purposely avoided dwelling on the more problematical aspects of Schoenberg and his work; I have made no attempt at an exact or careful estimate. No doubt, Schoenberg is still in many respects a problematical figure, as is every other contemporary master. But it seems more relevant to regard him as a source of energy and impulse; final estimates may well be left to posterity, and the habit of attempting them at every turn is one of the dangerously sterile features of our contemporary culture. It is a symptom of a rather nervous self-consciousness and above all of self-distrust.

What is essential now is to recognize the need our world has for the qualities that Schoenberg possesses, and how admirably he supplies our need. In a world-wide condition in which the rewards of facile mediocrity and of compromise are greater than ever, and in which one hears an ever-insistent demand that music and the other arts devote themselves to the task of furnishing bread and circuses to an economically or politically pliable multitude, the musical world yet celebrates in sincere homage the seventieth birthday of

[9] New York, 1942.

[10] Two books were published posthumously: *Structural Functions of Harmony*, New York, 1954, and *Preliminary Exercises in Counterpoint*, London, 1963.

an artist who not only, in the face of the most bitter and persistent opposition, scorn and neglect, has always gone his own way in uncompromising integrity and independence, but who has been and is still the most dangerous enemy of the musical status quo. This takes place in spite of the fact that his work is all too seldom performed, that it is exacting in the extreme, and is virtually unknown except to a very few who have made the attempt really to penetrate its secrets. It is in the last analysis an act of gratitude to one who has, so much more than any other individual, been one of the masculine forces that have shaped the music of our time, even that music which seems farthest from his own. It is not only a tribute to a truly great musician, but a hopeful sign that art on the highest level may still survive the bewilderments and the terrors of a mighty world crisis, of which so much is still ahead of us, and which contains so many imponderables.

Some Notes on Schoenberg and the "Method of Composing with Twelve Tones"
[1952]

ARNOLD SCHOENBERG sometimes said, "A Chinese philosopher speaks, of course, Chinese; the question is, what does he say?" The application of this to Schoenberg's music is quite clear. The notoriety which has, for decades, surrounded what he persisted in calling his "method of composing with twelve tones," has not only obscured his real significance, but, by focusing attention on the *means* rather than on the music itself, has often seemed a barrier impeding a direct approach to the latter. To some extent it has even, rather curiously, distorted the view of Schoenberg's historical achievement, of which the discovery of the twelve-tone method is only one phase.

Schoenberg's priority in the discovery of the "method" is assured, and he set great store by the fact of priority itself. One can understand why. He had the rare but often painful honor of remaining a "controversial" figure even to the time of his death at the age of seventy-six; the still more painful experience of seeing even his disciples used as weapons against him—a situation from which both Berg and Webern would have been the first to recoil. It can easily have seemed to him that this priority, being tangible, was at least historically a precious asset.

The significant fact is that—paradoxically—were the question of priority really important, the event itself would have little value. Once, for instance, we were taught that Mozart introduced the clarinet into the orchestra. Later, one learned that other composers had used the clarinet before him; this fact, however, did not diminish in the least either

From *The Score*, no. 6, May 1952, pp. 7-10. Reprinted by permission of Kraus Reprint.

Mozart's stature, or the historical importance of his immense contribution to the development of the clarinet. If the formulation of the twelve-tone method seems likely, in future estimates of Schoenberg, to assume a less central significance than it has done up till now, this is not because the system itself is insignificant, but because Schoenberg was a great composer, because his music, historically and otherwise, is greater than any system or technique.

For Schoenberg, far from being a mere "chef d'école," of whatever stature, embodied, more than any other musician of his time, one of the great critical moments of musical history. Dodecaphony—here used to mean simply the independence of the twelve notes of the chromatic scale —is the result of an impulse which has been inherent in Western music at least from the moment that musicians began to combine voices simultaneously. As students of music history we have become familiar both with the processes involved and the reasons generally adduced for them. At one period it is a matter of avoiding the tritone; at another, the strengthening of the cadence. Later, as forms become vaster and more complex, harmonies are thrown into relief by means of "secondary dominants"; the resources, both harmonic and linear, of the minor mode are made available within a predominantly major mode, and vice versa; and finally individual tones are raised or lowered, throwing the notes which follow into greater relief, and giving rise to sonorities previously unknown. Whatever their motivation, these processes are all in one way or another expressions of what may be called the chromatic impulse. Throughout the eighteenth and nineteenth centuries their use increased constantly, and penetrated more and more into the heart of the musical vocabulary. What began, in each case, as a means of emphasizing large musical design, later developed into an expressive resource, bringing contrast into the modelling of musical detail. Thus the "chromatic harmony" of Wagner and Liszt was born; harmony based largely on "alterations" which modified the ordinary "root chords," which tended to challenge the compelling force of the relationships between these chords, frequently superseded such relationships, and finally undermined, or at least, qualified, the unity based on tonic, dominant, and subdominant.

The process is one through which every vital inflection, every nuance, gradually imposes itself and demands development. The ear of the composer, in other terms, lingers over arresting or expressive detail, and follows the train of thought or impulse incited by it.

This story has been told often enough; but it still has to be re-told and re-pondered, since it relates a development that leads to the very center of the contemporary musical problem. The processes of impulse just described in purely harmonic terms, constitute, of course, only one phase of an integral musical impulse which embraces all elements, melodic and rhythmic as well.

Perhaps we should recall here what is meant by a musical problem. This must not be envisaged in technical terms alone. It is an *expressive* crisis that arises and demands solution. The technical solution is ex post facto, so to speak; the concept of technique, in fact, has to do with solutions, not with crises or problems as such. Furthermore, a genuine problem is the affair not so much of an individual composer as of music itself. It is a turning point in the development of the human spirit, and represents either the opening up of a new vein, or the exhaustion of an old one. Thus it does not lend itself to easy definition in words. How much easier, in fact, to take the technical ideas out of their context and define them, as it were, in the raw state—a process that actually reduces to absurdity any technical concept whatever.

The truly immense achievement of Schoenberg lies in the fact that his artistic career embodies and summarizes a fundamental musical crisis. More than any other composer he led the crisis to its culmination. He accomplished this by living it through to its furthest implications. But he also found technical means which could enable composers of his own and later generations to seek and find solutions. He opened up a new vein, towards which music had been tending; and the twelve-tone method is in essence the tool through which this vein can be exploited. Its discovery was a historical necessity; had it not been Schoenberg who formulated it, others would have done so, though possibly in a much slower and more laborious manner.

Nothing could be more wrong, in fact, or more unjust to Schoenberg and to his memory, than to regard the twelve-tone method as essentially limited to a single group or a single *Weltanschauung*. In too many quarters, friendly and hostile alike, a kind of orthodoxy has grown up—a convenience since orthodoxy offers both a safe refuge and an easy point of attack. But not only is dodecaphony constantly in process of development; precisely because it is a living process and not a dogma, it means something different, and shows a different aspect, in every individual personality. It has often been remarked that composers who, in the midst of their careers, adopt the twelve-tone method, do not essentially change their styles; they continue writing the music that is conspicuously their own—not less but, let us hope, more so for having been enriched by new elements.

What is the twelve-tone method, then? Obviously, within the limits of a short article one cannot give an adequate account of it and all that it implies, or can imply. Primarily it is a means through which the twelve notes of the chromatic scale—which, unlike the diatonic scale, is uniform and therefore neutral in harmonic implication—can be organized into a basic pattern capable of supplying the impulse toward extended musical development; and which, through the recurrence of the relationships implied in it, makes possible a unity, not unlike that yielded by the principle of tonality, which is implicit in the material premises on which a musical work is based.

The tone-series plays, in dodecaphonic music, somewhat the role played by the diatonic scale in music of the pretonal period. It is, naturally, not an identical role; the series differs from the scale in that it has an independent design, and thus a distinct character of its own—it represents a personal choice, that is, on the part of the composer. Instead of accepting it as a predetermined datum, the latter is guided by his own musical impulse in constructing it; it will, in other words, inevitably bear the stamp of his personality, and, as his command of the technique increases, it will more and more be penetrated by his musical thought. The composer's relationship to the series and to its treatment, in fact, is exactly the same as it is to any technique which he adopts. He will—as in any other technique— achieve spontaneity in proportion to the degree of mastery which he achieves; he will learn the resources of the technique through practice, and will formulate his own principles in accordance with his own needs. As with every other technique, he will heed, modify, or ignore the rules insofar as real musical necessities demand; there is no need to insist on this point. But he will be successful in this respect only in proportion to his mastery of, and insight into, the materials themselves.

It is necessary to emphasize these points because they have been so often misunderstood, and because this misunderstanding has interfered with the appreciation of Schoenberg's real achievement. He has, for instance, always opposed the use of the term "atonality," and this term, like the undue public emphasis given to the twelve-tone method in discussing his music, has for too long stood between the public and the music itself. The objection is that "atonality" is essentially a negative term, but also that it has led even sympathetic listeners to a forced effort to distrust all sensations which could be construed as "tonal"—and therefore to seek the real meaning of the music in some abstract concept which has little to do with what they hear. To be sure, dodecaphonic music cannot be analyzed in terms of tonality; and even areas in the music which one seems to hear in some sense "tonally," derive this quasi-tonal implication from relationships which, as can easily be seen, are inherent in music itself and are the product of no particular period or technique. A fifth remains a fifth, a third a third, in the twentieth as surely as in the fourteenth century. These relationships are felt, today as always, even though no way has yet been found by which the enlarged vocabulary of today can be systematized in a theoretical sense; and it is quite possible that no such systematization will be possible for some time to come.

What Schoenberg achieved, then, with the formulation of the twelve-tone method, was to show his followers a way toward the practical organization of materials. The true significance of the twelve-tone method, and of Schoenberg's immense achievement, cannot possibly be understood if more than this is demanded of it. No doubt, as music continues to develop, the "twelve-tone system" also will evolve—possibly though not necessarily into something quite different from its present form. The more it develops, however, the richer Schoenberg's achievement will have proven to be. For it is, precisely, *not* a new harmonic system: it does not seek to contradict or deny, but to make possible the exploitation of new resources. Its significance is the greater precisely for the fact of being something far more unpretentious, but at the same time far more vital, than a new harmonic theory or a new aesthetic principle could possibly be.

Thoughts on Stravinsky
[1957]

On the occasion of the composer's seventy-fifth birthday.

ONLY the blindest partisanship, it would seem, can any longer deny that Stravinsky has left a permanent and essentially indestructible mark on Western music. This is a distinction which he shares with Schoenberg and in a less obvious but nonetheless real sense also with Bartók, and as far as can be seen, with no others of his generation. No composer alive writes the same music today as he would have written had any one of these three not lived; their influence is widespread in its effect on composers of all styles and in all parts of the world where Western music is prevalent; and those who would deny it or try to escape it only thereby confess their provincialism. Each of them has played his appointed role in the drama of music in our time; each role has been a historically inevitable and necessary one, and each personality has summarized a facet of the problem of contemporary music as a whole.

Why must one speak so constantly of a "problem" of contemporary music? One might well answer: because everything is a problem nowadays—even human existence itself. In the field of music, nothing could be clearer today than the fact that the tradition on which the great florescence of the eighteenth and nineteenth centuries was based, has no longer any vitality so far as the present and the future are concerned. The music itself, needless to say, is as vital as it ever was; but the composer of today is the first to be aware, through his very love for this music, and loy-

From *The Score*, no. 20, June 1957, pp. 32-37. Reprinted by permission of Kraus Reprint.

alty to it, that it is precisely the most vital elements of the tradition that have led to a situation in which its basic assumptions are no longer useful. This is just as evident in the music of Stravinsky, from whom some people hoped at one time for a return to the tradition, as in that of Schoenberg and his followers. For in spite of its apparent break with everything that bore the imprint of "modernism" in the nineteen-twenties, and in spite of Stravinsky's very conscious and even outspoken development of impulses derived from certain styles of the past, in his music the familiar concepts have taken on quite different meanings. Tonality, diatonicism, chord-structure—even harmony, rhythm, expressivity—have quite another meaning for him than they had for Haydn or Brahms; and it is futile to apply to his music the analytical criteria which are valid for theirs.

Since the very beginning of Stravinsky's career it has been the custom to lay great stress on the perfection of his technique: on the mastery with which he has solved every problem that he has set himself. Of this mastery there is of course no doubt. But the criterion is a strange one, and its constantly recurring application is perhaps peculiar to our time. After all, technical mastery is, or should be, expected of every full-fledged composer, and it is possessed today by many others besides Stravinsky.

Is there then more in this matter than is readily apparent? The author still remembers very vividly a piano recital he heard in 1927, at a moment when he was, or believed himself to be, under Stravinsky's spell to the point of intense partisanship. The program contained pieces by nearly all the most prominent composers of that time. Stravinsky was represented by his Piano Sonata of 1924—a work which even then held little attraction for the present author. Two works, however, stood out for him quite unmistakably from the rest: this Sonata, and a couple of movements from Schoenberg's Op. 25—music which seemed to him as remote

377

as possible from his personal way of thinking at that time, and which, like the Stravinsky Sonata has never really had any very strong appeal for him. What struck him most forcibly, however, was the clarity and the authority of outline of these two pieces, which placed them in a category quite apart from the rest of the program, even though this included such names as Bartók and Hindemith. In both pieces it seemed that every note was exactly where it belonged, and the impression they made was unequivocal, unqualified, and completely focused. In other words, they were masterworks in the full sense of the term.

The qualities just described certainly involve far more than what is commonly called "technique." But it seems clear that today the concept of technique itself has acquired a new facet and a new meaning. One can no longer speak very significantly in terms of a mastery of craft. Genuine technique, today, is something quite different from this, and in fact lies on quite another level. It is inextricably woven into the composer's whole artistic vision, his style, his personality, and has to do precisely with the intrinsic nature of his musical thought and imagination. Every composer of course embodies somehow in his work the whole past, from which he inherits a degree of craftsmanship. But in a period like our own it is inevitable that these elements should become personalized to the utmost limits. In the work of a Stravinsky it is his very personal vision, whether of the past or of his own time, which becomes technically valid; what is generally called his technical mastery is really another term to denote what is in fact the essence of a clear and un-blurred, but intensely personal musical vision.

What was the nature of Stravinsky's so-called "contacts" with various styles of the past, and what did he gain from them? To answer the second of these questions in the most immediate sense: perhaps he freed himself first of all from being dominated by certain stylistic features that were threatening to run wild—elements that would inevitably have become purely and simply *devices*, had they not been assimilated into a broader concept of musical design. The musical conception embodied in *Le Sacre du printemps* or in *Les Noces* is quite sufficient so far as these works in themselves are concerned. But in terms of musical movement and articulation, even of harmony and acoustical organization, they represent a direction which can scarcely be pursued further without the serious danger of falling into *cliché*. In other words, Stravinsky apparently felt the urgent need of a change of direction.

At any rate, the past gave him a framework against which these elements—so personal and at the same time, in the light of his background and previous development, so imperious—could be subordinated to a larger and more impersonal design. Stravinsky took from the past what he wanted to take, what he could make completely his own. One may agree or disagree with the process itself—its effect is certainly often problematical. But at this date it is no longer possible to question its significance.

Stravinsky no doubt learned directly from the masters of the past, as other composers have done. But one must insist that this is not the real significance of his "neo-classic" works, which are as completely dominated by his personality as any of his other music. This fact was scarcely noted in the early twenties, when the Octet and the Piano Concerto were written; the departure they represented was too startling in its effect. Moreover, most of those who regarded themselves as Stravinsky's followers were pursuing a neo-classicism of quite orthodox conception, and these in turn helped to bring to the foreground the still more academic predilections of many others who heralded with glee the "return to orthodoxy" of a notorious—perhaps, at the time, the most notorious—exponent of the hated musical unorthodoxies of the twentieth century.

It is now clear to us that Stravinsky neither attempted to revive styles from earlier periods, nor in any real sense depended upon them. Rather—for reasons of his own which lay at the root of his artistic vision—he adapted some phases of the vocabulary of the past to his own purposes, and integrated them into his own style. It is his own personality which predominates at virtually all points—his very characteristic conception of musical movement, of tonality, of rhythm, even of melody; these are the elements which constitute the real activating force, and not those which seem evocative of other modes of musical thought. An attentive scrutiny of any page of Stravinsky, from the Octet and the Concerto to *The Rake's Progress* and beyond, should make this fact abundantly clear. This is not to say that the result is never problematical. The present writer must confess that for him at least it frequently is. But the problem does not lie in any real discrepancy of styles, or (as some have claimed) in any lack of security in his own style. It would be more relevant to note that the "past" which Stravinsky often consciously evokes is not the real past as it lived and was lived, but a very much frozen image of a past which itself never existed except as a kind of elegant fiction. The artificiality is entirely conscious, of course; one need only think of the Latin text of *Oedipus Rex* and of Stravinsky's own remarks about it, as evidence of this. The problem lies however in this artificiality and in the fact that often the music which results is evocative to such a degree that extra-musical—that is, quasi-archaistic—impressions disturb one's sense of the music itself, for all the genuine power which it embodies. It is the directness of impression which suffers; one feels at times as if the music were, so to speak, in costume, and wonders why that is necessary.

Yet this is not really a fair question, even though it may seem an unavoidable one. It is unfair because it leaves out of account the fact that the evolution of an artist is composed of a thousand elements, and that no single moment is definitive; also because it would seem to deny the right of any single work of art to be considered independently and on its own terms, rather than as a commitment for the future. It is true that any work contains, in a sense, this element of commitment; but the future to which it commits itself is one that will be realized only in other works, and in significant ones. Those who seem to follow an artist in the most literal sense prove often to be the worst obstacles to a real understanding of his art.

Had Stravinsky continued to compose only works like the Piano Concerto or the Sonata, one could speak with more assurance about a real "problem." But these works, like others, are phases of an evolution which is both complex and far-flung. It is natural that while an artist is in the process of full evolution, his public should look on with emotions which may at any time include a certain nervousness about the direction in which he may next move, and that among his followers will be found those for whom each successive phase immediately becomes a dogma. It is possible also that these followers may include really gifted individuals who will develop that phase to a point where it assumes a quasi-autonomous existence under a new hand. One thinks readily of Webern—and of Berg, for that matter—in relation to Schoenberg. But the phase of Stravinsky's work which has been called "neo-classic" can be clearly seen today as only one ingredient in a much larger picture; as an element which has played its role—neither a useless nor an essentially disturbing one—in forming a personal and integrated style which ranges far beyond the particularities of this phase itself. So far as that is concerned, it seems likely that Stravinsky was then preoccupied with problems of continuity, of movement, and of articulation, and that by letting his music develop at times along lines in a sense parallel to those embodied in certain forms out of the past, he was gaining new insights into these problems. It is hardly possible, nowadays, to see a closer relationship than this would imply. The Piano Concerto of 1924 is in sound, in idiom, and above all in conception, far closer to *Les Noces* than to Bach; and the "false notes" which aroused such comment in the twenties are now seen to be essential to the real matter, which is Stravinsky's own musical world, and not arbitrary deviations from the mirage, which in this particular case was often mistaken for the countenance of Bach.

For many years now it has been the rule to regard Stravinsky and Schoenberg as representing two contradictory, even irreconcilable, poles of contemporary music. Various adjectives are applied in this sense—Stravinsky: objective, diatonic, linear, volatile, rhythmically orientated in the direction of bodily gesture, etc.; Schoenberg: subjective, chromatic, essentially "vertical" (!), scholastic, addicted to the rhythms of speech and possibly song. Much of this is manifestly just talk. Though most of the adjectives, taken together, present a recognizable if by no means accurate composite picture, each one of them, taken separately, needs serious qualification. This is of course because to a large extent they are *mots de guerre*.

Such distinctions are unlikely to loom so large in the future, if only because the composers of the generations succeeding Stravinsky and Schoenberg (and especially the most independent among them) are in a very real sense the heirs of both. However remote the prospect may at present appear, it is quite possible that future generations will be at least as aware that Stravinsky and Schoenberg both faced fundamentally the same historical situation, as that one of them came from a Russo-Parisian background, the other from Vienna, and that they developed accordingly. The "polarity" is likely to become less and less of an issue, for the very obvious reason that future generations will probably be still more unwilling than ourselves to admire the one to the complete exclusion of the other.

At present, however, it does remain a considerable issue and in this context the admirable attitude of Stravinsky himself, especially in recent years, is a measure of his real stature both as man and artist. For many years the battles between the two poles were bitterly fought—perhaps as bitterly as any in the history of music; and the smoke of battle has by no means died away. Such battles are almost invariably fought more enthusiastically by disciples than by masters, and by and large this was true also of those in question here. But there was bitterness in abundance, and it was unhappily not altogether limited to the disciples. Stravinsky's warm-hearted participation in the tributes extended to Schoenberg in Los Angeles, both before and after the latter's death, will surely never be forgotten.

Such considerations as the above, peripheral as they may seem, are by no means irrelevant in a consideration of Stravinsky's music. "The greatest man," Emerson somewhere has said, "is the most indebted man"; and while it is obvious that indebtedness is by no means sufficient as a criterion, the fact remains that for an artist of real individuality it is a sign of particular strength when he is able to learn from his contemporaries. One thinks of Bach, of Haydn, of Verdi, and others. The important fact here lies not in the generosity of spirit which this implies, but in its artistic counterpart—the power of inclusiveness, the ability to achieve a new fusion and a new depth in a style already mature and self-sufficient.

To regard Stravinsky's recent adoption of serial techniques from a Schoenbergian point of view is quite misguided; equally irrelevant is it to note that Stravinsky has expressed an admiration rather for Webern than for Schoenberg himself. From any point of view whatever, Webern's music embodies the intensive cultivation of one phase of Schoenberg, to whom he always remained essentially and consciously subject, for all his extraordinary gifts. The important fact is that Stravinsky's Septet, his Cantata, and other recent works are at least as characteristic of him as anything that he wrote earlier on, and as easy to recognize as such. They afford yet further evidence of the span and assimilative power of a style which has absorbed elements from many apparently diverse and even theoretically contradictory sources, without the slightest loss of identity. As in the case of other works of Stravinsky, they also offer one more major challenge to the habit of easy classification of which our age is so fond, and which for all its obvious practical convenience can become an artistic menace if such challenges are not recognized and met.

The honest contemplation of the work of any one of a quite considerable number of composers of our century must convince us that we live in a period of immense productive richness and abundant genius. How this period compares with any other in the past there is no way of knowing; nor is the question in the last analysis at all relevant; every age is unique, and ours, with its universal mass media of communication, its highly organized material life, its vast population, and its unprecedented and infinitely far-reaching historical cataclysms—in the midst of which we are still living—has few points of resemblance to any other except in the continuity of man himself. In such a period defeatism in cultural matters is easy, and unfortunately it is rife in ours. This defeatism is engendered even by the very richness and variety of our cultural manifestations; it is easy to assume that these manifestations cancel each other out, and that they are of little importance anyway, since they apparently involve a mere handful of people in comparison with the great mass of listeners to music, let alone the population as a whole. In a world in which quantitative measurement has become a factor of vital importance, these matters loom large. For the vast majority of listeners today, Stravinsky remains the composer of *The Firebird* and Schoenberg of *Verklärte Nacht*—both early works quite uncharacteristic of the mature personalities in question, hardly related except in an academic sense to their real achievements, and not related at all to their far-flung impact on the whole of music.

A certain pessimism is therefore understandable; but whether it is justified from the long-range point of view is quite a different question. The answer will not be given in terms of music alone, or of the arts, or even of culture itself. It is a question of ultimate human resourcefulness; whether human beings can extricate themselves from the most complex and menacing situation that has ever faced them, and learn to live together in a manner which focuses their spiritual energies instead of scattering them, enabling the voices not only of artists but of all men of intelligence and genius and goodwill to be listened to by all, instead of by the few who possess the patience, the energy, and the dedicated interest to discover what they have to say.

It is this which makes the presence—the existence, in fact —of an artist like Stravinsky so important to every one, whether he cares to pay attention or not. For it is a testimony to the fact that the qualities of genuine imagination, of devotion, of deep involvement and of heroic single-mindedness that go into the making of great art are still in abundant existence, and are recognizable whether or not one is always in "agreement." As long as this is true, music is very much alive. For it is these qualities, and the composers who embody them, that keep music alive; not those for whom the market is the criterion, or those for whom music is simply a toy to be played with or the projection in one form or another of a purely individual neurosis. This is not to say that art need always be "serious" in the usual sense of the word, but simply that art of significance is produced by those who identify themselves with it, not by those who identify it with themselves or whose primary aim is to exploit it for purposes which have essentially nothing to do with it. The seventy-fifth anniversary of an artist like Stravinsky furnishes us with the occasion not only to pay homage once more to a great personality, but also to bear witness to the fact that great music still does, and can, exist among us.

In Memoriam Igor Stravinsky
[1971]

Igor Stravinsky died April 6, 1971.

STRAVINSKY's death came for all of us as a shock, not lessened by the fact that many of us had known, with deep concern, that for the last two years his health had been precarious. During all of our lives he had been present, and it is difficult and painful to realize that he is here no longer.

In these last two weeks many tributes have been paid to him, and many more are surely still to come. He was the last survivor of a very great generation, which has left its indelible mark on all of the music that has been composed during at least the last half-century. Above all he was the composer of many works which still retain their vitality undiminished, and will certainly continue to do so for very many years to come.

What I would like chiefly to express here, however, is the enormous debt that all of his survivors owe him. Without him, we would not be as we are—and there is no composer, perhaps no musician, living today, who could say otherwise. For us that have had the great privilege of knowing his music, from *Petrouchka* and the *Sacre* onward, when it first appeared; for whom each new work came as a fresh surprise; who enjoyed the zestful obligation of fighting for Stravinsky's music when it was still—to use the establishmentarian parlance of today—"controversial"; for us he has left the most precious of memories. He gave us no less than a part of ourselves, and it is for this we owe to him the high privilege of gratitude.

From *Perspectives of New Music*, vol. 9, no. 2/vol. 10, no. 1, Spring-Summer/Fall-Winter, 1971, p. 12.

In Memoriam Luigi Dallapiccola
[1975]

Luigi Dallapiccola died February 19, 1975.

L UIGI DALLAPICCOLA was, in the only valid sense of the word, a truly great composer. For me personally he was also a very dear friend, to whom I was profoundly devoted, and whose memory I shall always cherish.

To him we owe a succession of extraordinary works, of a style and character which is uniquely his own, and which developed steadily and resourcefully from the beginning to the end of his career. These works range in dimension from short instrumental pieces and song cycles, to large-scale choral and orchestral works such as the *Canti di prigionia* and the *Canti di liberazione*, and finally to his operas— *Volo di notte*, *Il prigioniero*, and his magnificent *Ulisse*. The music ranges in character from the utmost delicacy to enormous dramatic power, always with a constantly rich, and deeply sensitive, inventiveness, and a profile of the clearest definition. No composer of the twentieth century has written for the voice with greater eloquence, or with greater appreciation of its resources, than he.

As his music developed, it became increasingly concentrated, with the simplest means resulting in the boldest and most magical intensity of expression. An infinitely touching instance of this quality is revealed in the page which was found on his piano after his death, and which was reproduced in facsimile and sent, in the name of his wife and daughter, to many of his friends in his memory.

Unfortunately much of this music, including the monumental *Ulisse*, is still unknown in the United States except

From *Perspectives of New Music*, vol. 13, no. 1, Fall-Winter, 1974, pp. 244-245.

to those who have had the good fortune to hear it at one or more of the frequent performances in Europe, or who possess copies. Even the powerful *Il prigioniero*, though it has been performed more often in Europe than any Italian opera since Puccini, has had few and sporadic performances here.

Dallapiccola was not only a profoundly cultivated human being; he was also a rarely generous, compassionate, and humane one. He was vividly aware of the world in which we live, and was devoted to the cause of human liberty, both on the individual and on the political level. He was always ready to take the initiative in cases where he felt that injustice had been done, and to commit himself without reserve, as he always did to his personal beliefs. His nature was in essence a deeply religious one, which means, quite simply, that he was constantly aware of the human condition, in its profoundest as well as its most immediate aspects, and that he remained unfettered by limitations of a sectarian, narrowly partisan, or doctrinaire kind. This too is reflected, richly and eloquently, in the music he has left us.

Library of Congress Cataloging in Publication Data

Sessions, Roger, 1896-
  Roger Sessions on music.

    1. Music—Addresses, essays, lectures.
I. Cone, Edward T.   II.   Title.
ML60.S514   780'.8   78-51190
ISBN 0-691-09126-9
ISBN 0-691-10074-8 pbk.